WILLIAM PERCIVAL JOHNSON

*From a photograph taken by the late Mr. Richard R. Goulden*

# Johnson of Nyasaland

## A Study of the Life and Work of William Percival Johnson, D.D.

Archdeacon of Nyasa, Missionary Pioneer 1876-1928

BY

BERTRAM HERBERT BARNES, C.R.

*(One time of U.M.C.A.)*

UNIVERSITIES' MISSION TO CENTRAL AFRICA

CENTRAL AFRICA HOUSE, WOOD STREET, WESTMINSTER, S.W.1

1933

*Made and Printed in Great Britain by*
*The Garden City Press Ltd., Letchworth, Herts.*

Jesus said, " If any man would come after Me, let him deny himself and take up his cross daily, and follow Me. For whosoever would save his life shall lose it ; but whosoever shall lose his life for My sake, the same shall save it." St. Luke ix, 23, 24.

" I determined not to know anything among you, save Jesus Christ and him crucified." 1 Cor. ii, 2.

" The rooting out of evil does not take place without the labourer's bleeding and if you wish to answer the appeal of Christ met upon the road, you must give yourself up, head and hand, and be absorbed wholly in the ungrateful task, in the dim crusade against the powers of darkness, more cruel than Saladin of old ; you must consent to live by faith, without pay, without seeing the dawn of your harvests nor the ray of your victories. Nothing is accomplished, all is very difficult, and one can evade the task, escape the labour imposed, without even losing eternal salvation. . . .

" The great-hearted are not those who join the triumphal procession and scatter palm branches when all the world sings Hosanna. They are rather the realists, who, without illusion as to the severity of the obstacles, knowing well that the stones of the road will make their feet bleed, have deliberately answered the Redeemer : Everywhere, wholly and always." Pierre Charles, S.J., *La Prière de toutes les heures*, ii, p. 59.

# DEDICATION

*To all who love William Percival Johnson*

# PREFACE

IT is not easy to write the life of such a man as William Percival Johnson; but Father Barnes, who knew him intimately and worked with him for several years, has undertaken the difficult task, and I feel that he has been singularly successful in showing us the man as he really was. It is not a panegyric, but a life. We see Johnson with his "angularities" as well as something of his greatness; his humility, his intense devotion to his work, his entire sacrifice of himself in the service of his Lord.

Of none other that I have ever known have I seen so fully carried out in daily life the words of the Prayer of Oblation: "Here we offer ourselves, our souls and bodies, to be a reasonable, holy and lively sacrifice unto Thee."

Johnson was always reticent about himself; his letters and his speeches were obscurely expressed; the last subject he ever referred to was himself, or his own hardships, or his own experiences. To us who knew him in his daily activities and saw him living day by day and year by year his strenuous life, he seemed as one apart, different from all others, a solitary soul called to do a great work and doing it with all his might. He was perhaps a little difficult to work with, difficult to understand; to the world at large he was more or less unknown. He had no great gifts of utterance, he was no pulpit orator; there was nothing of the popular missionary preacher about him.

At a public meeting his words were often vague and hard to follow. Yet there was something so arresting about this man; it was he himself who impressed others and who appealed to them. There was a distinction and a sense of power in reserve which made him a notable figure in any company and marked him out as one who was cast in the mould of the saints. We might compare him with Ramon Lull in the thirteenth century, or still more with Francis Xavier in the sixteenth: men who mostly lived alone and worked alone and whose life was hid in God.

It fell to Johnson in the fifty-three years of his life in Africa (almost *continuously* in Africa) to have to work under six Bishops. He had a very high conception of the office of a Bishop, and the Bishops each in turn did their best to understand Johnson and to fall in with his ideas. But it was so difficult to find what exactly his " ideas " were. I fear we often failed ! He was one of those who seemed unable to put his thoughts into words, either in speech or in writing, so as to make it plain what exactly he wished to say. I remember Bishop Smythies at Likoma one day telling me, " I have had Johnson with me all the morning and I can *not* make out what it is he really wants."

If you asked Johnson for his opinion on any difficult matter, or for his advice on some mission problem, he would as likely as not begin arguing as if you were an adversary and you would probably get little or no help. Truly we may say he was " angular," " obscure," " difficult " ; yes! he was all that. Yet, apart from this, we all knew and felt that he was a man of God, utterly and entirely devoted to the service of his Lord.

It is sometimes said that the Church of England is the Church of the middle classes and can produce no saints. Yet when we look back over the last fifty or sixty years and recall the names of Father Benson of Cowley, of William Johnson of Nyasaland, of Frank Weston of Zanzibar, we feel encouraged to believe that sanctity is not unknown, even in the dull and humdrum Church of England ; that we may still find saints and heroes and martyrs not unworthy to rank by the side of the greatest of the saints of old.

I hope this book will be largely read, especially by candidates for Holy Orders and by the younger clergy ; that the example of such a life as William Johnson's may be the means of stirring up in some a desire to follow in his steps ; that some may hear the call to give up all and to follow Christ the King, that they may make other people Christians and bring others in lands very far off to the saving knowledge of His Name.

J. E. H.

# AUTHOR'S PREFACE

"THERE were giants in those days." That is what one may perhaps feel, as one reviews the work and life of Archdeacon Johnson. As long as that feeling helps to keep one humble, it is good and useful, but it should do more than that. If the example of a hero does not stimulate to heroism in things whether small or great, it is failing of its purpose.

In particular this should be the case with Archdeacon Johnson. Not that he himself would have it so in the very least, but that, in these days of civic and martial heroism, it is surely time that such a hero of the mission field of Africa should inflame the young men of our Church to-day with something like his own single-hearted ardour. We are too fond of our armchairs—very useful things in their place—and there is too little of the spirit that carried Johnson through fifty arduous years. His life should be a challenge to us who come after him, and it is to be hoped that the knowledge of what he endured and did will stir us to emulation.

It is a hard task so to tell such a story that this shall be the result and the writer is deeply conscious of his inadequacy for such a task. He can only plead in excuse that he did not undertake such a responsibility but at the invitation of those in authority, and, as with the pianist in the old story, it would be unkind to shoot him for he has done the best he could.

He wishes to thank those who have sent him letters of the Archdeacon's from which the extracts given in the end of the book have been taken. It has not been thought well to give many letters in full, but not one of those sent has been wasted, even if it has only contributed a line to the general picture somewhere.

Special thanks are due to Miss Nixon Smith, who has been indefatigable in assisting an absentee compiler to collect the necessary information which has been required from time to time, and on whom he has had to rely for the correction of the proofs and the preparation of an index.

That this little study may help to make William Percival Johnson something more definite than a vague legend is the writer's hope.

BERTRAM HERBERT BARNES, C.R.

*September 2, 1932,*
*Penhalonga,*
*S. Rhodesia.*

# CONTENTS

# LIST OF ILLUSTRATIONS

## MAPS

# PRINCIPAL DATES

Oct. : Johnson driven from Mataka's. Returns to
   Masasi, p. 40.
Nov. : Reports to Bishop Steere at Zanzibar, p. 41.
Dec. : Johnson and Charles Janson start from Masasi
   for the Lake, p. 45.

28  1882  Feb. 21 : Death of Charles Janson at Chia, p. 49.
March : Johnson settles alone at Chiteji's Village, p. 55.
   Faces an Angoni raiding party and later goes to their
   capital Songea to see their chiefs, pp. 55, 59.
Sept. : The Angoni raid Masasi. Johnson's visit to the
   Nyakanyaka, pp. 58, 59.

29  1883  Nov. 30 : Bishop Smythies consecrated in St. Paul's
   Cathedral.

30  1884  Johnson's successful appeal in England for a steamer,
   pp. 67-9.
June 23 : Johnson reads a paper on his Seven Years'
   Wanderings before the Royal Geographical Society,
   p. 67.
Oct. : Johnson sets out for Nyasa with the steamer in
   packages and a party of recruits, p. 69.
Johnson struck down by blindness near the Zambezi
   Mouth, p. 69.

31  1885  Johnson taken to England. Operated on. Sight partly
   restored, pp. 70, 71.
Aug. 24 : Bishop Smythies gets leave to settle at
   Likoma, p. 75.
Sept. 6 : Dedication of s.s. *Charles Janson*.

32  1886  June : Bishop Smythies with Johnson and party reach
   Masasi on the way to the Lake. Johnson has again
   to be sent back very ill, this time to Zanzibar and
   Cape Town, while the Bishop goes on to the Lake with
   C. Maples in Johnson's place, pp. 72, 73.
Oct. : Johnson at last gets back to the Lake and joins
   the s.s. *Charles Janson*, p. 74.

34  1888  April : Vice-Consul Buchanan and Johnson seized and
   held to ransom at Makanjila's, pp. 120-2.
Sept. : s.s. *Charles Janson* stranded at Matope for eight
   months.

36  1890  Johnson hustled, his dinghy seized and Stefano, his
   cook, killed at Mkalawili's, pp. 123-5.

37  1891  July : Boundaries of British, Portuguese and German
   Nyasaland finally settled, pp. 84-92.

38  1892  Disastrous fires at Likoma : library destroyed, p. 236.
Dec. 21 : Bishop Hornby consecrated, first Bishop of
   Nyasaland, p. 104.

| | | |
|---|---|---|
| 39 | 1893 | Unangu Station in Yaoland started under Dr. Hine, p. 40. |
| 40 | 1894 | May 7 : Bishop Smythies died at sea.<br>Aug. : Bishop Hornby resigns on account of ill health, p. 105. |
| 41 | 1895 | June 29 : Bishop Maples consecrated in St. Paul's Cathedral, p. 109.<br>Aug. 26 : Geo. Atlay murdered by Angoni, pp. 113-6.<br>Sept. 2 : Bishop Maples and Joseph Williams drowned, pp. 109-113.<br>Oct. 29 : A. F. Sim died of fever at Kota Kota, p. 116. |
| 42 | 1896 | June 29 : Bishop Hine consecrated at St. Matthew's, Bethnal Green, p. 117.<br>JOHNSON made Archdeacon, p. 119. |
| 43 | 1897 | Oct. : JOHNSON returns to England, p. 157. |
| 44 | 1898 | Nov. : JOHNSON returns to the Lake, p. 157.<br>Augustine Ambali and Eustace Malisawa ordained deacons. |
| 45 | 1899 | JOHNSON'S experiment of a " Peripatetic College," pp. 100-1. |
| 46 | 1900 | JOHNSON starts St. Michael's College for training teachers, p. 102.<br>Dec. : JOHNSON has blackwater fever. Is sent to New Zealand to recuperate, p. 158. |
| 47 | 1901 | JOHNSON at his brother's in New Zealand, pp. 166-9. |
| 48 | 1902 | Jan. 25 : Bishop Trower consecrated on Bishop Hine's translation to Zanzibar.<br>s.s. *Chauncy Maples* dedicated and launched, p. 158.<br>JOHNSON returns (April) to the Lake, p. 158.<br>St. Michael's becomes the Diocesan Training College, p. 102. |
| 52 | 1906 | Augustine Ambali and Eustace Malisawa ordained priests, p. 162. |
| 56 | 1910 | June 24 : Bishop Fisher consecrated.<br>Nov. : JOHNSON goes to England. |
| 57 | 1911 | June : JOHNSON given Hon. D.D. by Oxford, pp. 217, 241.<br>Nov. : Shooting of Arthur Douglas at St. Michael's, p. 243. |
| 58 | 1912 | JOHNSON begins work in German territory. |
| 60 | 1914 | The war suspends the work in German territory, p. 184.<br>Steamers both commandeered for war service. |
| 61 | 1915 | Work resumed in German territory, p. 185. |
| 64 | 1918 | End of the war. |

B

66  1920  Sept. : JOHNSON goes to England, p. 191.
67  1921  Oct. : JOHNSON returns to the Lake. Is priest in charge
          of Liuli (formerly Sphinxhaven), p. 192.
68  1922  Becomes Canon of Our Lady in Likoma Cathedral.
          Publishes *Nyasa the Great Water* and *Psalms in
          Chinyanja* ; *Chinyanja Proverbs*, pp. 189-191.
70  1924  Published *My African Reminiscences, 1875-95*, p. 191.
72  1926  JOHNSON made Hon. Fellow of University, his own
          College, p. 248.
73  1927  His last visit to Dr. Laws at Livingstonia, pp. 198-200.
74  1928  Sept. : His last illness, pp. 201-4.
          Oct. 11 : Dr. JOHNSON dies at Liuli, aged 74, p. 204.

# JOHNSON OF NYASALAND

## PROLOGUE

### 1874

HURRYING through the streets of Oxford is a young under-graduate, slim, slightly above middle height with an eager face, bright eyes and a resolute mouth. He is going to Professor Monier Williams's lectures on Sanskrit and is, therefore, one of a rather select band. His eye is caught by a notice on the notice-board as he passes, and he stops to read it. It is an invitation to men at Oxford to join the Universities' Mission to Central Africa, a Mission which has been struggling for recognition since 1860, when it began with a very small band. It has suffered the serious set-back of the death of its first Bishop and the with-drawal of the Mission from Central Africa to an island on the east coast, and has been bitterly criticized for having withdrawn. It offers nothing but hardship and the chance of preaching Christ to the people of Central Africa. The undergraduate goes to his lecture with a face more thoughtful than it was ; the idea of volunteering for this forlorn hope of the Church has taken root in his mind.

But there is much to be thought of before he decides. He is already booked for a career in the Indian Civil Service with great prospects of usefulness and promotion. His old school, Bedford, looks to him to win it more laurels. His mother, a widow, is expecting great things from him. But here is a new call.

He made his choice, and it was to Africa he went and poverty; not to India and the road of worldly success.

### 1911

Once more the scene is Oxford and this time the Sheldonian Theatre. A great assembly is waiting for the introduction of those whom the University delights to honour. Amid the enthusiastic cheers of the assembly Dr. Lock introduces a venerable figure, the Archdeacon of Nyasaland, grey, worn, but still upright, and straight as a dart, still with a gleam in the only eye that his hardships in Africa have left him, a heroic figure in robes of a Doctor of Divinity. Perhaps he remembers the hesitating undergraduate who chose the hard road and has stuck to it.

## 1928

Far away from Oxford on the shores of Lake Nyasa is a humble brick church, humble as compared with the stately churches and colleges of Oxford, but splendid by the side of the little houses of poles and thatch with which most villages are content in Central Africa. A crowd is gathered about the church in this far-off Liuli, a sorrowful, mourning crowd, for the Christian people from all around have gathered there to carry their Father to his last resting-place behind the altar in the simple church of the land for which he has spent himself to the very last. William Percival Johnson, D.D., Archdeacon of Nyasa, Hon. Fellow of University College, Oxford, has run his long race and is at rest in the Lord whom he loved.

# CHAPTER I

# The Call to Africa

WILLIAM PERCIVAL JOHNSON was born at Vernon 1854 Villa, St. Helens, in the Isle of Wight, on March 12, 1854. He was the third son of John Johnson, a lawyer of Ryde, and Mary Percival, his second wife, and their family consisted of four sons and a daughter, who died as an infant. The eldest son, James Magnus, died at the early age of 33; the second, John Charles, settled in New Zealand, and died there, and the youngest, Henry Robert, after an arduous life devoted to the Church in South Wales has returned to Ryde to spend the evening of his days near his birthplace.

John Charles was the only son who married and brought up a family of sons and daughters. Both of his sons, Magnus and Olaf, served with distinction in the Great War, and Olaf was killed in 1917. Their Uncle Will, fighting in another and greater war, was proud to tell his native friends in Central Africa of his two nephews " doing their bit " among the soldiers of New Zealand.

Harry Johnson, the youngest brother, was also ordained and spent most of his active life in South Wales, where as Warden for twenty-seven years of St. Michael's College (originally at Aberdare and now at Llandaff) he exercised a very great influence on the young men who came there to prepare for ordination, and who all over Wales and from many far corners of the world look back with love and veneration on him as the " Tad " who shaped them for God's service. Canon H. R. Johnson carried on this work of such importance to the Church in Wales until 1919, when on the death of Father Arthur Jones he was induced to shoulder the heavy burden of St. Mary's, Cardiff.

The Johnson family looks back to a great-grandfather, of the Orkney Islands, who ran away to London in his youth and settled there. The Scandinavian name Magnus, which occurs among the sons of each generation, is doubtless due to this connection with the Orkneys, and we may be permitted to think that the love of the sea, the skill as an oarsman and the indefatigable toughness of Will Johnson are traceable to his descent from the hardy fishermen of these northern islands.

1857

Will's father, John Johnson, died at St. Helens when Will was only three years old, and his mother, when the question of educating her three boys became pressing, removed from the Isle of Wight and settled in Bedford to be near its famous school. Emphatically in the case of Will Johnson this choice of a school must be reckoned as one of the main formative influences in his life. It is not easy to find details of the school life of a boy at Bedford in the 'sixties of last century, but one or two facts stand out. Will Johnson's skill with the oar was learnt on Bedford's Ouse and remained with him to the end. Also his old school takes pride not only in his work as a missionary over so many years, but also in the fact that the appointment to the Indian Civil Service, which he rejected for a higher call, was won by him as a boy in the school before he went on to Oxford to prepare for the work in India. One who knew him as a lad in those Bedford days recalls the remarkable straightness of his back, " as if he had swallowed a poker." There was never any flinching about Will Johnson.

Oxford,
1872-6

At Oxford his career was not undistinguished—a Second in Mathematics in " Moderations," and another Second in Theology in his Final Schools—but undoubtedly his own proudest memory of Oxford was his triumph when, as stroke, he carried his College Boat (University) to the head of the river.

In 1874 at Oxford occurred that small happening which changed and shaped the whole of his after life. The call to work in Africa was so great an event for Will Johnson that it will be best to describe it in his own words and those of his friend Chauncy Maples. Chauncy Maples, with whom Johnson's name will always be associated, entered University College in January 1871, while Johnson came up in 1872 to prepare for the appointment in India which he had won from Bedford. The two became great friends, as will appear from the accounts of their call to Africa.

Maples, in a letter to his parents dated December 5, 1874, tells them of his decision and of his negotiations with Bishop Steere, and he goes on :

BEDFORD GRAMMAR SCHOOL, 1874, NOW THE TOWN HALL

" As for Johnson, he is going with me, and, to tell you the truth, 1874 he was the first to say definitely that he was going. He went down to see his mother on Thursday last, and when he came back he told me, to my utter amazement, that he had thrown up the Indian Civil Service appointment which he held, and was going to become a missionary. In throwing up this he threw up a thousand a year, with infinite chances of promotion—altogether one of the finest openings (from a worldly point of view) a young man can have. Admiration for this act of his forbade me from being a coward—for to my own conscience, as I explained above, I *was* a coward—any longer, and I quickly followed his example. . . . If I have been more careful about religious observances and more earnest about spiritual advancement lately, it has, humanly speaking, been owing entirely to Will Johnson, and it is no little source of happiness to me to think that I shall at least set out for Africa with him for whose character I have so much admiration, and for whose self I have so much love."

Will Johnson in *My African Reminiscences*, written in 1924, when he was Archdeacon Johnson, D.D., and still pegging away in Africa, gives a fuller account of the things which moved him at this crisis of his life.

He says :

" Unless my memory deceives me, the first I ever heard of the Universities' Mission to Central Africa was a notice I saw stuck up when I was attending lectures on Sanskrit in Professor Monier Williams's rooms, after I had passed the examination for the Indian Civil Service. This notice, signed by leading men in the University, asked for volunteers for the Mission ; just as in 1914 notices posted up asked for men for the War. It seemed just the opening I had wished for, and I resolved to go.

" In those days there was much discussion about the fundamental truths of revealed religion ; *Literature and Dogma* had a great influence, and open scoffing was to be read in books and heard in talk. Therefore, many of us who believed in these truths were thankful for an opportunity of proving our belief practically.

" A word more as to this call. Afterwards, when I heard of men volunteering to fight for the liberty of Greece af er an harangue by G. W. E. Russell, I was thrilled, but the call of the Universities' Mission was different. The elders of Oxford had taken up Livingstone's appeal to the Universities, and called upon their alumni at the most sensitive time, the time when a man comes to realize a vocation ; called on them too, as they came to an ordinary lecture. Might one not naturally feel such an appeal, and rightly expect that it would be brought home to others in the years to come ?

" Our Master, the Rev. G. G. Bradley, reasoned with me about my determination. He was a real help and guide, but he argued that there would be more scope in the Indian Civil Service. Other authorities said roundly, ' You are mad.' As there was so much opposition, I thought that I had better go for advice to Rev. J. Burgon (afterwards Dean of Chichester), then Vicar of St. Mary's, an outstanding man of independent opinions whom I respected though I had never spoken to him. I asked him whether he thought my decision to go out to Africa was wise and he answered in a sympathetic voice : ' I suppose you mean, do I think you will ever repent it, if you make it.' And when I replied, ' Yes,' he said, ' No, I don't think you ever will.'

" My friend Maples felt as I did, and he too decided to go to Africa, which made a vast difference to me, and we had a bond with other men, some of whom were drawn to the Oxford Mission to Calcutta. Indeed, after I had written to resign the Indian Civil Service, I found a good deal of sympathy, very precious and valuable, but it had not come first to lead me on. Our determination to become missionaries was more criticized and discussed by the authorities than by the undergraduates, and I remember a man, who by no means agreed with us, saying to me, ' I heartily sympathize with you, and if I thought as you do, I should do the same.'

" After the plunge had been taken, our circle used to hold inter- cessory missionary meetings, sometimes very puny. Thus once Canon Christopher, who was very deaf ; Faithfull, who could not play much, and I, were the only three present, and the hymn went lamely. We even put out a number or two of a paper called *The Undergraduates' Answer to Livingstone*, a poor performance which Dr. Ince waded through patiently. Later we got into touch with Bishop French, with Aubrey Moore, and Copleston and Dr. King.

" Bishop Steere (Bishop of the Universities' Mission) had spoken in Oxford, but it was before our time, and we had not heard him. I can remember hearing another member of the Mission, who had gone out rather in devotion to his friend Bishop Tozer, Steere's predecessor, than as feeling the Mission call himself. He came and spoke to us in the Hall of my College (University College), but he hardly carried our awakening enthusiasm with him. But when one of us got hold of a short letter of Bishop Steere's describing his return from a visit to the interior of Central Africa, while Africa still had hidden parts, this letter was passed around among us ; we all read it, and every one was kindled. It was not the description of anything dramatic in the ordinary sense ; but his men had been starving on the way back, and he himself had had little to live on but coffee, and, if I remember right, he divided most of that

up with his carriers. Here was a leader whom, while yet unknown, 1874
seemed to call on us to share with him as far as we could."

Faced with this appeal, Johnson made the momentous de- Decision
cision to devote himself to the service of our Lord in Africa,
and having made it he never wavered. Few lives can have been
so long and unswervingly directed to one end as Johnson's was
from that day on. His prospects in the Indian Civil Service of a
distinguished career and rich reward were forgone for a hard
life of lonely devotion to what, in the eyes of the world, was an
obscure cause. Of course to no man is it given to see the end
from the beginning, but the decision Johnson made then meant
a great sacrifice for the first step and a facing of incalculable
demands in the future. Not always again does God grant to
such a sacrifice so long a period for its fulfilment in detail, and
such full recognition as the University and his College gave to
Johnson when, in 1911, Oxford gave him the degree of D.D.
*honoris causa* and, in 1926, University College made him
an Honorary Fellow. As with the apostles James and John
one served God by an early death while the other lived on to
serve Him by a long life, so with the two friends who, in 1874,
made the same choice; Chauncy Maples after a glorious
twenty years of service was drowned in the Lake he loved,
while his friend carried his indomitable heart and will
through another thirty-three years of such labours as few
have known.

Will Johnson's decision altered his career at once, and he
left the field of Oriental study to take his Final Schools in
Theology. The thoroughness and completeness of his self- 1876
dedication to Africa is shown by the fact that he refused the
offer of ordination in England, choosing rather to be ordained
in Africa. His own words are :

" Maples, who was a year senior to me, was ordained in England
and spent a year in a curacy ; he went out in the early part of 1876,
while still a deacon. I followed in the summer of the same year, a
summer which had included for me the Eights, the Schools and
Henley.

" I was not at that time old enough to be ordained save by the
Archbishop's licence, and when such a licence was kindly offered,
it seemed a privilege to be ordained in Zanzibar by Bishop Steere,
because he stood emphatically for the Universities' work in Africa ;
a blessed opportunity of showing some of one's loyalty. When, as

they often do, people point out the advantage of a period of work in England first, before going out, I feel that it is no use discussing the matter, as it all depends on one's previous conceptions and what one's particular values are. If no new movements took place in the spiritual world, obviously there would be loss."

## CHAPTER II

# Early Days in Africa

IN August 1876 Johnson sailed for Zanzibar in a British India Off to Africa steamer in what he called " comfort," but a comfort very much below the standard of mail liners of to-day. Some people he met at Aden while waiting for a steamer connecting with Zanzibar assured him that the English Church Mission at Zanzibar was closed down and that they had been engaged in repairing the mission house there and had handed it over to some natives. The news did not disconcert Johnson, whose eyes were fixed on Bishop Steere and his friend Maples, and he was not surprised on his arrival to find that these good men had made a quite natural mistake between the Universities' Mission and the Church Missionary Society, who *had* just given up their house in Zanzibar.

Johnson was not left long in Zanzibar, where the narrow streets, the Eastern bazaars in place of the modern shops, and a hundred other things make one feel there that one has stepped straight out of modern life into the life and atmosphere of the *Arabian Nights*. The Bishop was anxious to follow up that trip to Central Africa of which his description had so fired the little group at Oxford, and Johnson was to go with him.

But first on September 29 the two friends, Maples and John- Ordination, Sept. 29, 1876 son, were ordained, the first to the priesthood and the second as a deacon. Maples writing home on September 11 says : " It will be very strengthening to feel that my ordination will be in conjunction with that of W. P. J. . . ." September 20 he writes : " Johnson has arrived in first-rate health ; he is highly delighted with everything he has seen so far." And on October 13 he says : " We were ordained, Johnson and I, on the feast of St. Michael and All Angels, September 29—a holy and happy day for both of us."

The ordination did not take place in Bishop Steere's beautiful Journey to Masasi Cathedral at Zanzibar, for that was not yet built (though the site had been acquired and the walls were rising), but in the Chapel of St. Andrew at Kiungani.

Very soon after the ordination, the Bishop made ready for the long expedition into the interior which he had planned, and these preparations gave Johnson one of his first shocks. The pile of stores for the journey (mostly tins and boxes) gave him the impression that they were taking a small grocer's shop up with them. It seemed to him to amount to luxury, and he thought hardly for a moment of the man who had fired his imagination at Oxford by living " mostly on coffee " and not keeping even that to himself. His fears were needless—the food was carried for future use at some distant day and very little of it was touched on the actual journey up country. It must be remembered that the moderate needs of the three Europeans— the Bishop, Johnson, and Beardall, a layman—for an indefinite period going far inland with a view to making a settlement there if it could be done, would require a good many packages. Besides this, the traveller in Africa at that date had to carry barter goods, cloth, beads, soap, salt, and odds and ends in order to buy food in the villages on the way, and to make gifts to chiefs whom it is needful to propitiate. And, of course, the food to be bought would include all that was needed to keep a party of carriers happy and fit. The party of carriers on this expedition were led by that David Chuma who was one of the people who travelled with Livingstone and brought his body back to the coast through many difficulties after the great explorer's death at Chitambo. To Johnson these men seemed like " hardy ruffians," and not at all the sort of people that imagination associates with a missionary expedition.

Two reasons existed for this expedition. In the first place it must be remembered that the original aim of the Universities' Mission as indicated in the title of the first Bishop, Bishop Mackenzie, had been " the tribes dwelling in the neighbourhood of the Lake Nyasa and River Shiré." Dr. Livingstone accompanied the first Bishop and assisted in the first effort to reach Nyasa by way of the Zambezi and based great hopes on that Mission sent out by the Universities to which he had appealed in his famous speech at Cambridge in 1857.

The death of Bishop Mackenzie and so many of that first party was a great blow to Livingstone's plans and hopes, and a great grief to him personally. The withdrawal of the Mission to

Zanzibar under Bishop Tozer, the second Bishop, was an even 1863
greater blow to him than his own recall with the expedition he
had undertaken for the British Government. " He could hardly
write of it ; he was more inclined to ' sit down and cry '."[1] He
wrote to Bishop Tozer, imploring him to reconsider the matter,
using these words : " I see that if you go, the last ray of hope
for this wretched, trodden-down people disappears and I again
from the bottom of my heart entreat you to reconsider the matter, and may the All-wise One guide to that decision which will
be most for His glory." At that date, 1863, no other prospect
had opened, and it was not till 1874, after Livingstone's death,
that the Livingstonia Mission of the Free Church of Scotland
was formed and settled on the western side of the lake.

The withdrawal of the Universities' Mission to Zanzibar was  Criticized by
hotly criticized at the time and cost the Mission many friends.  Dr. Livingstone
To-day it is likely that very few in the light of the later develop-  and others
ments would doubt the wisdom of that withdrawal. It is worth
while to quote the words written in 1865 by Livingstone in his
*Zambezi and its Tributaries* to show the strength of his feeling,
even after two or three years.

" Bishop Mackenzie had in a short time gained the first step, he
had secured the confidence of the people. This step it often takes
several years to attain ; and we cannot but regret that subsequently
the Mission of the Universities, when contrasted with others, should
appear to so much disadvantage. In fact, though representing all
that is good and manly in the chief seats of English learning, the
Mission, in fleeing from Morambala to an island in the Indian Ocean,
acted as St. Augustine would have done, had he located himself on
one of the Channel Islands, when sent to christianize the natives of
Central England. This is, we believe, the first case of a Protestant
Mission having been abandoned without being driven away."

These are some of the hard words that Bishop Tozer and the  Criticisms
Mission behind him had to bear. They are, of course, grossly  answered
unjust, because first, the withdrawal was not an abandonment
but strictly a strategic withdrawal, from one way of approach
in favour of another. Secondly, the relation of a remote Channel
Island to Central England was very different from that of
Zanzibar to Central Africa. Anyone who has followed Livingstone's own travels will know how closely the remotest parts
were connected with Zanzibar and the great Seyyid or Sultan

[1] W. G. Blaikie's *Life of Livingstone*, p. 270.

there, whose word ran very far from his island base. Again, every traveller in Central Africa for many years after the date of Bishop Tozer's withdrawal had to make Zanzibar his starting-point and base of supplies. Zanzibar in fact was the capital of Central Africa and by withdrawing there Tozer acted as a wise and far-seeing strategist. The remonstrances and entreaties of Livingstone, the loss of friends in England, did not shake the Bishop or the Mission ; but it must have acted as a sharp spur to Bishop Steere, Bishop Tozer's successor, and to such eager recruits as Johnson and Maples. In the light of such criticism as I have quoted it is easy to see how strong was the pull towards Nyasa, and how keen was Bishop Steere to make that new leap towards the Lake for which the Mission had been preparing and looking forward ever since the retirement in 1863.

Problem of the freed slaves    But there was another reason. Since the Mission had consolidated its base on the Island of Zanzibar it had undertaken the care of many of the slaves set free by British gunboats, and had as one part of its work a large settlement of these freed men, many of whom came from somewhere vague in the neighbourhood of Lake Nyasa. It seemed the obvious and simple thing to take a number of these back to the Lake in the hope that they would either find their homes and people, or form there a colony of freed slaves, at any rate amongst people more akin to them than the mixed multitude of Zanzibar. In practice it proved to be far from simple, but the hope of such repatriation was among the reasons justifying the expedition of 1876. The Bishop, Johnson and Beardall with their large party of carriers and freedmen were conveyed to Lindi, some 300 miles south of Zanzibar, on H.M.S. *Flying Fish*, by the kindness of Captain Cohen, who was engaged in the suppression of the slave trade on that coast. From that port, then an Arab port of no importance, except for the slave trade, the party of over 150 men journeyed inland for some fifteen days along the road that slave caravans from the interior followed. The pace of an expedition like this with a large body of people to be fed depends largely on the food supply. On this journey Johnson recalls that at one point they had to encamp for two days while Chuma sent his " hardy ruffians " of Zanzibari porters to search the countryside for food. Even when a good price is offered, food cannot always be got if the holders of it see no immediate prospect of renewing their own supplies, and this is more often the case in Central

1876

Africa than one likes to remember. Altogether this expedition,
taken in the end of the year when old food was running out,
and the new rains and their promise of new food were still in the
future, gave the eager recruit a new light on the real conditions
of missionary work. It made a difference that at this early stage
any expedition, whether missionary or other, had to depend on
the hired labour of heathen or Muhammadan people of not the
ideal type. Johnson, in his *Reminiscences*, speaks of the shock
to his sensibilities when it became necessary to give a formal
beating to one of these Zanzibaris who had been convicted of
stealing from the stores which were being taken up for the purpose of bartering for food. The enthusiast from Oxford was
beginning to come in contact with the realities of African travel,
and to realize the difference between dream and fulfilment.
Looking back, he admitted the inevitableness of this contrast,
and, whatever it held of disillusionment for him, it never
embittered him or made him swerve from his aim. The Bishop
made a stay at Masasi, a fertile district where the food supply Founding of
was fairly safe and where water was handy. He had possibly Masasi
noted this spot on his earlier visit to Mwembe, a long way
farther on, for Masasi was a well-known halt on the road to the
interior. Beardall was sent on soon after their arrival at this
temporary stopping-place to Mwembe, 200 miles west by south
of Masasi, and he came back from there with lurid accounts of
the burning alive of men at Mwembe on various charges such as
witchcraft and intrigues with the chief's wives. There was also
disturbing news of raids and tribal wars in the country more
immediately between Masasi and the Lake. All these things
made the party glad to stay at Masasi and make a station there
as at least a first outpost on the road to the Lake. The Bishop
stayed till the end of the year and left Johnson and Beardall to
carry on. He had himself already made some necessary buildings for a beginning, and had laid out the plans of the first
Masasi, for the raiders some years later reached this site and
destroyed it, and the Mission was restarted on a new site. It
was during these days at Masasi that Johnson began to suffer
from terrible ulcers, one of the common ways in which malaria
manifests itself, and from a curious sensitiveness which makes
its victim feel sure that he hears long conversations between
supposed enemies plotting against himself or others.

He told the Bishop of these supposed plots and talked boldly Supposed plots to Chuma, one of the supposed plotters, about the matter, and in general took it with great seriousness at the time, though he was aware that his knowledge of the languages in which the talking took place was very slight. One may be permitted to parallel this with the wonderful experience (in fiction) of the young man in Buchan's *Prester John*, with this difference, that Buchan's young man, emanating from the author's fertile brain, lived through and took a great part in the plots which he had gathered from the whispers of the countryside, whispers which no one else could hear but which he could pick up and understand after a month or two in the country. Buchan's young man provides the reader with a jolly good thriller, but Johnson, on cool reflection, dismisses his discoveries as hallucinations. Anyway, they did not disturb him in his efforts to get as nearly as possible into real understanding of the people he had come to serve. When the Bishop returned to Zanzibar, he left Johnson and Beardall at Masasi, with Johnson, still only a deacon, in charge as " spiritual head of the Nyasa Expedition." We see that still the Bishop calls it the Nyasa expedition, though it might be some time before a further step in the direction of the Lake was taken.

In August 1877 Maples and Joseph Williams (that Williams who was drowned with Maples in Lake Nyasa in 1895) arrived at Masasi and Maples took charge. After a few months of happy work together Johnson had to go back to Zanzibar for medical treatment. He had to be taken down to the coast lying on a native bedstead because he was not strong enough to walk. It has sometimes been asserted that Johnson never consented to be carried, as lesser beings have had to be, in a *machila*, the common hammock conveyance in the tropics. This is, of course, untrue, but it is quite true that he never submitted to this unless it was absolutely necessary, and his ideas of what constituted necessity were different from those of softer men. From Lindi he went to Zanzibar in a dhow (an Arab sailing-boat, such as was used in the slave trade) and the trip which the skipper hoped to accomplish in five days took eighteen. As Johnson had provided food for five days he had some experience of hunger before the trip ended. He found, characteristically, ways of whiling away the time. He says (*Reminiscences*, p. 31) :

" Our daily routine was varied by the necessity of filling up the water-box by fetching water from the shore, and I started an entomological collection, securing some twenty-seven specimens of 1877 water insects and vermin on the dhow. As on other occasions in African trouble, the prophet Isaiah's description of dreaming that one was eating and waking up with nothing to eat, came home to me with a new sense of his power. I used to have visions of ice-machines and other foolish fancies."

They were stopped and overhauled by a British man-of-war's boat one day under the suspicion of carrying slaves, and the ship's doctor, who was in charge of the boat, told them that the morrow was Christmas Day, and sent Johnson a bottle of port, which was unfortunately smashed to atoms before they opened it. At last they reached Zanzibar, and the Mission quarters at Mkunazini, simple enough in all conscience, seemed like Heaven to this worn traveller.

It is difficult for us, who have only known W. P. J. as, even in old age, a man of marvellous strength and proved toughness, to realize that at 23 years of age he struck observers as delicate. One fellow passenger, a doctor, of Indian experience, with whom he travelled as far as Aden on his first journey out, assured him cheerfully that he could not possibly live long in the wearing heat of Central Africa. It is probable that he wasn't as discreet as an African traveller should be, and, moreover, the science of keeping well in the tropics was not nearly as far advanced as in later days, hence these ulcers that plagued Johnson at Masasi and many times afterwards.

He was kept some time at Zanzibar, for ulcers are slow to heal when the blood is vitiated by malaria, and he was put in charge of Mbweni, the settlement of freedmen from which the Masasi settlers had been drawn. It was at Mbweni that he earned the nickname of " the man that never sits down," a name which those of us who only knew him some twenty years later never heard save as a legend handed down among the members of the Mission.

Before Johnson returned to Masasi in 1879, he was ordained 1878 Ordained priest priest (September 21, 1878) and had a spell of work on the mainland at Magila, where the Rev. J. P. Farler had laid good foundations. This last experience was useful to him as being his first work among free men and not simply freedmen. At Masasi and later, on the Lake, and in Yaoland, apart from the care of the Mbweni settlement at Masasi, his work outside as it extended

c

1878

would be almost wholly among free-born men, and it was in such work that the main hopes of the Mission lay.

1879
Return to
Masasi

Johnson was sent back to Masasi in May 1879 to take charge while Maples was on furlough, and he was conveyed with his party as far as Lindi, on this occasion in one of the steamboats of the Sultan of Zanzibar, which was being sent by the Sultan to the Ruvuma to enquire into a rumour of workable coal said to be obtainable there. The Sultan's brother was also on the

Charlie Nasibu

steamer, and among the Mission party was one man, Charlie Nasibu, who went later with Johnson to the Lake and was for many years well known to everyone who had anything to do with Likoma, as the Mission's invaluable " steward " and store buyer. I have vivid recollections of Charlie's coming in the evening to report his very mixed morning's purchases of eggs, milk, vegetables, mats and suchlike, all paid for in such currency as spoons of salt or beads and lengths of cloth. One was amazed at the way in which he carried the complicated details of these numerous transactions in his head, for he couldn't write nor, I think, read. His sterling honesty and ability were invaluable to a harassed priest-in-charge.

On this occasion, too, Johnson took up a party of the Mbweni freedmen to join the Masasi settlers or go farther as should be possible, and at that time or shortly after, John Swedi, the earliest of the African deacons in the Mission, joined them at

1880
Return of
Maples to
Masasi

Masasi and was very useful. Maples returned from his furlough in England in the course of 1880, and thus set Johnson free for his first adventure towards Nyasa. We must summarise the story of this first considerable expedition, referring readers for fuller details to Johnson's own account, *My African Reminiscences 1875-1895*.

W. P. J. sets out
for Mwembe

Barnaba
Nakaam

Johnson left Masasi in September 1880, taking with him only five or six men and two young teachers. Barnaba Nakaam, a headman of some importance in the Masasi neighbourhood, went with him as guide and " *capitao*," i.e. overseer of the porters, etc., and general purveyor of supplies. His experience and influence among the not too friendly tribes was invaluable to the solitary white man.

We have to realize what such an expedition meant in those days. We are too apt to assume that a certain almost magical prestige attaches to the white man as such, and that he goes protected amid the most savage tribes by their clear knowledge

of the might of civilization. Actually this is a fable. The people 1880
of the interior of Africa, among whom David Livingstone earlier
and W. P. Johnson in the 'eighties moved without any show of
force, knew little more of any power behind them than the wild
beasts did. A man, whether white or black or brown, was estimated by the strength and importance of his visible and present
connections ; and accordingly the presence in Johnson's expedition of a known man, owner of a name and rank among
kindred tribes, gave him more help and security in his travels
than any notions of a white race out of sight could give him.
No doubt the calm fearlessness of the white man, alone amongst
warlike people of so different a race, would count for much ;
even a dog distinguishes between those who fear him and those
who do not ; and I suppose Johnson was as fearless as any explorer that Africa has ever known. It must be difficult even for
an infuriated savage to kill a man who obviously doesn't expect him to do anything of the sort.

Again, in the later degenerate days of easy security (with perhaps a dash of anxiety about wild beasts) we travelled in great
comfort the short definite journeys between known and friendly
villages ; and, if the villages of our destinations were too far, a
tent or two, a gang of cheerful porters, carrying even through
the wilderness the necessary apparatus of civilization, took
away every appearance of hardness from the traveller's life.
It was not in such conditions as these that Johnson travelled to
and fro over the largely unknown lands lying between Nyasa
and the Indian Ocean. Even the humble " push-bike " was
unknown—I remember the first appearance of a bicycle at
Likoma in 1902 or 1903 and the excitement it caused—and the
only beast of burden was Shanks's pony, where now bicycles,
motor bicycles, motor cars and lorries and even aeroplanes are
fairly familiar objects.

When Johnson with his small party set out from Masasi—
itself an outpost—they were venturing into a relatively unknown land, in great uncertainty as to their reception along the
path, and at the mercy of sudden tribal wars or forays over
which they had no sort of control. Nakaam, the *capitao*, seems
to have had his own gun, but no one else had one. For food, instead of the well-supplied caravans of later years, they carried
only bare necessities and the minimum of the indispensable
barter goods, such as salt, beads and cloth, without which it

1880

would be difficult to buy for men or master such food as the country was able or willing to supply. I don't think Johnson ever carried a tent on his own expeditions before 1918—it means three extra porters, three extra hands to pay and mouths to feed—but that was no great hardship. If they camped at a village the local chief or headman would put a house at the disposal of the traveller and very likely bring gifts of food. If the camp was in the bush country through which the path led, then a halt would be made near enough to a water supply ; porters and attendants would quickly make a clearing, put up necessary grass shelters, surround the little camp with a hedge of boughs, as thorny as possible for the better discouragement of wild beasts, and gather logs of wood to keep fires burning through the night both for warmth and protection. This would be the daily routine with an experienced traveller like Johnson. I remember well his upbraiding a younger traveller, many years later, whose raw inexperience of the ever-present danger of wild beasts made him what W. P. J. described as " foolhardy."

Slave caravans

In 1880 on the road to Mwembe there was the likelihood of meeting slave caravans. In a letter to Bishop Steere, written from Masasi in December 1881 on his return from Mwembe and the Lake, Johnson said : " I met two caravans of slaves as I returned up the Lujenda, I came down from Mwembe with a third, passed a fourth on the way, and a fifth passes here to-day, who have come by the road by which we hope to go to Ngoi."[1] Johnson, like David Livingstone before him, had to live and travel among the slave-trading Arabs and Yao raiders, and even on occasion to accept the escort of a slave caravan, without being able to do anything beyond example and occasional gentle words of remonstrance to individuals. There was no room for Exeter Hall in the heart of Africa.

W. P. J. at Mwembe

At Mwembe, the capital town and residence of Mataka, the most important chief of Central Yaoland, Johnson settled and lived for nearly a year. Mataka gave him a hut to live in in one of the " suburbs " of Mwembe and a second hut in Nakawali, his " country seat." He gave him a boy to wait on him and showed himself quite friendly. It may be that he saw some gain for himself from having a white man under his wing. Johnson started a school to which Mataka sent his nephew and other boys, and in the course of his first stay there he admitted nine male

First catechumens, 1881

[1] See also letter p. 41.

catechumens, giving them crosses, as is the Mission custom, but these were cut by Johnson's own hand out of the top of an old biscuit tin—which is not quite the custom.

He made one long circular journey in the direction of the south end of the Lake with Barnaba Nakaam, returning up the Lujenda River, with a view to preaching possibilities and making notes of what he saw as to the direction of the rivers and the general lie of this uncharted land.

Scarcity of food was one of the troubles of this time at Mataka's ; not merely the shortage of imported provisions— that wouldn't have troubled Johnson much—but actual famine in the land that made it impossible to buy food even when the barter goods were renewed from Masasi. This famine was a very sore thing to live in, without any power of relieving the sufferers by any but the most trifling gifts. Johnson did what he could and literally shared in the hunger. Barnaba Nakaam was sent back to Masasi to get new supplies of barter goods, etc., and returned with these and a donkey—which proved useless— some few books and letters, including one from Bishop Steere. It may seem strange that people in a not unfertile land should be short of such food as the labours of their hands could produce. It is to be remembered that tribal wars and raidings for slaves can interfere very seriously with hoeing and all the year's round of field work. Moreover, in a peaceful year, the slightest failure of the crops on account of poor rains or too heavy rains makes it quite likely that the harvest will not keep people in food till the next harvest comes in. Why not store food from the fat years to carry over the lean years ? It is impossible to store food satisfactorily even for a year in these lands where damp, weevils, termites (white ants) and other pests find their way to the best-guarded store.

Nakaam was sent on a still more adventurous trip in search of food later in the year. He went 200 miles from Mwembe to the south of Lake Nyasa and round the end and up the west side some seventy miles more to the headquarters of Dr. Laws of the Scotch Mission of Livingstonia ; the station was then near the south end of the Lake and not, as now, near the northern end. He even went a good distance farther to the south-west from Livingstonia to an Angoni chief, who sold him some oxen and sheep. With these, and the supplies that Dr. Laws's credit had enabled him to buy, he returned to Mwembe, passing all along

1881

the way through a country inhabited by one robber chief after another. His pluck and influence are shown by this very great performance.

Thieves

Even in Johnson's mission station under the very wing of Mataka there was at one time suspicion of thieving by night, and Johnson tells how he watched one night by his open back door till a face appeared silhouetted dead black against the moon. He struck out and the intruder disappeared. Next morning one of the missionary's most forward pupils appeared

Ulcers

at class with a swollen eye. More serious still was an awful visitation of ulcers, due to the famine, the flies, and bad drinking-water. Before Barnaba Nakaam got back from Dr. Laws, Johnson had " used up all his available surplices and shirts " for bandages and, moreover, had got his own hands infected so that they got very bad indeed, and he had to flee himself to

1881
W. P. J.'s first
visit to Dr.
Laws

Dr. Laws to have medical treatment. On the way down he had his first sight of the Lake, but, he says, " I was too intent on the attitude of the natives and my own hands to feel enthusiastic." He spent a month with Dr. Laws and experienced the " wonderful hospitality " of the doctor and his wife, not

and in 1927 his
last

for the last time. Some forty-seven years later at the new Livingstonia which is the standing monument to the zeal and energy of Dr. Laws, these two " grand old men " of the Lake met again for a fortnight of happy and understanding intercourse only a year before W. P. J. died. Of this first visit he says, " Could Dr. Samuel Johnson have visited there he would certainly have lost all his prejudice against the Scotch." He was not at that time himself Dr. Johnson, but only a ragged, hungry wolf of a missionary. Dr. Laws said that if he had come much later his fingers would have been permanently crippled.

He got back to Mwembe gloriously refreshed by this trip and by the healing of his hands, but almost at once a slight coolness began to arise between him and Mataka. Mataka had up to this time been quite friendly and helpful and Johnson had had considerable influence with him. For example, a letter came to Mataka from Abdallah bin Amri, the principal Arab trader of Lindi, bidding him get rid of his *Mzungu* (white man) in the interests of the slave trade. Mataka disregarded this letter and remained on friendly terms with his white man. Even after the coolness had begun he backed Johnson up in building a log church, and his support meant a great deal for, in those days, a chief, especially a great chief like Mataka, counted for a very great deal with all his people. Mataka's frowns would have hindered all the work of the missionary seriously.

All this happy prospect was upset when a caravan that had set out from Mataka's some months before returned with the news that on the coast they had been interfered with by one of the British men-of-war and had, in fact, driven a small party of the white sailors off. The actual happening was that Captain Foote of H.M.S. *Ruby* had had the idea of sending a landing party to release the slaves of this large caravan on shore instead of keeping to his proper element and intercepting them in the sea passage. He had no idea of the size of the party and fondly supposed that the slaves would be eager to be released and would reinforce his efforts. The slaves, filled with stories of the white men eating those whom they released, instead of helping, fled from their would-be protectors into the bush, only to join the caravan again when the greater danger was past. Captain Foote, meanwhile, had to draw off his little party and get back to his ship, and the effect of this affair was seen in the changed attitude of Mataka when his people got back from the coast. He was now convinced that those were wise who had told him that the white man was a spy in their midst and would let the warship know of the movements of that particular caravan. The feelings, which were acute on the first return of the caravan, seemed to die down, and Johnson thought that the cause of peace and good understanding would be best served if he went off for a while on a projected preaching tour, and he got Mataka's approval of his plan. He stayed away ten days or, he says, " it may have been a month," and when he came back he found that his sheep and oxen had been taken by Mataka, his church and other buildings destroyed, his little hut at Mwembe itself sacked and burnt, and that there was nothing left to him but what he had taken with him on his preaching tour. Friendly messengers with most of these tidings had met him a little before he got back, presumably to give him a chance of avoiding the lion's mouth. Immediately on hearing the news, he pressed on at his own rapid pace, leaving his more feeble porters and companions to follow at theirs, and went straight to Nakawali, where the chief was. He could not get to see him for a day or two and had to keep inside his hut for most of that time because an initiation dance was going on and Mataka and a great many

Mataka cools

His caravan attacked by British

W. P. J.'s buildings burnt

1881

of his people were too drunk to attend to his business. When his few porters reached Nakawali's with his loads, they were at once set on under his eyes as they came down the last slope into the village, and the baskets they carried were thrown down and the contents, including Johnson's letters of Orders,[1] were

and himself driven away

scattered here and there. After some days of waiting, Johnson saw Mataka and arranged with him that he should join a small caravan going to the coast under the care of a headman whom he knew well. It was clear that no more could be done at present at Mwembe and, in fact, no settlement of a missionary at that particular capital has ever been made since that day. (Another town of the Yaos was chosen for the next experiment in Central Yaoland, when Dr. Hine in 1893 started work at Unangu. When Dr. Hine became Bishop of Likoma, this station was carried on for years by the first native priest in Nyasaland, the Rev. Yohana Abdallah, stepson of that Barnaba Nakaam

His return to Masasi

who served Johnson so well.) On his way home with the caravan from Mataka's, the food for his own little section of the troop being mainly a large bag of red beans that he was able to buy with Mataka's last gift to him of twenty fathoms of cloth, he carried with him a lame slave boy whom he had befriended at Mataka's and two more broken-down men, so feeble that they " were not up to carrying anything, hardly themselves." The lame boy had to be carried in a rough hammock, and for a good deal of the way Johnson took his share of this load. As he would say, the boy had to be got along somehow, so what else was there to do ?

At this point it is right to notice that this and other experiences of the slave trade gave Johnson a right to speak as one who knew things at first hand and when we consider his views and feelings about slaves this must be borne in mind.

When the caravan reached the villages on the Ruvuma River the supply of beans was already giving out, so Johnson, knowing himself to be the most physically fit of his party, decided to push on alone, leaving the caravan and his few men to come on at a more ordinary pace. The first day, after walking hard all day, he was " entertained with porridge in the evening, in a native hut, by a total stranger." Next day he heard on the road

W. P. J. meets Janson

that a white man was coming to meet him, and soon after came

---

[1] The letters of Orders were found later by Bishop Hine in a locker on the *Charles Janson*.

upon Charles Janson, camping by a small stream. It was the 1881 greatest possible joy to Johnson to meet one of his own friends after his long exile in the wilds. But Janson was not at all well, and the next day, borrowing two men from his friend, Johnson set off again faster than ever and did about sixty miles in the day, arriving at Masasi in the evening to find Maples and his friends and " something like home." There followed a short stay at Masasi and then he went down, travelling light again, to the coast at Lindi for Zanzibar, where he would report to Reaches Zanzibar Bishop Steere.

Here it is appropriate to set a letter he wrote from Masasi to Bishop Steere while the incidents of the trek were fresh in his mind.

MY DEAR BISHOP,

I sat down to this when I had read your letter in the May number Nov. 1881 of *Mission Life*, it seemed to open up such a field. I could have wished it had been longer. Perhaps what I wished to see discussed was of too particular a nature for a general paper on Mission lines.

My mind is, of course, just now very full of the slave—and anti-slave—interest ; anything akin to desire for vengeance does not come in. So little am I tempted that way that I may not have guarded against such a construction sufficiently in my last to you. It is for Mataka's sake, I wish him to see the true state of the case.

As it is this country swarms with slave caravans[1] conducted Slave caravans more or less by coast agents, with little wanton cruelty, and little of the bitter feeling on the slave's part one is apt to associate with it. "*Ndoa*," i.e. using charms to cause death, and cases of grievous wrong determined by ordeal, witchcraft of any kind, helped to some extent by raids, and more by the war captures of the Maviti beyond Mponda's with a proportion of discarded women furnish the material. The whole map of bad life goes on without fearful brutality or the least chance of a slave rising.

I met two caravans of slaves coming down as I returned up the Lujenda, I came down from Mwembe with a third, passed a fourth on the way and a fifth passes here to-day, who have come by the road by which we hope to go to Ngoi.[2]

---

[1] Some measure of the havoc wrought by the slave trade in Nyasa may be gained from the following quotation from W. G. Blaikie's *Life of Livingstone* : " Dr. Livingstone was informed by Col. Rigby, late British Consul at Zanzibar, that 19,000 slaves from this Nyasa region alone passed annually through the Custom House there. This was besides those landed at Portuguese slave ports. In addition to those captured, thousands were killed or died of their wounds or of famine, or perished in other ways, so that not one-fifth of the victims became slaves—in the Nyasa district probably not one-tenth."

[2] Probably Ngofi on the Lake.

All the men engaged in the trade directly or indirectly, all the wealthy and business men connected with it object more or less strongly, not to the European himself, but to his settling where he knows all about it, and they will continually strive to induce any chief who has welcomed him to drive him away. They all continually make representations founded more or less upon facts, so that they act as a continual dropping ; they do not try open opposition at first, they say, " No one resists these ' *Wazungu*,' for they will pay ; they pay the Seyyid lakhs of rupees, and so they live beside him, and we cannot take slaves under the guns of their men-of-war, but all the coast wants slaves, the Seyyid included, if they can blind these Europeans." Then presents of ivory pass and some slaves are returned and the Missionary must give very freely, if he is to seem as profitable as his rival. If something could be done by the Governor of Kilwa, i.e. clearly by the Seyyid, to one of Mataka's caravans as infringing the proclamation against importing slaves, it might seem that there was no profit in getting rid of Europeans, and that the coast people themselves are not in favour of the traffic, though those actually engaged in the trade are.

Mataka's "mind" on slavery

Mataka has so little of a mind of his own in the matter that a very little, I think, would make him discountenance slavery ; he resisted Abdallah bin Amri's letter against me, but this attack on his caravan, as he hears of it, just confirms the coast way of putting things. There was no sign of the Seyyid's co-operation.

Slave routes

I have heard from many that Mponda (who holds the east of the Shiré from the Lake) does not personally buy many slaves but he does a wide business in ivory, yet a vast number of slaves cross the Shiré on his ground ; others cross the Lake at Kota Kota, or at Makanjila's and they pass by the line of the Lujenda or by Mwembe to the Ruvuma, some branching off to Kilwa, others to Machemba's (a very lawless chief near Lindi), or from the Lujenda by Mtalika's to Chisanga close to Ibo. Between us Maples and I seem to have observed one large caravan all the way from the Nyasa to Chisanga, in Portuguese territory.

Advantages of Masasi as Mission centre

Coming again to Masasi after traversing in all directions the country between it and Nyasa and round to the south, I thank God that you were led to settle there ; its productiveness is known everywhere, not only contrasted with towns such as Mwembe or Kisiunguli, but with the banks of the Lujenda and Ruvuma and the shores of Nyasa. All the way down from Mwembe, from Livingstonia to Mwembe there was little water and less food, while on our last morning march into Masasi we passed five capital wateringplaces, and all the fowls and food needed by the settlement are brought to it, when elsewhere the neighbourhood has to be scoured for anything that can be got at any price. In so many parts the clearings have to be shifted every year, here at Masasi, at the end of 1881 years, here only, if here, can we hope to do without migrating in the native fashion. The population round, though very scattered, is as large as in any part of this country outside the three big towns, e.g. Mwembe, Kisiunguli (Makanjila's) and Mtalika's, while to work the Mwera, Machemba's, etc., and for all Lake work an independent station, one or more was thought by you, and still seems, absolutely necessary. By a happy combination of tribes we are welcomed by the dominant people, yet so as to be able to defend ourselves, and the road for all in advance ; our presence is so valued that many of the youth round hear the truth without continual check from their masters' pleasure. This check is a necessary feature of all work with the big chiefs. The Masasi people, with all their faults, are really a light in the land ; when they came to Mwembe and everywhere on the route they left a good impression, and the fact of its existence, and its good report, is the one good fact known in our favour until you get near Livingstonia. A fair number of people of Masasi have now paid visits to Mwembe, and all conversed with the four Livingstonia people that came down here, yet there have been no traces of wishing to push on to Nyasa partly because they value the place so much and all its advantages, partly because the shores of the Lake would not be their exact home and hardly two come from the same place, while the Maviti bar their old homes if they wished to go there. All the caravans agree that when they get near Masasi all their " *wajinga* " think this must be the coast.

*Good repute of the freedmen at Masasi*

I am delighted to see how firm a hold Maples obviously has on the people. The willing obedience is itself a wonder, and a lesson amidst such loose governments. While I am here, as I trust on but a flying visit, I think it must be right to express a hope, which I find Messrs. Maples, Janson and Porter feel as strongly as I do and which formerly Clarke and Goldfinch shared. Could but you see with your own eyes the tree you planted not so long ago, I am sure you would see its strength of religious influence and the importance of its independence in all internal matters while the owners of the land so thoroughly value its presence on this very condition, that the Nyasas obey the European. I see myself, and Maples authorises me to say, how much Episcopal work there is for your Lordship, and you will find a stone church to consecrate, a worthy thing to follow the house which you left us and we still use, and worthy the fine fellows who come to worship in it.

Yours sincerely and obediently,

W. P. JOHNSON.

Maples, in a letter home, said of this expedition and of Johnson's unexpected return :

" It is such a real treat to see Johnson again, and hold converse together as in old days. For months together at Mwembe he was sorely pressed by famine, with only one meal a day, and for many weeks that meal consisted only of leaves and herbs and grasses—not even pumpkins. Many people died of starvation there, and many shocking deeds were perpetrated. If ever missionary endured hardships in modern times that missionary is my friend Will Johnson. He tells us the tale in his own simple, unadorned manner, but it is thrilling enough, however told. He tells of his sitting down eating whatever there was, and then looking hungrily at the empty plate, and waiting till next day to waylay the women coming in from the fields with the herbs and leaves. The very skins of the last goats he killed were gnawed and eaten by poor skeletons who came by night to steal what they could for food. God has preserved Johnson's health in a wonderful way, though his poor ulcered hands were in such a state when he arrived at Livingstonia that Dr. Laws told him had he arrived a few weeks later he could not have answered for his life."

In another letter of the same mail, he says : " Johnson is the real hero of the lot of us, and of this there can be no shadow of doubt." Writing in December, he says :

" I assure you the fame of his " (Johnson's) " wonderful courage and bravery, and moral earnestness in all his privations and dangers, had struck deeply into the mind of, one might almost say, the whole Yao tribe. The country-side rings with the tale of the wonderful ' *Mzungu* ' (European) who endured so much so dauntlessly. For my part, I feel that the whole affair " (i.e. the expulsion from Mwembe) " will prove eventually to have done wonders for the work."

This is the sort of thing that his friends said about his exploit ; to himself, it just came in the day's work and was not a bit wonderful. In his *Reminiscences* he recalls how, when he got to Zanzibar and made his report of his escape from Mwembe to the Bishop at work on his cathedral, the Bishop said, with a twinkle, " You should send an account of it to the *Field*," and then it " flashed upon him " that much of his talk had been of covering distances in quick time. In his own estimation there was great room for thanksgiving to God for having enabled him to endure, and for bringing him through a tough time, but he saw no ground for boasting of sufferings which could not be avoided. Some people seem to love adventure and danger for their own sake, but that was not Johnson's way. Anything he endured was solely in the interests of the Master he served, and

he never thought he could do or suffer too much, so long as
his end was forwarded. Neither then nor at any later time did
he pretend to be indifferent to comforts, or even to luxuries,
but he could never see why he should have them while his
friends and neighbours went without and suffered much more
with grim patience and no sort of a halo thrown to them.

On the evening when he met Janson before his arrival at
Masasi Janson was on the way to join him at Mataka's, and they
had much talk before they slept of plans for the future. Johnson found Janson every whit as keen as himself on pressing on to
the Lake now that the Mataka settlement was out of the question. It was a great refreshment to Johnson to find an older
man so ready to join him in further adventure in the great
cause, and he was delighted to find the Bishop very ready that
the two should go off together as soon as they could make the
necessary preparations. This Johnson did without delay in
Zanzibar, and got letters from the British Consul there, Colonel
Euan Smith, to send to Mataka. Johnson spent Christmas at
Masasi with his friends and got away as soon as possible. The
party this time consisted of himself and Janson, one half-
trained teacher, two married couples from Masasi who were to
settle on the Lake, and thirty Masasi men, mostly Christians,
who were to act as porters and to return to Masasi when they
had settled the party on the Lake. The route chosen was farther
to the north than the track that led direct to Mataka's, and the
party went a good deal farther up the Ruvuma, i.e. as nearly
west as the paths allowed. Johnson had hopes of going on in
the same westerly line till they reached the Lake, but the stories
of raiding parties of Magwangwara made them decide to turn
south at the village of a chief named Mponda and make for the
hill of Unangu, following the direction of the Luchulingo
Valley.

They had some donkeys with them and one of these was
carried away as they crossed the Msinji river on a bamboo bridge
of such a sort that it is almost inconceivable that a donkey
could ever be got to face it. The other donkeys which did get
across must surely have found some other way than a bamboo
bridge. The donkey boy who fell from the bridge along with the
donkey was happily saved. Another accident which involved
the death of a boy occurred when they were crossing the Ruvuma and is recorded in the letters now following, which are

Johnson's report to Bishop Steere and have never before been published.

The iron strength of Johnson himself is brought out in the contrast with his equally keen and devoted friend, whose physical strength, alas! was not equal to the tasks his will laid on him. The memoir of Bishop Steere by the Rev. R. M. Heanley makes no mention of this report and it may have been too late for the Bishop to receive it, though it was written on February 21, and the Bishop died in August of that year. The death of Janson probably delayed the settlement of the others on the Lake side, and it may have been necessary to keep the men who were due to return to Zanzibar for some time longer than the dates of the letters. One may hope that the Bishop was spared the pain that such an apparently fatal blow to this second attempt on the Lake would have caused him.

Appended to the report are two other letters written during Johnson's solitary years on the shores of Lake Nyasa after Janson's death.

1. *Pachia, February* 18, 1882—*W. P. J. to Bishop Steere.*

MY DEAR BISHOP,

I fear the men will make rather a demand on the funds, they will hardly get back to Zanzibar under five months at least ; however, I hope there will not be much unnecessary delay here. I am feeling the news I have to give you that Janson has had a very severe attack here with nearly all the symptoms of cholera ; I wondered to see him get along from the first, so evidently oppressed and sickened by some of the work, he was always up to the point again, and ready to push on—however, I fear the strain the last part of the time has put on his stomach was too great. Maples had warned me as to many of his distressing symptoms, but this attack he considers himself more severe than any before. I am thankful that his age, etc., preclude my being called on to judge of his being able to do this or that. We were making for Chiteji's town, represented as three days (with loads) from here, when he was suddenly seized with fever, then immediate diarrhoea and vomiting totally uncontrollable, and now vomiting for four days, I cannot leave him for an hour. This casts a gloom over us, otherwise we have found everything more favourable to our plans than could have been expected. Much as I gathered at Mwembe, these Nyasas are only too glad for a European to settle amongst them, and this natural disposition makes it much less of a strain on one's patience to live amongst them than in a Yao town ; then, though friendly in every way, they seem quite to understand that a sick man will be annoyed by staring. It might seem want of spirit, yet apparently here alone of this part of the country a deter-mined opposition is made to the Magwangwara, and numerous head-dresses and shields of the latter attest their prowess ; none carry guns ordinarily, but they tell me they have some kept by public authority with all the gunpowder they can get for time of war. The people here speak Chinyanja, the same as is spoken at Living-stonia, and as most of the Masasi Nyasas speak. At Masanje's there are at least 700 houses, here not so many, while two or three other places before Chiteji's are said to be about as large, and Chiteji's much larger ; by land it is said to be three days from here with loads, by canoe only one day. So we have plenty of harvest field open, if we can get a good site and a well-manned canoe; perhaps, the latter would be after all our best way of getting about. Masanje was very eager we should stop with him, and food was very plentiful, fowls, eggs, ducks, goats, fish, but few oxen ; to help us he lied most firmly ; he made a great point of the different tongue at Chiteji's, i.e. the same as Chitonga that I understood Dr. Laws to say he was learning ; it now seems that this is only spoken on beyond him.[1]

The places we have hitherto passed on the shores of the Lake are little fitted for European residence, a flooded river behind and Nyasa in front ; the people are fairly cleanly, i.e. it is much better than some Eastern towns, yet, of course, sanitation is a desideratum. Chiteji's is said not to have water immediately behind, all say there are plenty of oxen there, goats, etc., mahogo [cassava], a fair lot of rice and Indian [? Kaffir] corn but hardly any maize, but there is plenty here if not nearer. However, I must not speculate more about Chiteji's till I can go there ; as Janson much needs milk, we hope some cows will be brought here in a few days. I hope forty couples can come up next time. Nobody (*pace* Chiteji) will be vexed as the strength we bring is the first thing to attract them. We passed plenty of stone that contained lime, or what the lime chewers [Lime is commonly added to tobacco by those who chew] took for lime, at a capital situation, perhaps one and a half days from Losefa and four from Masanje's, thorough up-and-down walking, it might be occupied some day. Yaoland seems much wider now with the Ruvuma people, then Unangu. The houses there are round the hill, and look like grey stones in the distance. We got to it by a long walk, part through a pelting rain and two rivers, so that it was inexpressibly depressing to get to deserted clearings, etc., and on, and on, not a house to be seen and the drear peak in front, till we (who were on

---

[1] Masanje's statement wasn't altogether a lie. His villages came more under the language influence of the Tonga of the west side of the Lake than under Masanje's, until steamers and missionaries made the intercourse north and south easier and more constant. Masanje is chief of Msumba.

ahead) began to suspect houses, and soon we could see, and then hear the hum of a town. One might take it as roughly triangular and I counted 500 houses on one side (1,500 in all). We were nobly housed in the chief's deserted house, and all were very kind. Then Chiwagulu, still more of an eagle's nest and a large place ; our legs were worked next morning to get up to the invalid chief's ; so far it was all Yao. It was just before Chiwagulu that we saw the Lake. You will see as to our route, we go fairly straight up the Ruvuma and beyond, but then should cut across to Chiteji's ; instead of this all make a detour near due south to Unangu for fear of the Magwangwara. Most people had heard of a *Mzungu* at Mwembe, those who understood what had been done seemed to think Mataka had made a mistake, perhaps as good a way of regarding it for us as any.

Unangu had been harried and Chiwagulu threatened by the depredators, the Magwangwara, these in turn are now being driven along by the Nyakanyaka and we ought to go to them. These Nyakanyaka as far as I can learn speak Chitonga or a kindred dialect.

As to the men, they have behaved very well, though at first there seemed positively no one man of influence among them—I have already informed you two ran away at Kilwa and one on the road to Masasi. Of course this running away was not to be dreaded from people who had been long with us ; the Nyasas seemed glad and proud to see Nyasa but fully aware of coast advantages. We had

one other loss. Mabruki, who had accompanied you in old times, was drowned in the Ruvuma at Mponda's. A cry was heard in the darkness as the river rushed by and over its black rocks, but the lamp could show little but darkness on the high steep banks, and one man clinging to a tree—his companion in a canoe was not with him ; we searched next morning but found no trace of the body.

You know what is due to the porters ; Selimu, I think, is perhaps the best, but several carried good loads and no word of grumbling or ill-feeling. Mabruki had been engaged nearly two months and we took charge of a half-dollar's worth of amerikano, and a half-dollar mat, if these items could be paid to his heirs.

I forgot to mention that we hear that canoes often cross at Chiteji's ; our guide, an Unangu man who joined on to our large party, was going to cross there. If we could get the road direct from Chiteji to the Ruvuma villages, one of them, Chipajola's, would make a good half-way house to Masasi, and one would be a great boon to the country. As yet I can hardly see what use a large vessel would be to us here even if we could man her. Canoes seem to pass and repass sufficiently to keep up intercourse on this side and even to cross at Chiteji's. There is no salt just here but that again is obtainable from places on the coast farther south.

I do hope as soon as possible some Mbweni couples will come to settle. I fear the unsettled state in which the men leave us will 1882 militate against this. However, I hear that some forty are only waiting for a settlement to come up if they might.

I hope to get some power in Nyasa [*Chinyanja*] these rains and to get about enough to preach and choose good site, also to get into touch with Livingstonia. I want to hear if possible the fate of the letters to Mataka's—Mwembe did not seem on friendly terms.

### 2. *Pachia, February* 21, 1882—*Shrove Tuesday.*

MY DEAR BISHOP,

Little did I think when I penned the few lines I send with this that so soon would our fears be realized. Dear Janson fell asleep about noon to-day after a terrible morning of suffering, yet, I thank God, victorious ; he seemed to cling to our Lord from within, though, I think, scarce able to hear a word of the Church Office when one could snatch a moment to supplicate. We arrived here last Monday [February 13] and, after taking quinine, he was seized with the old painful symptoms. We were both, however, more thankful for having got to a place where we could halt than fearful of the future ; towards night he seemed easier, and in the morning somewhat stronger. Our house was fortunately waterproof, as the rain rushes on us every day here ; Wednesday and Thursday promised recovery, though sickness ever and anon prostrated him. I begged him to take oil and laudanum, but he from former experience trusted to chalk and opium. On Thursday we had the lamp all night, but I still ventured to lie down ; alas! one too often takes a man at his own valuing, and in his wonderful fortitude he had walked through, and joked over, the pangs of continuous diarrhoea, through rain and rivers and long sitting in wet clothes waiting for porters behind, till I involuntarily supposed he must be cured with rest. Friday found him so terribly prostrate, and, as we sat listening for the first cock, it seemed torture to him, and from that time he could not be left a minute. I think it was Friday his vomiting began to show that he had not digested *anything* at all ; it was fearful, and the pain of bringing it up evidently telling, all the symptoms as in cholera. He found some relief from rubbing the stomach with oil and laudanum ; and beef tea, tea and tonic were ready at hand ; brandy, generally the tonic, always produced nausea, but he naturally fought to get strength. The floor of the house, mere sand, was in its way a boon. One Thursday he longed for air, and we thought of getting a house looking out on the sea, we feared the move, but Thursday morning found us under water ; a little barrier at the upper door had given away and the lane above drained in to us. Fancy him, poor fellow! We soon found ourselves in the house looking out on the Lake, and again it seemed a question which would give out first, his strength

Feb. 21, 1882<br>Death of<br>Charles Janson

D

or the undigested matter; continual vomiting led to hiccoughs, only relieved by continual rubbing with oil and laudanum, and a mustard plaister. Yet we were doubtful and hopeful, but this morning a new feature came on; from earliest dawn to 11 a.m. he insisted on being raised alternately and lying down; as often before we had hot-water bottles to his feet, and rubbed them; he had five or six paroxysms of a fearfully painful description. I tried everything I could think of, as he called out in his pain, yet throughout he seemed to be praying until it was drowned now and again by the paroxysms of the outer man; he took, about ten, some brandy and 25-30 drops of laudanum, with for a time no apparent result; then he grew violent in action, his lower jaw working spasmodically as he begged us to "move about" his legs, which since early morning, he said, were, as it were, paralysed. Ever and anon he uttered ejaculatory prayers, now and again wishing he might die, yet always adding as from the heart some qualifying petition; so we prayed together, and then so peacefully it was over; the men came in almost directly and hardly a voice struggled through the Lord's Prayer, and we felt we could indeed call on the Lord as over one who had conquered in much weakness. Without a word, and reverently, they did up the body and dug a grave, and so Janson and I are for the time parted, but I don't think God leaves gaps long in such work as this.

3. *Bandawe (opposite to Chiteji's Town), September 4, 1882—W. P. J. to Rev. E. S. L. Randolph.*

MY DEAR RANDOLPH,

You write so very kindly of me and our work, that I must try to give you a view of the work on Lake Nyasa.

After my great loss, in Janson's departure, I settled at Chiteji's; he like all the other Nyasa people has taken refuge behind reeds, marsh and fence, and his teacher's location is necessarily not a healthy one. However, I think that three Englishmen could with a sailing-vessel occupy his considerable village, and *visit* a large number of coast villages, and occupy a place with plenty of lime and slate, in the hills not far above Losefa; a first-rate place (only two days overland from Chiteji's). All who know the Lake say that there is no place close to the shore that is really healthy, yet there is a large population.

Strange to say, I have not heard from Zanzibar or England for seven months, so I have not the vaguest idea if my continual appeals for help have had any response.

The Livingstonia people, Dr. Laws and his wife, are now my kind hosts, they have pressed me to visit them as I did last year, and after my return from the Magwangwara I needed a change.

They have parted with their steamer, *Ilala*, to the Glasgow trading company under certain restrictions, and another steamer is coming out, to be carried overland to Lake Tanganyika for, I think, the London Missionary Society. Those men are busy laying down the road from Nyasa to Tanganyika. Surely we can have a sailing-boat. Here everybody recommends the new steel boat. I really hope the Glasgow company will at last supply me regularly with most things required, and with a bi-monthly mail [*i.e. two-monthly*], such as the Scotch Mission get with fair regularity.

As the arrival of their steamer last week was the first I had heard of them since I gave their agent an order for cloth, etc., in January, and now but few of the things ordered have come, I have room to hope for better things.

I must refer again to the proposed Mission Station in the hills. Plan for a We could with the lime that works easily and the stone that breaks proposed easily too, build a station that would laugh at the Magwangwara, hill-station and be a secure spot in the country, and we could get a road down to the Lake one and a half days' distance, just between two Yao towns of 4,000 and 5,000 each. It would itself serve as a missionary station, a sanatorium, and I have reason to believe there is good soil for growing crops. Janson was quite fascinated with the neighbourhood. Single-handed, I do not like to leave Chiteji's without a teacher, and indeed to carry out the plan effectually we need a vessel to work the Nyasa villages, as well as the upper country. Lime everywhere else is scarce.

Yours very sincerely and obliged,

WILL JOHNSON.

4. *To the Rev. W. H. Penney, Secretary of the Home Committee, for the new Bishop—St. John the Evangelist's Day, 1882.*

DEAR MR. PENNEY, Dec. 27, 1882
Thank God, I have no precedent to teach me to whom I should write at this time. I know not if another Father[1] has in God's will been appointed over us or even if it be so, whom to address. I trust then this may be placed in his hands as a report from his obedient son in Christ.

A visit of the Livingstonia steamer on her return voyage gives me opportunity to write at the above date. Mr. Moir promises this or next month to give us full particulars of freight charges, etc. Personally, I had wished for a visit to England *if* the work here could be maintained. Yet I have ordered again and again a large supply of things such as would be necessary at a large station, taking for granted that our Mission hopes to plant such. For such there is a great opening on this east side of the Lake. Things here though not Great opening rose-coloured yet do give hopes ; the population is very large, the on east side of Lake

---

[1] Bishop Smythies.

1882

Need of
sailing-boat

and a hill-
station

How to reach
the Angoni

chief a sensible though worldly man ; the Lake shore offers other large villages, which one European could easily and *healthily* systematically visit ; for this purpose a boat such as I described in a note to Mr. Heanley would, if approved by your Lordship, be *admirably suited, especially if a mariner of steady character were engaged to sail her, train a crew and guard her.* An upland station would be useful in the fertile country above Losefa (say one and a half days from the Lake shore), we should want a European to settle there, he could tour among the big Yao towns, while a fourth European clergyman, if we could get him, could relieve the sailing missionary as well as the up-country missionaries and would also be able to relieve the missionary in charge at Losefa and thus prevent too much strain on the staff. A Kaffir catechist would probably soon be able to open communication with the Angoni. Bishop Steere speaks of having applied to some South African Bishop for a volunteer for this work. Very likely many at Mbweni or elsewhere might like to form a settlement above Losefa ; there is a fine country, here there is no land to hoe worth hoeing, and daily fear of war. As to work here, I fear to speak ; the black side is very black ; how much an affectionate schoolmaster for small boys who would stick to that work might do! A regular supply is very important, and there are many friends as well as adversaries.

Ever yours obediently,

W. P. JOHNSON.

It is no surprise to any of those who knew Will Johnson that in all these troubles and difficulties he says nothing of his own sufferings and is obviously entirely preoccupied with plans for the future work. It is interesting to note the development of his ideas ; at first he is inclined to think that the native canoe, a huge log hollowed out by axe and fire, will serve all his needs ; then he begins to see that a large boat with a British mariner and a native crew trained by him will be necessary ; in the end, after his two years of lonely work on the east side of the Lake, he finds that nothing less than a steamer, to be a sort of floating mission village, will serve his turn ; as the work in later years grew he began to dream of a second steamer, larger and better than the first, which should be a floating college, and, as we shall see, he dreamed his dream true.

Before leaving the subject of Charles Janson's death, we would refer to Johnson's account of it in his own *Reminiscences*, written long after these letters, and quote one or two short passages. He says :

" The huts at Pachia and other places were of the smallest, and

nursing him was a humbling process as showing my complete and 1882
hopeless ignorance." " Once, in agony, he cried out ' Maples and I
have spoken of how you could not sympathize with others' pain ' ;
so I lifted up my voice and wept, and he melted and said, ' What's
the use of making yourself miserable ? ' Except for this he was
perfectly patient, making every now and again an ejaculatory
prayer. . . . So Charles Janson left us on Shrove Tuesday, 1882
(February 21), and I went on up the coast alone in that Lenten
season, and Isaiah's words, ' He withholdeth his north wind in the
day of his east wind,' came to me with comfort."[1]

[1] Isaiah xxvii, 8.

# CHAPTER III

# Johnson Alone

1882

LEAVING at Chia the grave of his companion, Johnson went forward on his intended trek up the Lake side to visit the large village of Chiteji, where he hoped to settle for some time, as he had done before at Mwembe under the Yao chief Mataka. The name of Chiteji was known as far away as at Kilwa, and was the only name of a local Nyasa chief which had come to the ears of the Mission looking along the road to the Lake from Masasi.

Comparison of Wanyanja and Yaos

Chiteji was one of the most important chiefs of the Lake people known to us as Wanyanja,[1] which name indeed means literally " Lake people." They were a very different race from the Yaos of the hill country and with a very different language. While the Yaos had the virtues of the hunting, warlike hill people in most parts of the world, they had also their defects. The Wanyanja had the virtues, and, no doubt, the defects, of agricultural and fishing people ; and it is foolish to class either as higher or lower in the scale of civilization, though it is difficult to refrain from comparison. I think it would be admitted that the Wanyanja have, on the whole, shown more intelligence than the Yaos, of whom for many years after Johnson's settlement among them they still went in dread. Yao houses and tribal organization were both better than those of the Wanyanja and from both these neighbouring tribes splendid fellows have been produced in the years that have passed since mission effort was begun among them. It will be remembered that in Johnson's letter of February 18 to Bishop Steere he notes that in the coast strip alone of all that country some determined opposition had been made to the raids of the Magwangwara and that shields and feather head-dresses of the Magwangwara remained as witnesses of the prowess of the generally unwarlike Wanyanja. In face of raids, both Yaos and Wa-

Refuge from raids

[1] Wanyanja = Nyasas.

THE NYASA CHIEF, CHITEJI

nyanja took refuge as best they could, the hill people in the more 1882 inaccessible rocks of their hill-tops, the Lake people actually in the water, of which a very little width was an almost insuperable obstacle to either Magwangwara or Yao raiders, so that houses built on piles a few yards only from the shore, or on rocks surrounded by water, made a quite adequate refuge from the enemy.

Johnson found Chiteji's village quite a large one and the chief's house good. To his surprise he was given the free use of that house and then discovered that the whole village was A raid moving in to a stockade two miles away. They were, in fact, expecting a raid and indeed very soon after a party of the Magwangwara came and raided villages within the bay, near enough for Johnson to be roused quite early in the morning by the long wail of " *Koto! Koto!* " and to see the villagers fleeing with all they could carry from the burning villages where the W. P. J. goes to see the raiders spears of the raiders awaited them. Johnson went with the chief and his nephew to parley with the enemy at the villages where they were, and where they found dead bodies and wounded men to whom they gave such aid as they could. Here are some of Johnson's own words :

" It seemed that the enemy had moved out of the village when they had spoiled it, so I followed after them to their camp, taking in my hand Keble's little book on the Eucharist, which I had been reading in the canoe. There did not seem to be a large party of them, I imagine well under a hundred, and when they saw me they came dancing out in a rough semicircle. I wonder whether it was my little book, or my face, or my clothes, or what else, was employed by God to check them ; whatever it was they gave up dancing and sat down and I sat down too, and then we had a rather lame talk, for we had not any serviceable common lingo ; but they gave me to understand that they had come across white men in old times and did not want to quarrel with them. They said that there were memories of their having been beaten in battle by the white men and that there were evil people up north whom they called the Nyaka-nyaka, who had wantonly burnt the villages in the north of their own country, adding : ' Where could we raid now, except in the south ? ' I think I promised these Angoni to come and see them and, if possible, to go on to the Nyakanyaka with a view to reconciling them ; anyhow we parted in a friendly spirit and I went back to the village. I was greatly hindered all this time by my very elementary knowledge of what was said around me."

He began at once to gather round him a few people willing Work at Chiteji's

1882

to listen to his message, and to take good walks in every direction to explore the possibilities and get in touch with the people
in neighbouring villages. He got across to Likoma in the chief's
canoe and found there a large population attracted by its free-
Visit to Likoma dom from raids. Chiteji was chief also of all that island, now the
headquarters of the Mission in Nyasaland, but he would on no
account give him permission to settle there at that time. He
wanted him to stay in his own village where the presence of a
white man would be some protection, he felt, in the event of
fresh raids taking place. An elephant hunter, Mr. Fenwick,[1]
some forty miles north along the coast, wrote on hearing of the
arrival of a white man so near him, and invited him to come up
and stay with him because of the Magwangwara who were, he
said, on the war-path. Johnson declined the invitation ; he
says, " it did not seem to be worth while to leave my big village
and go up north to live under a hunter's shadow."

Johnson soon found that the crossing from Chiteji's via the
stepping-stone islands of Likoma and Chizumulu to the west
side of the Lake was used like all the other crossings as one of
the feeders of the slave trade. As the visiting trader from
Kilwa got his caravan filled up and was thinking of going, even
some of the local people were seen selling some of their own
W. P. J. rescues slaves to him. Johnson could, of course, do nothing ; but when
a woman from they were actually proposing to carry off the wife of one of the
slave-traders two men he had brought with him from Masasi, he simply went
up to them and took the woman back. The trader got very much
excited and pranced about with a drawn sword ; the natives
on each side held back the combatants, though it is certain that
Johnson would have used no weapon more deadly than a very
useful fist, and the commotion subsided. The woman remained
with her husband, and, doubtless, the little affair increased
Johnson's prestige with the chief and his people. Johnson felt
sure that the chief would in the last resort stand by him and
not allow this robbery of the woman. He speaks very highly of
the chief and relied greatly on his influence with his own people,
White visitors both at the time and in subsequent occasions of friction. While
at Chiteji's Johnson was living at Chiteji's he had at long intervals the
pleasure of seeing a white face and hearing something of the
outer world, for the steamship *Ilala*, belonging to the African
Lakes Company and captained by one Captain Gowans, called

---

[1] Fenwick was subsequently killed by natives south of Blantyre.

occasionally and even brought letters and books. Mr. John
Moir, that early manager of the African Lakes Company whose
glasses won, first for him, and then for the Company he represented, the nickname of Mandala, by which the A.L.C. is known
everywhere among natives of Central Africa to this day, also
paid him a visit once or twice on the *Ilala*. In fact, when we
speak of Johnson as working alone on the Lake shore for the
years after the death of Janson, it is well to remember that the
solitude was only on the east of the Lake, and that even that
was mitigated by such rare visits as those of the *Ilala* and by
the possibility of getting in touch with Dr. Laws at Bandawe,
almost immediately opposite Chiteji's, by canoe. Lake Nyasa,
however, is so large and so wide, at its widest part by Chiteji's,
that one solitary white man could be very much indeed alone
and at the mercy of many kinds of mischance. The Scotch
Mission had been founded in 1875, in the wave of enthusiasm
that followed the death of Livingstone and his burial at Westminster. Dr. Laws in 1881 when Johnson visited him from
Mwembe, as related above, was at the first station that bore the
name of Livingstonia on the peninsula which ends in Cape
Maclear. That site proved unhealthy, and he moved to Bandawe where he was stationed in 1882. Later still he moved, with
Livingstonia, to Kondowe, much farther north and there the
Mission is till now, and has put forth strong roots. At all these
places Dr. Laws was visited by Johnson, especially when he
needed medical attention or a time of recruiting his health, and
it made all the difference to him in his lonely pioneer work on
the east side to know that some sixty miles away across the
rough waters of the Lake there was another pioneer working
also at the foundation of a mission for the christianization of
the lakeside people. Johnson was the pioneer of the east side
of the Lake and of the wide country of the Yaos between
Masasi and the Lake, just as Dr. Laws and his associates were the
pioneers of the west side and of the Angoni hill tribes. The east
side has remained in the care of the Universities' Mission until
to-day, but the stream of trade passed up the west side of the
Lake as the best road to Tanganyika, and, for a long time, to
Northern Rhodesia, of which the development began in the east
from Nyasaland and not from the south. There was very little
traffic, except by natives, up and down the east coast even
after the Portuguese made a government post there in 1901,

*Margin notes:*
1882
" Mandala "

Trade routes
went up west
side

1882 until the Great War, when it became a highway for South African and Rhodesian troops to the north-eastern part of the Lake where German territory began. The trans-continental telegraph wire followed the trade route up the west coast in due course and the bulk of the U.M.C.A. work has been well away from the line of European travel. Its developments have been generally to the east and to the south among the Yaos of the highlands and the Mang'anja of the river valley. But in 1882 Johnson was content to do what he could from the single centre of Chiteji's village, and all his efforts were liable to interruption and defeat

The Magwangwara or Angoni

through the continual danger of raids from the hills. The Magwangwara were the greatest danger in the villages near Chiteji's and farther north, and accordingly Johnson as usual made an effort to deal with the evil at its source. He planned and carried out a visit to the Magwangwara in their own strong-

1883

W. P. J. visits the Angoni

holds in the hills to the north early in 1883. He had the chance of using the services of some men from Masasi who had been sent up to him with letters, and who were induced to take Johnson to the Magwangwara, even though it was a more or less untried route and there was the evident danger of being captured or killed by the " shield men," as the Magwangwara were often called, in allusion to their characteristic use of shields in war. It says a good deal for the confidence of these men in their " white man " that they ventured thus to walk with him right into the lion's mouth. Johnson took also a few boys from Chiteji's to bring him back, as the Masasi men would go from the Magwangwara country by the most direct route to their

Masasi men detained because of projected raid

homes. At least that was what they intended to do, but, in fact, after they had left Johnson to make his way back to the Lake with his Nyasa boys, the Magwangwara actually detained these Masasi men for some months without ill-treatment, while they made their plans for the raid on Masasi itself in September 1883. Johnson they sent off with honour and a present of an ox, at the very time that they had in mind this raid on distant

The Masasi raid

Masasi and the mission station there. As is fully recorded in the *History of the U.M.C.A.*, and in the life of Chauncy Maples, this raid resulted in the destruction of Masasi and the capture of many of its people, and in the death of some seventy people in their immediate neighbourhood. The Magwangwara are said to have told the leader of the detained Masasi men that their raid was a trial one to see what sort of resistance the Europeans there would put up. William Porter of Masasi (afterwards 1883 Canon Porter), during the incapacity through sickness of Chauncy Maples, had the task of following up the raiders and making terms with them for the redemption of the captives.

Long before this raid Johnson had got back to Chiteji's with his little band. The only loss they sustained was the death of their cook, Tomaso, who was caught one night by a lion. They missed him at the usual roll-call, and followed up the trail, recovering in the end enough of the body to give his remains the decent interment which matters so much in the estimation of the native people, whether heathen or Christian. This happened while they were among the Magwangwara and some of these people helped to recover and bury the body. In this expedition Johnson reached the quarters of Songela, or Songea, north of the Ruvuma. He had with him some Bible pictures, and tried to give some idea of his message to the headmen, including the chief Songea, with the aid of the universal language of the pictures. *A lion kills the cook*

After his return from this attempt to get into friendly relations with the Magwangwara, Johnson went north again on a still more distant and dangerous expedition to visit, as he had promised the Magwangwara, the Nyakanyaka people beyond them, who were raiding the raiders or the villages near them, which they regarded as their private raiding-ground. The *Ilala* took him and his party to the north end of the Lake on the west side, to that Karonga which was the scene of the first brush with the Germans in that part at the beginning of the War. *W. P. J. goes north to see the Nyakanyaka raiders*

From the Karonga landing-place they went through the country of the Wakonde—a rather fine race notable for their courteous manners, their scanty clothing and their diet of milk and bananas—round the north end of the Lake and away to the north-east in a rather fruitless quest for the people whom the Magwangwara had spoken of to Johnson as the Nyakanyaka. As is quite usual this same people were known by different names among the different tribes that surrounded them and it was difficult for Johnson, approaching them through the Wakonde, to discover what was the name by which they were known to that tribe. Ultimately he seems to have identified them as the Bena people, but even that is most likely not the name by which they called themselves. These people were very shy, and, although Johnson saw a good deal of the common people, it *The Wakonde*

*The Nyakanyaka prove to be called Bena*

1883
They are
suspicious of
W. P. J. and his
party

seemed impossible to get into touch with their chief. They were suspicious of Johnson's men because their ears were bored, a custom that they associated with their enemies, the Magwan-gwara (whom, of course, they did not call by that name, but by a nickname meaning " The stickers "), and they were inclined to think that Johnson himself was not a new European but rather the French explorer M. Giraud, who had gone by shortly before and who was, they supposed, returning because he had failed in his object. They were at last convinced as to the " newness " of Johnson because he wore a different style of boot, but they remained convinced that his people were spies of the Magwan-gwara and insisted on their returning the way they had come. Johnson decided not to go round the north end again as there was no certainty of a steamer, but to follow down the east coast

W. P. J.'s
Wanyanja
" strike "

of the Lake by a hitherto untried track. His men " struck " at this, preferring the evils that they knew something of to those they did not know, and they all bolted into the bush except one. Johnson sat down and waited for them to come back, and, though he was torn between hopes and fears, he showed no sign of wavering. They came back and followed him down the east

but return

side, passing through two or three tribes unknown to them all. Everywhere he tried to explain to the people he met the object of his coming, but as he says, " one can but wonder if any single person took in anything." It was Johnson's set plan to bear his witness wherever the chance presented itself, and to leave the results to God. Like the watchman of Ezekiel, if he gave the warning " he had delivered his soul."

Over the
Livingstone
Range

It was on this trip down the east side—when they came to it across the Livingstone Mountains and down a steep hill path like a ladder—that Johnson saw a great number of villages built on wooden piles a short distance from the shore to which the people retired for the night by swimming or by canoe. Still farther south round the headland of Mbamba Bay the hill comes close to the water and huge rocks dot the narrow beach. In

Lake dwellings
on rocks or
piles

those days every one of these rocks that had a top as big as a table carried a little hut, which could often only be approached by ladders capable of being drawn up at night. On one island quite close to the mainland the people had their villages and cattle kraals, but the cattle had to swim every morning to the mainland for pasture and to swim back at night for safety. Some of the lake dwellings were on platforms four to five hun-

dred feet long and thirty feet broad, all carried on piles. Hoeing 1883
for food could only be carried on in continual fear of raiders and
it can easily be imagined that the crops not infrequently failed
long before new food was grown. Many years later, the Archdeacon, as he then was, had the chance of asking a man who
knew the old days of pile-villages whether the hunger in the
war years, when the countryside was swept clean by the
clamorous needs of large armies, was as bad as that of the old
days. The man consulted declared that the hunger of old was
far greater, because every district was dependent entirely on
what it could raise, while in the war days supplies could be,
and were, fetched from very far away. Even the natives themselves in these districts were able in the newer days of European
help to go far afield without fear in search of food from districts
less stripped of their crops.

On this trip down the eastern shore of the Lake, Johnson
and his party had sometimes to make perilous crossings of big
rivers (e.g. the Ruhuhu river, where during the war a bamboo
bridge had to be built). Crossing a river in flood in a dug-out
canoe was no joke, but Johnson says, " One's nerves held then
as they do not now." It is significant of the isolation of places
along the Lake shore that they had difficulty in getting any
certain information as to the whereabouts of the important
village of Chiteji, for which they were making. However, they
found their way back at last to what was in a sense home for Gets back to
Johnson as for the others with him, but, as he pathetically re- Chiteji's
marks in his *Reminiscences*, " a home without home comforts."
This journey was really a very remarkable one, as a glance at
the map will show. Without reckoning the trip up the Lake to
Karonga in the s.s. *Ilala*, he had travelled close on 500 miles
through country entirely unknown, among tribes that were
strange, warlike and quite likely to be definitely hostile. His
own porters were as ignorant of the best route as he was, and
quite certainly could not have undertaken any such enterprise
on their own or for any ends of their own. What was Johnson's Objects of this
object ? In the first place, to follow up the curse of the Lake, trip
the raiding parties of hill warriors, to their source and to try to ex- (i) To influence
ercise some restraining influence by appeal to those whose orders the raiders
started the pressure. He had already been to the Magwangwara
at Songea and found that they pressed on the Yaos and the
Nyasas because they in turn were being driven by the Nyaka-

1883

nyaka farther north. In accordance with his promise to the Magwangwara he went straight to the Nyakanyaka on this very difficult and venturesome expedition. The visible fruits were slight, for the heads of the Nyakanyaka kept themselves out of the way and he could not make direct contact with them.

(ii) To proclaim his message

In the second place, here as always on his travels, he " proclaimed his message." He regarded himself as an ambassador, not of the great Queen, but of the King of Kings, and he made his proclamation. The language difficulty must have hampered him, but he did what he could and he quite clearly must have managed to make some of his words understood or he could not have continued his journey. One of his men was a Zanzibari, and Johnson himself knew Swahili and it is likely that in every village, then as now, there would be one or two people at least

(iii) Exploration and observation

with some knowledge of that language. Lastly, he occupied himself all along his route with those observations, geographical, botanical, and ethnographical, which made the substance of the paper which in the following year he read before the Royal Geographical Society. He passed through the country of some of those tribes for whom in the later years of his life he translated the scriptures, and among whom he died.

It is not surprising that on his return to Chiteji's he soon

W. P. J. ill

found himself ill, indeed very ill, and was glad to get across the Lake again to the kindly care of Dr. Laws and the Scotch

Visits Dr. Laws at Bandawe

Mission at Bandawe. These friends again set him up in health and lent him a boat in which to recross the Lake, and Johnson remembers how on that trip as early in the morning he left Chizumulu, which, with Likoma, is one of the stepping-stones

A great comet

for the passage of the Lake at this wide part, they saw a great comet " subtending an angle of at least forty degrees " high in the eastern sky and pointing straight down over Johnson's house at Chigoma.

Rumours of raids, east and west

These were days of many rumours ; the stories of the raids on the mission at Masasi were filtering through and in the absence of any direct information from Zanzibar or home this was very disturbing to the lonely missionary on the Lake shores. Again it was reported that the Angoni on the west had actually raided the Scotch Mission, from which Johnson had just returned. This Johnson knew to be quite within the bounds of possibility, for on his recent visit he had found the missionaries almost shut up within their own bounds, not by raiding Angoni, but by their own native friends, who looked on the presence of the missionaries as a safeguard for them against the raids they were continually fearing. Meanwhile, Johnson got to work on the language and with the help of a little book by Mr. Riddel of the Scotch Mission at Bandawe he began to understand what was said to him and to be able to make rough translations of the Gospels. This was the beginning of his work in Chinyanja, the third language that he had had to tackle in Africa. He already had considerable acquaintance with Swahili and with Yao, but Chinyanja was the language in which he was destined to do his greatest output of work. It was, of course, not his plan to sit down at a comfortable centre in order to learn the language, and indeed that is not the best way in any case. He tramped about the district near Chiteji's village and made acquaintance with all with whom he could get into contact. He was laying the foundations of the immense work which has been done in that part by the Universities' Mission down to the present day.

W. P. J. works at the Chinyanja language.

During these solitary days, he naturally spent a great deal of time considering how best the work could be done as soon as an adequate staff was provided from home. At first, as may be seen from his letters, already quoted, he did not think of anything more elaborate than the large native canoe in which the natives did most of their trafficking. These canoes are what are called dug-out canoes, because they are made of a single huge log, cut down in the hills, brought to the Lake shore with singing and dancing, and there shaped and hollowed out with traditional skill till it becomes a safe and navigable vessel. They make them of all sizes and there may be seen anything from the small canoe in which one man goes out to look at the nets he has set overnight, to the large war canoes carrying a formidable crew of twenty stout paddlers ready to exchange the paddle for the spear as soon as they land. In nothing better than these dug-out canoes men venture to cross the Lake at its widest and to go on trading ventures up and down the Lake shores. In such dug-out canoes the pre-Roman British of the West of England traversed the first waters round the isle of Avalon, and to this day such a canoe, literally dug out from the peat in the flats of Meare, can still be seen preserved in the Museum at Glastonbury. But they did not seem on reflection to be adequate to all the work demanded of them for the missionaries working on Lake Nyasa. Very big canoes of this same kind are in use to-day

His plans for the future work

Canoes ?

1883

on the big waters of inland Africa and it may be your lot to be conveyed, goods and all, up and down the Luapula river, which divides N.E.Rhodesia from the Belgian Congo, in such a canoe fitted with an outboard motor instead of the ten or more paddlers. But such a wedding of the primitive and the modern did not occur to Johnson, nor to anyone else in those days.

A sailing-boat?

Next, the need seemed capable of being met by a good sailing-boat, and that involved a good seaman to train a crew of natives in the more complicated ways of a boat. But already there was beginning to dawn on Johnson's mind the very great advantages of a steamer, and he wondered if it could be done.

or a steamer ?

Some time in 1883 he went down to the south end of the Lake and up to the Scotch Mission at Blantyre, where he was warmly welcomed by Dr. David Clement Scott and his fellow mission-aries, and where he found a good batch of letters from friends in England and Zanzibar. He had already heard of the death of the great Bishop Steere, in whose steps he had trod in his first African journeys and who had encouraged and inspired his ad-vance to the Lake. Among other things awaiting Johnson at

W. P. J. is called to England

Blantyre was a telegram from home, calling him to England to report and consult with the headquarters Committee. He de-cided that before returning he must make one more round of the country that was now becoming familiar to him, and set things in order for the period of his absence. Accordingly he set out on foot with a few porters and went round the south end of the Lake and up the hills on the east side visiting again those lands in the south-east of the Lake which he first saw when he went from Mwembe to Cape Maclear and the Livingstonia Mission. His porters were a very scratch lot and one had come

1884

straight out of gaol at Blantyre. "Some of them bolted on the way," he says, "but we left part of our baggage behind and went on without them." In order to be able to report fully on the whole area to the new Bishop (Charles Alan Smythies, con-secrated on St. Andrew's Day, 1884), Johnson went well up into the hills east of the Lake visiting again Mtonya and Unangu and descending to the Lake again at Losefa. There he waited for the s.s. *Ilala* and went up to Chiteji's village to say good-bye to that friendly chief and hold out hopes of returning with a party of missionaries.

Travelling in 1884

Back to Blantyre he went, and thence overland to Quilimane, the then port of the Zambezi mouth, on foot through a country

which was claimed by the Portuguese, but in which there were 1884 compared with travelling to-day
no signs of Portuguese occupation. The modern traveller sees
nothing of this kind of journeying—he gets on a train at Beira
and is in Blantyre the next evening. In the intermediate period
before there was any railway the happy traveller landed at
Chinde, a new and better entrance to the Zambezi discovered
by Mr. Rankin, waited there a day or two till a stern-wheeler or even in 1900
could take him up the river, and then spent a delightful week
going up the Zambezi and the Shiré through the most charming
scenery, viewed panoramically from the grand stand of the
steamer's deck. One more day overland brought him to
Blantyre and the headquarters of the transport companies, one
or other of which had been in charge of him from Chinde on-
wards. He would have no alarms and uncertainties but would
be working, as well as the state of the river allowed, to a time-
table. All the natives he would come in contact with would be
men hired by the transport company for their job, and as safe
and steady as the carriers in any civilized part of the world.
At this date it requires an effort, which ought to be made, to
realize the dangers and difficulties of the pioneer traveller of
Johnson's day.

It is enough here to say that by these ways Johnson got home W. P. J.'s reception in England
in the summer of 1884 and made his first reappearance in
England since he had set out for Africa in 1876. Naturally, he
was given a great reception everywhere—not least by his old
school—and he speaks gratefully of the " interest in the Mission " which he found in England, " an interest," he says,
" which I have never seen paralleled in later years." He took to
England with him three " boys " whom he hoped to get trained
in seamanship at Brixham. One of these " boys," Hamisi, was Three " black men " at Brixham
the Zanzibari who had been with him on his trip to the
Nyakanyaka, and was the only one who did not run away when
their master determined to go back the new way along the east
side of the Lake instead of returning the way they had come.
Hamisi shared with Johnson the anxious day when they waited,
and not in vain, for the runaways to come back. The others,
named respectively Manweri and Tumani, were Nyasa boys
whom Johnson picked up at Blantyre and who had been porters
with him on the last trip before he left for England. The Rev.
A. G. Stallard, of St. Peter's, Brixham, had always taken a
very lively interest in the U.M.C.A., and Johnson found in him

E

a friend for these " boys " who introduced them to some of his trawlers, found them homes for the time and the chance of going out with the fishing fleet. Mr. G. S. Johnson, who was one of the crew of the trawler *Competitor* (Skipper, Eliezer Johnson), and is now the only one left of those crews of 1884, writes :

" The Blackmen were to be boarded by Mr. Stallard at his house, attached to which was a large Guild Room provided with books and games for the members of St. Peter's congregation who would spend their evenings there when in from sea. The younger members made it their duty to associate with the Blackmen on their arrival in Brixham and to be escorts for them while in Brixham."

Manweri was the " Blackman " allotted to the *Competitor*, Mr. Johnson's boat, and he says :

" The lad seemed willing to give a helping hand, but through lack of knowledge he would usually get into the wrong place, and not being used to the motion of the vessel would often find himself upside-down on the deck, which seemed to bewilder him."

They sent him to bed after tea, fearing lest in the dark he should fall overboard. About midnight the noise of getting the trawl aboard, coupled with that of the winch, woke Manweri up and " suddenly we noticed Manweri crawling along the deck on his hands and knees, very excited ; after a while we understood from him that the noise had frightened him, as he thought it was a lion. He was glad when the first week was up to get on shore ; he was a little sea-sick, but he soon got over it, and after a few weeks he began to be a bit useful ; he was soon able to row a boat and to steer and occasionally we put him to fry the fish." Mr. Johnson thinks that he learnt things nautical fairly well for the time he was there, but that he and his fellows were very glad when the time came for them to go back to Africa. They all parted the best of friends and the interest awakened by this visit has never entirely died down in Brixham. In 1886 George Sherriff, skipper of one of the boats that took on a "Blackman," himself joined the Mission and worked there till his death in 1891. Since that there have been others, Matthews, Partridge, Brimecombe, who have come to help the Mission as a direct result of the work of Mr. Stallard and the impulse given to their interest in Africa by these three " boys " from Nyasa in 1884, and by Johnson, whom they held in veneration.

Johnson himself, during this visit, made his famous appeal 1884
for a Mission steamer and in a wonderfully short time over £4,000 W. P. J. appeals for a Mission steamer
was raised for this purpose, the steamer was designed and built,
and by October was shipped in 380 packages for transport to the
Lake. Miss Woodward, who joined the Mission in 1885, says
that she saw the Archdeacon for the first time at a meeting in
London, where he was pleading for the first Mission steamer.
" His eyes were so sunken that I wondered whether he was an
old man or a young one," and he was only 31 at the time!
Many well remember seeing him during this memorable visit,
and everyone was struck by the simplicity, sincerity and devotion of the man. One said, remembering St. Stephen, " His
face was ' as it had been the face of an angel.' " He spent a good
deal of his furlough at Aberdare, where his brother Harry was
curate, and it was at Aberdare on October 29, 1884, that the
three sailor boys from the Lake were baptized by Will Johnson
himself. Our friend Manweri became Elvani and the other two
Harri and Yohana only a day or two before they said good-bye,
to their joy, to the increasing cold of England and set off on the
return to their own sunny clime.

It was during this furlough that Johnson gave to the Royal W. P. J. reads a paper before the Royal Geographical Society
Geographical Society the result of his seven years' travels in the
regions east of Lake Nyasa, in a paper read before the Society
on June 29, 1884, and printed in full in the *Proceedings* for
September. The paper itself, with which we shall deal when
treating of Johnson's work as an explorer, is a wonderful record
of travel and observation and shows the extent of his work.

The great work of this furlough was the successful appeal for Reasons for asking for a steamer
a first steamer for Mission work on the Lake, and it is worth
while to dwell on the reasons for this particular development.
Few people realize what a tremendous expanse of water Lake
Nyasa is, or what a great part it inevitably plays in the life of
the peoples who live around it. Its length is about 360 miles, Size of the Lake
that is to say, the length of a straight line from Berwick to
Exeter ; its breadth varies from 15 to 50 miles and its depth,
which doesn't enter exactly into the picture, reaches a maximum of 2,316 feet. Though the Lake is narrow in comparison
with its length it will easily be imagined that there is room
round its shores for a large and varied population of diverse
tribes. In those early days of imperfect communications these
tribes were much more separated from one another than is the

case now. In particular, communication between east and west (for the Lake runs practically north and south) was possible only at two or three regular ferrying-places at the narrowest parts, or where islands like Likoma and Chizumulu made a sort of stepping-stone for the canoes. The lands round the Lake consist of a fairly level belt leading to the foot-hills of mountain ranges which rise to the central plateau and form another barrier to communication, except where some pass winds up into the hills along the valley of a river. In several places on the east coast (with which we have most to do) the mountain range comes close to the Lake and leaves hardly a path for a goat round the base of its cliffs. Such a point on the shore was in fact in the early days a greater barrier to intercourse between the people lying north and south of it than the width of the Lake itself at Likoma, where it is widest. Again, the villages round the Lake were built as close to the water as could be, and, if possible, with a river or lagoon or at least a reedy marsh on the landward side. This was necessary for protection against the raiding warriors from the hills, who, whether Magwangwara or Yao, hated and feared the unknown waters of the Lake. A few feet of water was a sufficient bar to those hillmen. As late as 1899, when the chances of raids from the hills were greatly reduced, from one cause and another—the British in effective occupation to the south-east, and the Germans beginning to make themselves felt in the north-east—the lakeside villages were built in such sites and consisted of a close huddle of huts inside a stockade. To-day the stockades are gone and the large

villages have broken up into little hamlets scattered along every bay and inlet. Very few even of the larger old villages know anything of the stockade, except that the name of it survives to indicate where it once was. Such crowded villages, placed in the worst possible situation from the hygienic point of view, were ill suited for the homes of the missionaries, though it was in such conditions that Johnson had been living in those lonely years at Chiteji's. But, on the other hand, the Lake itself, if it could be used, was an unrivalled means of communication between any and all of the places along its shores. Johnson's first thought, a large canoe to carry him from place to place, was rejected because it did not provide a home. The second plan, of a good sailing-boat, was open to the same objection, and, besides, a good sailing-boat, even if large enough to provide a

home for a missionary or two and his belongings, was liable to 1884
great interruption of its usefulness by the violent storms which
frequently prevail on the Lake, and its navigation presented
considerable difficulty. The natives are well accustomed to
water and are from their earliest years almost as much at home
in the Lake as the fish that people its depths, but they are accustomed only to the canoe and the paddle, and only for special
needs venture far out into the Lake. So Johnson came naturally
to the steamer plan as the only solution and this was the plan
which he put before the friends of the Mission during his furlough in 1884. The new Bishop, whom Johnson must have seen
in Zanzibar on his way home, took up the idea with warmth,
and encouraged Johnson to appeal for it. The idea was that the
steamer would enable one or two missionaries to cover the whole
ground of the lakeside villages without endangering their health
by residence in the unsanitary conditions described above, and
that they would gain the maximum of influence with the
minimum of disturbance of native social conditions in the
villages to which they would minister. As we shall see later on
this idea of minimizing the European's influence on native
conditions was always fundamental in Johnson's conception of
missionary work, and there is no doubt at all that his plan was
absolutely the only possible good one for those days. There is
no disagreement at all on that point.

His advocacy of the steamer in England, backed by the mani- The quick
fest devotion of his character and by the glamour that sur- response to his
rounded his exploits, met with a most ready response and he appeal
was able in October to start back to the Lake with his steamer,
so to speak, in his hands. It was in fact transported in many
pieces made up into packages such as could be transported
overland by the only available means of transport at that date,
namely, the heads of sturdy porters able to march twenty miles a
day with a load of 60 lbs. These packages were landed at Quili- The new
mane and conveyed up the Zambezi, with Johnson in charge of expedition
the whole Nyasa expedition. He had with him Leonard Frere, a Quilimane
deacon who had spent some time in Zanzibar, Captain Calla-
ghan, Mr. Bellingham, who had been in the Mission since 1879,
and one or two carpenters and engineers. This party had W. P. J. struck
hardly started on the journey up the Zambezi when the leader down by
Johnson was struck down by a violent ophthalmia, which blindness
rendered him entirely blind. He had to return at once to

Quilimane to a Portuguese hospital there (the Portuguese doctor recommended rose-water), and wait till the return of the tug which was conveying the parts of the *C.J.* up the river. As soon as it got back he was conveyed (in its hold) to Mozambique, where there was a hospital with a big reputation for those days. But there was no eye specialist and little nursing. One might suppose that, under such a blow as this, and with these painful delays, and the greatest uncertainty as to the future of his sight, Johnson would be very impatient and chafe horribly. There is no evidence on the subject, but those who knew Johnson best as a patient in later days will, I believe, agree with me in thinking it not at all in keeping with his character that he should so behave. He always had an extraordinary power of adapting himself to inevitable circumstances, whether it took the form of a serious food shortage or of blindness or disabling illness. As long as he could fight against an evil, he fought, but when it was no longer possible to fight he yielded in almost a spirit of fatalism, in what *would* have been a spirit of fatalism but for the great difference that it was Christian acceptance of whatever God might send. The testimony of those devoted women who nursed him so often in his later days, when he had to fly to Likoma for nursing and treatment, is unanimous in this sense. Nurse Townsend came down from Zanzibar to take charge of him and take him to Zanzibar. Again, there was no eye specialist and poor Johnson had to be carried right home to England. His own words shall be quoted here :

"We arrived in England, and the specialist in London said that I must go home and be fatted up for an operation in some three months or so. Thus I continued to be a trouble to every one and so discovered treasures of kindness. Then came the first operation, performed in lodgings by Mr. Nettleship. It is wonderful to think what I owe to him, and not I only but hundreds of others. He was operating on many patients daily, and I was told that he could not venture to play ball games, as he had to keep every muscle in perfect control. It was touching to hear a woman who was travelling up with me from South Wales, on the same errand as myself, say : ' What a pity it was we couldn't put five pounds together and get him to come down to us.' I think I am right in saying that if he took anything from me it was positively one pound only, as a formal thing,—prodigious! I suppose he let this poor woman off any adequate fee.

A BEDFORD GRAMMAR SCHOOL BOY

WILLIAM PERCIVAL JOHNSON

1885

"A second operation was in St. Thomas's Hospital, and here, as 1884 during all the time I was in London, kind messages and presents of flowers and fruits came from many and divers people, as unseen as angels. . . .

"Then there was the operation itself. Mr. Nettleship, as I came Second into the room, introduced me formally to his assistant, who had the operation same name as myself; 'Mr. Johnson—Mr. Johnson.' And then successful two nurses sat on my head, for the operation was performed without chloroform, and I thought, while I prayed, how futile this precaution was, for if the agony had come they could not have prevented a jerk; but it did not come. Then came the time of waiting to have my eye tried, and when it was tested, I remember the concentration of every fibre in me to read some yet smaller letter. 'He will be able to read with his head close to a gas-jet,' said the man who made others see, and so it is to this day. I felt ashamed when a friend asked the wonder-worker whether he could not do anything for my other eye, and sympathized with the way he rapped out : 'I can take it out.'

"He was so genial when I consulted him again ages afterwards; he said he remembered the case before he looked it up in his book, and I shall never forget him, or the studies by his brother of lions for his great picture of Daniel in the Lions' Den."

Dr. Howard gives the following account of the blindness and the operation in more exact language than a layman can do, and though it was not till years later that Dr. Howard had medical charge of Johnson, he had abundant opportunities of learning exactly what had happened. He says :

"As a result of the intense ophthalmia he got corneal ulcers and Limitations of iritis and returned to England quite blind. One eye was quite blind W. P. J.'s sight from corneal scarring and iritis, but in the other eye, though the central pupil was blocked, there was some clear cornea on one side, and it was possible to do an iridectomy and so make an artificial pupil opposite this clear part of the cornea. The operation was successful and he could see. Such an artificial pupil has no power of contracting and dilating. In consequence, when looking at near objects (when the normal pupil contracts) the artificial pupil let in too much peripheral light, and so the Archdeacon[1] used to put his two fingers together and make a narrow slit through which he looked to read, then the fingers cut off all the light above and below. Conversely, at dusk, the normal pupil dilates widely to let in all the light possible. The Archdeacon was very blind in the dark because his

---

[1] Mr. Johnson was always THE Archdeacon to many of those who knew him as such after the death of Bishop Maples and before the growth of the work had led to the appointment of other archdeacons.

artificial pupil could not dilate any more. The result was that he was apt to kick against stones or to stumble into the Likoma ditches and he would always accept a proffered arm to get from the Cathedral to the *Mezani* (dining-room) ; indeed, at night was about the only occasion when the Archdeacon ever asked for help. The retina and the optic nerve were quite sound, all the trouble had been in the front part of the eye. He could read small print if he had a good light, and I do not think that even with long hours of translation work his eye got tired and I don't think that he got much headache."

It will not be necessary again to make more than slight allusions to Johnson's blindness, but it should be carried in mind throughout that all his work had to be done under this terrific handicap, and that, as far as possible, he never allowed it to interfere, and indeed rather preferred not to have it noticed. One learnt to treat him exactly as if he had no such handicap and that is certainly what he wished.

It was on his second return to the Lake that he took with him George Sherriff, the first of those Brixham men who have since that day done so much for the Mission and have kept green the memory of Mr. Johnson in Brixham.

At Zanzibar, he had further conference with Bishop Smythies and renewed acquaintance with old friends, native and European, there. Of course, he visited Mbweni, which had been his first charge in the Mission field and where now his friends Archdeacon Hodgson and his wife were in charge.

From Zanzibar he went on with the Bishop, who planned to make with him the overland journey to the Lake for the first time (he had already visited the Lake by the Zambezi route, and had returned overland). Sherriff went with them as far as Lindi and thence to Quilimane and up the rivers Zambezi and Shiré as far as Matope, where the *Charles Janson* was being put together.

The Bishop and Johnson and a party, including five priests and a native deacon, went up from Lindi to Newala. Here their troubles began. Johnson, on the point of getting at last to the Lake and to his steamer the *Charles Janson*, now actually afloat on the Lake, was laid low a second time with a large abscess under the arm, and had to be sent back to the coast under the charge of the Rev. Spencer Weigall, a priest who had some medical knowledge. Johnson in his own *Reminiscences* seems only to recall this abscess, which would in the nature of things be a more vivid recollection to him than to others, and pos- sibly more vivid to him than less poignant sufferings of greater actual importance. His friend Chauncy Maples, who was then in charge at Newala, speaks much more seriously of Johnson's illness. He writes on June 10, 1886, that :

" Dear Johnson is very, very ill and while we are arranging for him to be carried to the coast we have also to rearrange our plans about Nyasa. The result is that I proceed at once with the Bishop and Wathen to the Magwangwara, and the Lake. . . . I feel I have lived all too long here in ease and comfort while others—so notably my dear, dear friend here, now lying so low, and so very weak and ill—have been bearing the burden and heat of the day ; therefore, I hail this opportunity gladly."

A few days later he writes :

" Dear Johnson was carried away yesterday terribly weak and ill, and we hardly dare to speak of his departure. It seems so doubtful whether we shall hear of his safe arrival at the coast. . . . Still, he was a trifle better when he started. . . . I fear that he will never gain strength enough to return to up-country work, but he has prepared the way and gone through privations and hardships that none of us had either the physical or spiritual strength even to face, much less to go through."

Little could Maples foresee the years of continued hardship gallantly borne that were to be his friend's lot.

This second break-down was far less serious than the blindness of 1884, but it had the very important effect of once more cutting Johnson off from the initiation on the Lake of the work for which, as Maples says, he had prepared the way. Maples himself was torn up from the roots he had sent down in the Masasi country, and was sent to the Lake to take charge of what would otherwise have been Johnson's natural work and responsibility. Johnson speaks of this with characteristic modesty when he says in his *Reminiscences* : " I was not yet out of the wood as regards my health and had to turn back ; happily, perhaps, as Maples thus came into his own, for he was put in charge of the party going up to the Lake instead of me : clearly his place." That Johnson should twice have been thus hindered is so remarkable as to appear almost a providential overruling of the blind purposes of men. The partnership of Johnson and Maples was an ideal arrangement and both men were entirely happy in working together. They were largely

1886

complementary, the one to the other, and each had the fullest sympathy with the other's point of view. But this partnership was for the present delayed by Johnson's absence.

W. P. J. in hospital at Cape Town

He went not to England this time but down to the Cape, ministered to all the way by " angels in the form of doctors," to use his own words. There, when convalescence allowed his removal from the Hospital, he stayed with the Cowley Fathers at their Mission House, where so many missionaries passing through Cape Town from those days to these have found the friendliest welcome. There he met Father Puller (who, like Bishop Smythies, was associated with the parish of Roath in Cardiff, and whom Bishop Smythies had ardently desired to see preferred to the Bishopric of the U.M.C.A. instead of himself), Father Shepherd and also Bishop Knight Bruce just then going up to Mashonaland. The Archbishop (Archbishop West Jones) showed him great kindness, too, and he returned from the Cape as soon as he was well enough with a happy feeling that his visit had enabled him to forge new links between the Universities' Mission and the Church of South Africa, from which the first Bishop, Mackenzie, had been sent to his perilous adventure of 1861. Johnson is sure to have seen at Cape Town Ann Daoma, one of the African people whom Bishop Mackenzie rescued from the Yaos, and who was brought to Cape Town by Mr. Waller when the Mission withdrew to Zanzibar, and who lived there to an honoured old age, dying in 1930.

There was some danger of further delay when Johnson reached Quilimane, for there was a native rising which blocked the river for a short time. Happily the delay was not long nor

W. P. J. at last on the new steamer, the C.J.

was it at all due to Johnson's health. On reaching the Upper Shiré or at some point on the Lake Johnson had the happiness of joining up with the new steamer, the *Charles Janson*, named after one friend, and now at work in charge of another friend, Chauncy Maples. The two journeyed together up the Lake to Likoma and doubtless had many long talks about the work which in future they were to carry on together. By this time a definite settlement had been made on the island of Likoma, opposite to Chiteji's village, where Johnson had lived and from which he had visited the island and marked it as a suitable site for the mission base.

Likoma

The island was under the suzerainty of Chiteji and Mataka of Kobwe. It is about four or five miles long and more than two miles broad and its outline is diversified by many jolly little bays, of which the very best for an anchorage became the property of the Mission, with a good piece of the land behind it rising to the hilly backbone of the island. The island is not fertile, but carries, and has probably always done so, a good population, which in 1885 was estimated at 2,600. A formal sale of part of it to the Mission was made by Chiteji, and the docu- ment with the precise consideration in various articles of barter for which it was sold is still in existence as the title-deed of the Mission. The agreement secured to the Mission its own location, with defined boundaries, gave it exclusive right to the excellent harbour and the slope down to it and guaranteed that in future no witches should be burnt on the island. This purchase and agreement were made with the native chief of the island on the recommendation of Mr. Buchanan, the British Vice-Consul for Nyasaland. When Sir Harry Johnston in later years came to the Lake he astonished Maples and Johnson by sending to them one day a deed in which the island, with some limitations, was handed over to the two missionaries and their heirs for ever in fee simple. Thus the right of the Mission to a controlling posi- tion on the island rests on two agreements and is unshakable. Sir Harry Johnston's action was, of course, solely determined by the desire to secure protection for the natives. To complete the account of Likoma and its position politically, it may be added here that, when the delimitation of boundaries between British, Germans and Portuguese was made, the fact that an important station of the Mission was placed on Likoma Island led to its being placed under the British Flag,[1] though the ad- joining mainland was in the Portuguese sphere. It would, no doubt, be after this that Sir Harry Johnston made the deed of gift already mentioned. Until recent years no Government official came regularly to Likoma to judge cases and no taxes were levied on the people. The burden of settling minor cases fell on one of the Mission and any serious matters were sent to Kota Kota for judgment. The priest-in-charge, who judged the smaller cases, naturally acted in conjunction with the local headmen, and in most cases referred matters to them and re- vised their judgments. As the population increased this became an excessive burden and for some years now there have been

[1] Sir H. H. Johnston put the "Nyasa archipelago" (i.e. all the islands on the Lake) under the British flag.—J. E. H.

1886

Its growth and
population

W. P. J.'s work
on the C.J.

the inestimable blessings of taxes and the periodical visits of a
Magistrate from Kota Kota, but even now one of the Mission is
actually appointed as the headman of the island under the
visiting Magistrates. From a variety of causes the population
has steadily increased and at the present date the number of
baptized Christians on the island is nearly double the whole
estimated population of 1885, and there are 1,800 children
in school, of whom some are included in the total of
Christians.

When at last Johnson reached Likoma he found the settlement there already established with Maples as Archdeacon, and
a staff of clergy and laymen. The s.s. *Charles Janson* was working to a fairly regular time-table. Based on Likoma it made
weekly cruises to the stations south—there were already Mission
stations established at several points, of which the farthest was
fifty miles south of Likoma—and once a month crossed the
Lake to Bandawe (the Scotch mission, where Johnson had
already once or twice had to repair in his solitary days for the
hospital treatment and nursing of his kind friends Dr. and Mrs.
Laws), there to pick up the mails and leave those that were to
be sent off to England by the first passing steamer. Very soon
after Johnson's arrival Archdeacon Maples preached his first
sermon in Nyanja without an interpreter, which shows that the
new people had promptly set about the important task of getting into touch with the natives around them. Maples was
already proficient in Yao and probably in Swahili, but neither
of these languages would do for Likoma and the lakeside
villages. Mr. Swinny, a priest, and his wife, Mr. Charles Alley,
a carpenter, Mr. Bellingham, whose *Diary of a Working Man in
Africa* gives a vivid account not only of the transport and
building of the s.s. *Charles Janson*, but also of the earliest
efforts of the Mission in school work and building at Likoma,
together with Mr. Frere were the mission staff at that date, and
it will be easily imagined that, from that time on, the return
to Likoma after steamer trips and excursions into the hills was
indeed a " coming home " for the pioneer missionary Johnson,
and that too not " without home comforts." The work of the
*Charles Janson* naturally fell mainly to Johnson and he was now
able to carry out his plans of extending the work along the Lake
shore and establishing in as many places as possible a school
and church, very often the same building, under the care of a

native teacher. On his way through Zanzibar in 1884 with the
*Charles Janson* party, he called on the native teachers in Zanzibar to volunteer for the pioneer work on the Lake. Several re-
sponded, among them Augustine Ambali, whose work on the
Lake, especially at Msumba, earned for him the love and esteem
of all who had the privilege of knowing him and whose death in
1930 left a gap that can never be filled. He was the first, and
so far the only, native priest of Nyasaland to be given by his
Bishop the honour of a canonry in the Cathedral, and the
appointment was everywhere hailed as a most proper mark of
dear Augustine Ambali's worth. One of the earliest youngsters
to come under the Mission influence on Likoma was Yohana
Tawe, now a priest himself. Mr. Bellingham gives an amusing
account of how in the absence of chalk and blackboard the
missionaries got five small boys, of whom Padre Yohana was
one, to take an interest in the mysteries of reading and writing
by using cassava root for chalk and the brown bodies of the
boys for a writing surface, and performing what seemed like
magic tricks with mysterious marks on the bodies by one man,
and then interpreting these into some desired action by another
European, who had no other guide as to what he was to do.
Padre Yohana Tawe has long since been a master of all that
magic business.

CHAPTER IV

# Halcyon Days

FROM now on the more striking hardships and dangers which Johnson had known may be said to have come to an end. On the Lake itself there is a central base, safe from all raiders, practically independent of the caprices of local chiefs, and centrally placed for probable developments. There is a strong base and a very mobile flying column in the shape of a steamer entirely devoted to the work of the Mission, manned by employees of the Mission and run by a priest-in-charge, Johnson himself, with Mission workers under him capable of navigating the vessel. Johnson's hopes and dreams have come to fruition. On Likoma, Maples, appointed Archdeacon by Bishop Smythies while it was still uncertain whether Johnson would ever be able to come and resume work on the Lake, with a growing band of workers, was laying the foundations of the Mission headquarters.

A station was laid out, a church was begun and built as soon as possible, and evangelizing work was begun, not only on the island but on the mainland opposite. Maples was an admirable head for such a work and kept his little band cheerful through his social and other gifts. His interests were many and varied. He would pass from making a pudding to the writing of a hymn in the Nyanja language, and then go on to composing the music for it.

He did, with energy, the immediate task of starting schools and classes, preaching to the heathen in the villages of Likoma, and at the centre under what became famous as the " preaching-tree," and has figured in many photographs of that part of the work. It was a fine tree with spreading shade and was practically evergreen. Its fruit, like an acorn with the cup red and the contained nut black, is frequently used for bead necklaces and is quite beautiful. He was exercised in mind at the sight of the hordes of little girls running about in all the villages, and he bemoans the helplessness of mere men to grapple with the

78

problem of their education and training in Christian ways. He 1890
and Mr. Frere did what they could and Mrs. Swinny, during the
short time that she was at Likoma, doubtless helped. It has
always been a problem in Mission work everywhere, and the
U.M.C.A. has been happy in the solution of it in most dioceses
one after the other. It is inevitable that men should begin the
pioneer work, and it is only when they have made some sort of
habitable settlement that it is possible to invite women to
volunteer. That plan has been followed with most notable success at Likoma, where to-day the girls' schools are extraordinarily good and very well attended. It was not till 1888 in
November that more ladies came to take over from Archdeacon Maples the uncongenial task of care for the little girls
and teaching them needlework. Mr. and Mrs. Swinny, who came
from Natal and knew Zulu, had been intended for work on the
mainland and actually made an expedition to the Magwangwara
country, and got permission to settle there, but God willed
otherwise. First their little child died at Likoma in 1886, then
Mr. Swinny in 1887 at Bandawe and lastly Mrs. Swinny at sea
on her way home to England in 1888. One knows that such
sacrifices are never in vain and it may well be that the later
growth of the Mission in those lands owes a great deal to these
pioneers who served so short a time but gave their all.

Miss M. E. Woodward, sister of Archdeacon Woodward,[1] so **Women**
long identified with Magila, with Miss McLaughlin came to **workers at**
Likoma in 1888 and from that day to the present with but a **Likoma**
short interval Likoma has been the field of work of one after
another of a line of devoted women who have done wonders
for the native women and girls. Teachers and nurses alike have
given unstinted services, and in addition to serving the native
people they have been invaluable as bringing into the hard
life of missionaries some at least of the amenities of home. We
shall see from some of his letters how even the heroic Johnson
valued the presence and work of women, not merely for its
influence on the native women and girls but also for the whole-
hearted devotion and skill with which they looked after the
creature comforts of all the missionaries and nursed and tended
them when they were sick. Anyone who knows anything of
missionary work will agree that, as the British army is said to
march on its stomach, so British missions may be said to make

[1] Died at Zanzibar, June 17, 1932. R.I.P

1890

their steadiest advances in the same sort of way. It is not merely a matter of physical health, but of spiritual well-being too, for the two are more intimately connected than we sometimes like to admit.

Johnson was mostly at work along the Lake side, extending in all directions south of Likoma and as far down the river as Matope, where the *Charles Janson* had been put together. So far all the mission work was on the east side of the Lake and on the river south of the Lake.

Work started on the Upper Shiré

A temporary disablement of the *Charles Janson*, which required its repair once more on the Shiré river, gave Johnson the opportunity and the call to start work down there with, as usual, the aid of native teachers. There have been more than the usual ups and downs in that particular sphere of work, but at most times there has been something doing along the river, and now there is a priest-in-charge stationed at Matope to look after all the work on the river and in its neighbourhood.

It is needless here to describe the actual work of the *Charles Janson* in detail through these years. Are not these things written in the chronicles of the Mission by Miss Anderson-Morshead ? We shall see more in a later chapter of Johnson's missionary principles and at this date, and for a long time after, these principles governed the work of the steamer. Nor can we chronicle the long list of men, priests, engineers, artisans and seamen, who came to measure their strength alongside that hardy pioneer, for whom no task was too hard, and to fall out again through sickness, death or resignation. A native of some intelligence said years later to a member of the Mission who formed one of that string, " You know, *Bwana*, that if the Archdeacon were a native we should say that he was a wizard because so many people who come to work with him die or go away." It is true that the conditions which Johnson stood without flinching were even in these better days enough to test the endurance of the toughest, and it is little less than amazing that one of whose health his friend Maples wrote so despondently in 1886, at the time of his second set-back from the journey to the Lake, should in subsequent years have proved so very tough. Dr. Howard, who knew him very well and attended him through some serious illnesses, says of him :

See p. 73 1886–90 W. P. J.'s toughness

" There is no doubt at all that the Archdeacon had a marvellous constitution, and he put the greatest possible strain on it in his work, but I don't think that he was deliberately careless of his health or 1886–90 deliberately rash. His idea was to do his duty regardless of consequences, he did not count illness and never made a martyr of himself. He was distinctly a good patient ; when ill he regarded it as a duty to do as he was told, so as to get back to work as soon as possible. (N.B.—In this he was the exact opposite of Bishop Hine, who would insist on carrying on in spite of fever and took three times as long to get well.) . . . As a young man, I imagine, he had great strength and amazing power of physical endurance, and even when quite old he could outstay the average younger man. He was a good walker but owing to his blindness he was apt to jar his toes, and he suffered a lot from jiggers, as he could not see where they were or take them out."

As to his walking, one nickname that he earned in Nyasaland in his days of defective sight was a word that means " the old blind elephant," descriptive of his pressing on through whatever might be in the track without paying much attention to the obstacles. This seemed to the native imagination to hit off well Johnson's manner of striding resolutely along with rather high steps and a disregard of exactly where he was going. For the next eleven years, i.e. from 1886, when he got back to the Lake, until October 1897, Johnson carried on steadily this work on the Portuguese mainland, both in the purely Nyanja-speaking strip that lay from Losefa to well beyond Likoma Island and in the Yao lands that are found around the southeast end of the Lake.

The Bishop, who, it should be remembered, was still the one Bp. Smythies Bishop of the Universities' Mission with his seat in Zanzibar, made his third, fourth and fifth visits to the Lake in the years His travels 1887, 1889 and 1891, journeys involving the long walks across from the Indian Ocean via Masasi which rank among Bishop Smythies' greatest achievements in that line, and which it was clear were latterly becoming too much for him. This fact and the great and steady development of the work on and around the Lake convinced the Bishop that a division of his diocese was necessary on every ground. During his last visit to Nyasa he had found himself unable to stand the strain of such journeys, and he had corresponded with the Committee at home on the necessary plans for his relief. He had at first inclined to the idea of a suffragan or coadjutor for the Nyasa work, but before he got away from Nyasaland (he was unfit to return overland Agrees to and went instead by the river and sea route) he had agreed to division of the Diocese

F

a division of the diocese, and made his farewell to the great work which he had seen spring up from its beginnings in 1885, when the *Charles Janson* was consecrated and set on the Lake.

The time of beginnings

Those years were a time of steady progress, when nearly all the great works of the Mission were started. It was a time of beginnings and had all the interest for those living at the time that the sense of sowing seeds for the future always has.

1880 Dispensary started

In 1880 a regular dispensary was started on Likoma, though, of course, some sort of medical work had been carried on from the beginning. We have already seen how Johnson in those early days at Mwembe used up all his spare shirts and surplices to provide bandages at a time when there was a serious outbreak of sores. In 1889 Dr. Hine joined the Mission and after a short time at Zanzibar came on to the Lake, and for the first time the Mission at the Lake had a doctor of medicine to look after its sick—and a man who was not only a doctor but also a warm-hearted missionary priest who was later to prove his wisdom and worth in both dioceses of Zanzibar and Likoma, in starting and carrying on for some years the work at Unangu in Yaoland, and later in ruling as Father in God over successively the three dioceses of Likoma, Zanzibar and Northern Rhodesia, and whose unique experience and wise judgment are happily still at the service of the Church and of the Universities' Mission in particular.

1889 Dr. Hine, doctor, priest and bishop

Likoma Printing Press, 1888

In the same year 1888 that saw the first dispensary there was started the first printing press at Likoma, the beginning of a very great work. The 1931 catalogue of publications of the Likoma Mission Press runs into over thirty pages and includes works in Chinyanja, Yao, Chimpoto, Kipangwa and Chimanda, and informs the would-be purchaser that the publications in Chimpoto must be ordered from a daughter press at Liuli in the northern district. At first its works were small and few, and its chief value was in producing tentative versions for trying out in the schools and villages before they could be offered to the great publishing Societies, the S.P.C.K. or the B.F.B.S., for final printing in large quantities. This work was one most dear to the heart of Johnson, whose labours as a linguist must be described more fully in a later chapter. The work has had a string of superintendents in mission-hearted printers from England, and for many years the foreman of the printing shop was Nicholas Mkwarasho, who came, probably in 1888, from

Zanzibar as a skilled printer and continued in charge of the 1886-90 large staff of native printers for many years, until his eyes became unequal to the work. I believe he is still living pensioned at Likoma.

Carpenters were needed from the very foundation of the mis- Carpenter's shop sion station at Likoma and again there has been a long series of good men and true who have set going and carried on there a school of carpentry, turning out useful skilled workmen to meet the needs of the diocese and to carry their skill in the later years into such far countries as Rhodesia, North and South, the Congo and possibly still farther.

# CHAPTER V

## Political Questions : Delimitation of Territories

1886–90
No-man's Land

JOHNSON'S work, as has been already indicated, was mainly in the villages of the east side of the Lake and the narrow strip of fairly level lands lying between the Lake and its encircling mountains. When he began his journeys all this country was No-man's Land, but, as early as 1882, there were movements on foot, if not to grab land, at any rate to prevent others from grabbing it. This developed into something like a scramble between the British and the Portuguese, with the The Portuguese Germans later taking a hand up north. The Portuguese had been the earliest explorers of East Africa over a good stretch of latitude and in a few places they had penetrated some distance inland. But at the time we are dealing with there was nothing that could be called effective occupation anywhere beyond a very narrow strip of coast in the neighbourhood of such towns as 1885–90 Mozambique and along the Zambezi Valley. When Johnson was in hospital at Mozambique at the time of his blindness one of the English friends who visited him there and read to him told him that there was so little control even there at the centre of government of a large province that it was quite usual to see the natives on the mainland (Mozambique is an island) fighting with one another undisturbed by the authorities. As for the distant interior there was no pretence of administration and control. Along the line of the Zambezi there were some stations with a Government official, but these were ineffective beyond the radius of their camp. The readers of Livingstone's *Zambezi and its Tributaries* will remember how the explorer found that one of his chief difficulties in regard to the slave trade was the open or secret connivance of the authorities, generally on account of the profit it brought them.

84

The " scramble for Africa " concerns us because it had a very 1885-90 real influence on the work of the Mission on the east side of Lake Nyasa, and Will Johnson had very definite views on the subject of the delimitation of spheres of influence between the British and the Portuguese. Bishop Smythies, who had been closely concerned in the Anglo-German settlement on the east coast, had also to take a hand in the similar difficulties between British and Portuguese on the Lake. In 1885 he had written home his impressions of affairs around the Lake as follows :

1885
Views of Bp.
Smythies on
the relations of
British and
Portuguese in
Nyasaland

The whole of these great populations which people the shores of the Lake seem to live in utter terror and misery from the continual raids of marauding tribes. The motive of these raids is chiefly to feed the slave trade. For many years British subjects, at the risk of their lives, have tried to help these Lake tribes. Mr. Moir has just returned from visiting them, and was welcomed by all, and takes to England from most of them petitions for English protection. . . . Such a state of things (i.e. English protection) on Lake Nyasa would do more to stop the slave trade than all that is done to capture the miserable remnants of caravans away from shores 300 or 400 miles off, and I believe that all men who have experience of this part of Africa will entirely bear out what I have said. But I firmly believe that, if once the English Government allow another European power to occupy the ground before them, all the efforts and sacrifices of Englishmen will have been in vain, and the great opportunity will be lost, probably for ever. And if anyone should object that this is underrating the humanity of other nations, I would ask, " What members of other nations have made any efforts or any sacrifices for the tribes of Lake Nyasa ? What other European nations have shown any earnestness or any enthusiasm comparable with that of England for the suppression of the slave trade ? "

When the Bishop was at Likoma in 1889 he was asked to lend the s.s. *Charles Janson* to Mr. H. H. Johnston, then Consul at Mozambique and shortly after Commissioner for Nyasaland, who was sent up to the Lake by his Government on an important mission. From the *Life of Bishop Smythies* we take some account of this important mission and its results :

The desire of the English Government for years had been to keep this part of Africa open for trade, to maintain peace with the native tribes, and to prevent " abrupt seizure " of land by other Powers. The African Lakes Company, established for trading purposes on The A.L.C. Lake Nyasa, found their business constantly hampered on the one hand by the Portuguese of the Zambezi, and on the other by certain powerful Arabs at the north end of the Lake, whose cruel slave-raiding wars produced a continual state of terror and unrest among the natives, and threatened indeed to exterminate the Europeans. It was to make peace with the Arabs to conclude treaties with the

Mr. H. H.
Johnston,
H.M. Consul at
Mozambique,
goes up to the
Lake

Mr. natives, and above all to keep watch over the Portuguese, that H. H. Johnston (afterwards Sir H. H. Johnston), already well known by his services in Africa, was appointed H.M. Consul at Mozambique.

To understand the claims of Portugal to the shores of Lake Nyasa, we must remember that ever since Vasco da Gama's famous voyage round the Cape in 1497 the Portuguese had fostered a tradition that they possessed the southern half of Africa. Basing their claim on this tradition and on the actual occupation of Mozambique and a few other coast towns, they continued to publish maps in which a trans-African empire was coloured as their own, and to maintain that their settlements at the mouth of the Zambezi entitled them to prevent traders of other nationalities from entering the country by means of that river. No other European Power regarded Portugal's claim to the Hinterland as serious, and for years—indeed since Livingstone's discovery of Lake Nyasa in 1859—British traders and missionaries settled in increasing numbers in the healthier parts of the interior. Friction between the two races was inevitable, for, in spite of frequent warnings from the British Foreign Office, the Portuguese officials on the Zambezi continued to obstruct as much as possible the ingress of " foreigners." In vain their attention was called to the terms of the Berlin Conference of 1886, by which no claim of sovereignty in Africa could be maintained without effective occupation. Though there was not, and never had been, effective occupation by the Portuguese on the Lake shores or in the Shiré Highlands, they continued to claim and to obstruct, until at last in 1889 matters came to a crisis.

Mr. H. H. Johnston's little party going up the Zambezi met with a large " scientific " expedition of Portuguese under the distinguished Major Serpa Pinto, proceeding up the river with a staff of white officials and a force of several hundred armed natives—all so much in keeping with the declared " scientific " purpose—and no clash occurred. Mr. Johnston went up to the north end, assisted by the loan of the *Charles Janson*, and made a satisfactory peace with the Arabs up there, and treaties with the native chiefs. He did this very quickly, no doubt thinking

of the problem he had left behind him. The " scientific " expedition soon developed into an attack on the natives and a determined effort to seize the Shiré Highlands, a district that had already become entirely identified with British interests.

The African Lakes Company had its headquarters there, the Mission of the established Church of Scotland was settled there, and an increasing number of British coffee-planters were working to bring the soil under cultivation.  Mr. Johnson had warned Mlauri, the chief of the remnants of Livingstone's Makololo, not to lift hand against the Portuguese.  But when Mlauri found Clash with the<br>Portuguese his villages raided by the Portuguese, he retaliated by attacking them, and was completely defeated by the " scientific " expedition.  He then claimed the protection of Mr. Buchanan, Acting-Consul at Blantyre, made a treaty with him and received the British flag.  Pushed by the Portuguese aggression, the Acting- Sept. 21, 1889<br>British<br>Protectorate of<br>the Shiré<br>Highlands Consul proclaimed a British Protectorate over the Shiré Highlands Province on September 21, 1889.  Serpa Pinto, faced with this Protectorate, went to Mozambique for further instructions from his Governor there, leaving the " scientific " expedition under the charge of a young lieutenant, whose zeal outran his discretion and led him to tear down the British flag, which Mlauri had hoisted on his territory as the sign of his treaty with the British, and to advance on the Shiré Highlands.  His activities were finally checked from Lisbon when the British Government sent an ultimatum to Portugal demanding the repudiation of these acts.  From the *Life of Bishop Smythies* we take the final results of all these troubles and the settlement made internationally between Britain, Germany and Portugal.

" The final result of Mr. H. H. Johnston's mission is well known. Final<br>settlement The whole of the western shore of the Lake became British Protectorate, joining on the west the territory of the Chartered Company, and on the north German East Africa ; the Shiré Highlands of course remained British, together with the islands of Likoma and Chizumulu, while only a part of the east Lake shore fell to Portugal, with the Zambezi valley and an extensive coast territory."

The part of the settlement that concerned Johnson and the W. P. J.'s views<br>on the<br>settlement U.M.C.A. was that dealing with the east Lake shore, and it was not regarded as wholly satisfactory.  Some extracts from his letters of this date will show how he felt about it and what were the grounds of his dissatisfaction.  The British Protectorate 1889–90 over Nyasaland was declared in 1890, but the details of delimitation and the final signing of the treaty were not completed till July 1891.  Hence these letters represent an attempt to have the details settled in the way that seemed to Johnson best for the natives and most likely to check the slave trade.  As far as may be determined from the occasional dates and the internal evidence the following extracts are in chronological order.

*Probably* 1890.

Letters to
Maples in
England

The Bishop writes kindly and interestingly July 27, *re* the islands, German down to Mbamba, Portuguese thence to Makanjila's, either inclusive or exclusive, thence British right away. One feels what is the use of making *masanje* (children's play huts) here on the shores of the Lake when the wholesale business is going on else-where—I mean *qua* politics. Here we are in possession, anchorages and wooding stations bought for thirty miles, Mluluka and Losefa and doubtful people from Mkalanila pressing us to return, Likoma half-bought, and anchorage becoming first-rate under our work. The Portuguese cannot compete overland with a stream of com-merce up the great Lakes ; if that is to come, let it come as a river to both its banks. Mr. Moir said to me at Likoma, " we give the *Jumbe* (chief of Kota Kota) this money just to get a footing and pay our way, and this is what will go on (viz.), Yaos will do some bit of treachery and escape to Portuguese friends on the other side (the boundary) ; English stop the trade in spirits on the west where the ivory arrives, and Portuguese bring it (or fail to stop it) . . . to the east side and then smuggling revives ; Makanjila will absorb the Nyasas when Germany has broken their present keepers, the Magwangwara. What extra expense is involved in Consular juris-diction and trading operations on the east, if they are once adequate on the west ? "

W. P. J.'s
proposal

He proceeds in this letter to argue for a boundary line on the east side of the Lake which would have given all the Lake shore to the British, leaving the Portuguese and German dependants looking to the Indian Ocean for their coast line while those under the British faced to the Lake on their west. He complains that the line actually drawn then (and upheld to this day) is " a slapdash line depending on no knowledge of natural divisions or tribal feeling." He maintains with heat that leaving the Portuguese a strip of the Lake shore prevents any effective dealing with either the slave trade or the importation of spirits, because it leaves the harbours used by the slave-traders in the hands of the very people who will do least to interfere with that trade. Undoubtedly the control of the whole eastern side of the Lake by British or by British and Germans (whose sincerity as opponents of the slave trade Johnson never doubted) would have, as he said, " closed the Lake to the slave trade." More-over, the development of trade on both sides of the Lake would also have had beneficial effects as providing the people with a 1889-90 trade route and so diverting them from that intercourse with the Indian Ocean coast which was so closely bound up with the slave trade. His line would have run roughly ten miles east of His ten-mile line the Lake through its whole length, or at any rate from the German boundary southward, thus keeping the Portuguese territory right away from the Lake shore and making it impossible for the slave-traders to make use of any harbours on the east side for their traffic. Johnson had no other aim than that of making the best arrangement to crush the slave trade, and there is obviously a great deal to be said for his contention. To-day the question is purely academic, for the methods actually employed, of holding the west shore, of capturing any vessels that tried to cross with cargoes of slaves, and of imposing peace on the raiding tribes of the hills who supplied the material for the trade, has put an end to slave-trading on the Lake. The British and the Germans have worked together to this end but the Portuguese have done practically nothing either in the way of hindering the trade or of finding other outlets for the activities of the natives.

Here are a few more extracts from Johnson's letters to Maples (who was in England) on this burning question.

*November* 17, 1890.

Let England command the Lake harbours, sharing the east with Germany, for Germany won't wink at the slave trade, and in the name of these poor people whom we profess to wish to protect let us know where the division is.

Now for the Delimitation, can't you speak about it and not just 1890 hug yourself over Likoma, or I shall be thinking of Esther and Mordecai's language, only I wish you would come, even to be selfish, in Likoma.

. . . Why in the name of Boundaries, divide Makanjila's and Mkalawili's, so throwing the Yaos north on the Nyasas. Makanjila doesn't care for his sandy beach ; Losefa will do as well, he is master of Mkalawili's, Losefa, Mluluka and almost of Chingomanje's, for we have seen him smash them all, or do it by deputy. Who will stop him up north ? At present he is too far off to do much, what shall we say if he is driven upon Masanje's (at Msumba) and our Christians seized and our boys sold and teachers of the hated Englishmen shot ? Who is to stop him ? Chingomanje, etc. is said to have leagued with the Angoni against Msumba, and coming down we saw two dhows at Mtengula.

Two gunboats, I hear, are at Chiromo opposite Katunga ; Buchanan talks of visiting Makanjila, but do protest against a white raid of any sort or bombarding. Makanjila would not care a rap for thirty Nyasas killed and straw roofs burnt ; he would only hate the white man more, and he would have all Yaoland, all the slave-lined Makuas behind and effete Europeans at the coast to fall back on.

Here at Mponda's to-day there are to be seen two flags, Portuguese and English, two English steamers close by, and one of them paying him £25 this trip, and the Portuguese with NO representative. . . . These Yaos neither fear nor respect us, and now England is going to try and settle Nyasa, leaving the chief slavers in possession of their old harbours from Mkalawili's to Chiwagula ; the valley of the Msinje still to be inaccessible and Magwangwara-raided ; Yao headquarters behind Mkalawili, Madimba, Losefa, Mluluka, Chingomanje, the old Yao harbours ; pay the *Jumbe* (at Kota Kota) £300 a year to exchange western ivory for eastern Nyasa girls,—this is not a distant vision. The thing is to extend the British sphere and encourage Yaos in it, then every village is a hostage for keeping the peace and the people see we are not only *nkondo ina* (another war host). Now good night from the midst of river damp, mosquitoes, sleeping teachers, tea, etc.

*December* 15, 1890.

A July *Times* speaks of ceding the Shiré Highlands and I hear from no one this mail. Buchanan is down river with gunboats, last time he said Makanjila was in the British sphere and I wrote a last pleading for the Msinje R. line of longitude right away as east British boundary, a last vain cry.

*February* 5, 1891.

I do hope to hear from the Bishop to-day—at last in the paper is found reference to the British limits of the Protectorate. It seems to me that you all have thrown up our cards on the east side by not making use of your humble servant ; people, e.g. Consul Johnston, have been at Likoma and know how much and how little you know of the country. Belcher ran me down as not knowing anything, so all I write or say is regarded as that of a very second-rate authority, and the conditions of the east coast are treated as hardly known. It is the business of men like Buchanan to listen to heads only, and I have had no hearing. I have no hesitation in saying that in native affairs we know the east coast and have more hold on it than any one can boast of the west.

*March* 1891.

We hear H. H. Johnston is Commissioner for Nyasaland. Cannot you even now press for the Msinje or ten-mile limit ? If he comes in force as Commissioner he could as easily deal with all as with part 1891 of the east coast.

It was in vain for Johnson to cry in the wilderness, his voice His cry in vain was not heard where the settlements were made and the east side of the Lake was distributed among the three Powers according to the arrangement which is familiar to us. The Germans had the north end and a strip down the east as far as the line of the Ruvuma ; the Portuguese became neighbours to the Germans to the south of the Ruvuma and controlled the east coast nearly down to Makanjila's village. That turbulent Yao was indeed placed, as far as his lakeside village was concerned, in British territory, but with so narrow a strip behind him that he enjoyed the great advantage of being astride the boundary and able at will to settle on whichever side was most convenient for the plans of the moment. Johnson's fears for the great village of Msumba under its Nyasa chief Masanje were not realized, and it has continued to be a stronghold of the Mission, blocking the invasion of Islam from the south.

We said above inadvertently that the Portuguese " controlled " the east coast strip allotted to them, but that word was by no means appropriate for at least ten years after the settlement. It was not till Christmas 1900 that any Portuguese force at all appeared in their piece of Nyasaland, and then they came as emissaries of a Nyasa Company which has till very lately continued to administer the territory.

From 1891 the work of the Mission on the mainland, i.e. pre-eminently Johnson's work, was carried on subject to these international arrangements and the greater part of the work lay in what was at first nominally and since 1900 effectively a foreign domain. Treaty rights safeguarded the interests of the Mission, which, as has been shown, was actually in that strip of territory long before there were any European overlords to reckon with.

Bishop Smythies, for one, judging the matter in a purely abstract way, always rejoiced when the Mission was put into the position of working in foreign territory, because he thought it a good protest against the notion that the English Church can never do anything beyond the range of influence of an English-speaking nation. This would be cold comfort, however, to poor Johnson, deeply concerned for the safety of the people among whom he was working, and who were not abstract to him, but very much indeed concrete. However, he accepted the settlement, as he accepted his impaired sight, as one of the conditions under which he had to work, and it was his invariable rule, so long as Portugal had a king, to pray for him by name in the place of the English sovereign when he was celebrating in Portuguese territory. He regarded it as important to teach the people to pray for the powers set over them.

# CHAPTER VI

## Mainland Villages

It is worth while at this point to give some idea of the kind 1890
of work that Johnson and his helpers, lay and cleric, had to do
on the mainland. To begin with, the steamer was viewed as a
floating station and had, just like the stations ashore, its priest-
in-charge who was responsible for all decisions. But unlike the
stations ashore there was a captain associated with him whose
position was one of more power than would be usual on a fixed
station. The work of the *Charles Janson* depended on the mo-
bility of the steamer, and on that point the engineer or captain
(generally one man) naturally had a deciding voice. I believe
it is proverbial among ships' engineers that the top of the
cylinder can always be relied on to secure a delayed start, if the
engineer wishes it. The whole ship is at the mercy of the one
man, who can say absolutely, " It is impossible to move for
twenty-four hours." It was inevitable that there should sometimes be difficulties between a priest-in-charge who must move
with his ship, and a captain who might have to refuse on perfectly good grounds. On the whole, the partnership between
priest and captain worked very well, but it must be remembered
that the situation had always in it the elements of strain. Johnson was one of the hardest taskmasters imaginable, and it did
not really make it much easier for those associated with him to
know well that he drove himself harder than he drove anyone
else. The crew consisted at first of whatever men could be got
to join on, but, as training developed, there grew up in the villages a good supply of men who were extremely capable, both
as sailors with the boats and in the management and steering
of the steamer, and also as firemen and engine-drivers. The
steamer has quite frequently had to run for months under the
nominal captaincy either of a man who knew nothing about the
sea, or of one to whom the working of a steam-engine was a
complete mystery. Probably it was very rare and quite occa-

sional for it to have been in charge of a man who knew nothing of either. In 1896 the Rev. Christopher Benson Eyre joined the Mission and came to Nyasaland. He was a seaman as well as a priest and held a master's certificate in the British Mercantile Marine. He had also been everywhere and seen everything—at least that is the impression he left on those privileged to know him and to listen to his yarns and he was of so genial a disposition that he endeared himself to all his fellow workers, and to the natives with whom he had to deal, and whom he knew how to rate in no unmeasured terms. I think his strongest term of abuse was no worse than " Blooming jackass! " but even that can be made very expressive. Naturally, he came at once to the work on the *C.J.*, and was identified with it for years until 1901, when the *C.M.* appeared on the scenes ; considerably later (1906) he was withdrawn from the *C.M.* and was sent well inland to Mtonya as Archdeacon of Yaoland. The long association between Johnson and Eyre was a very happy one, none the less

so because they were men of very different types. Johnson lived long enough to mourn for the loss of his old companion and fellow Archdeacon, and it may be permitted here to quote some words he wrote of him soon after Eyre's death : " To him his Lord must always bring beauty, bravery, fortitude, comradeship and fire of righteousness, but he was very gentle with the absence of these in anyone else. . . . To him every place, a hill, a canoe, a camp was full of the chariots and horses of fire. He lived in the One Presence." One who read these words said at once, " Why, that is exactly true of Johnson himself! "

The *C.J.*, for most of us who have known it, means very largely these two men, and that is why their association and relations with one another need to be set forth at this point. Eyre was, with his sea experience, much more tied to the steamer; Johnson and any other priest who might be working with him used the *C.J.* rather as a floating base of operations on the mainland—but both when the steamer reached a village would go ashore to take services. The flying-column people often were dropped at one village after another and last of all the steamer moored off a third village and Eyre made it his duty to minister to that village, and in the morning after breakfast to make connection again at agreed points with the other two. Thus even with three priests on board there was no overlapping and no

A TYPICAL NYASA VILLAGE

lack of important work. Eyre was naturally the ship's husband, 1890 looking after its stores, its provisions, its supply of the firewood without which it could not run, engaging the steamer hands and paying them. He was also generally responsible for paying the teachers ashore, and that was no simple operation. Each had to be paid, at least until the later days, in such things as cloth, soap, salt, beads, possibly in books for their private use, and the paymaster had to know what was the value in cash of each of these things in kind, and to work out a teacher's pay fairly. Later it became the rule to pay only in money, but that was not till the days of Bishop Fisher, by which time traders had established stores in a good many places and the teachers could go and buy what they chose with their money.

Let us suppose ourselves travelling as passengers on the *C.J.* Life aboard from Likoma. The steamer whistle has called us, perhaps with the *C.J.* a little impatience, to get aboard with our baggage and our boy, or it may be boys. Eyre welcomes us aboard and tells us to make ourselves at home, and, this was his regular jest, to ask for anything we wanted if we did not see it provided. On the main deck is a sort of house which provides a small saloon, with an arrangement of the cupboard kind that converts it at short notice into a small chapel. Somewhere below are tiny cabins, but not more than enough to justify the use of the plural number. Above is an upper deck on which most of the life of the steamer is lived by the staff and the missionary passenger. Amidships and visible from the upper deck is the galley, if that is the correct word for the cook's realm, and when the boat is rolling a bit it is possible to sit on the upper deck and to watch a cook making vain efforts to keep a milk pudding from swishing round and round the oven. A little forward is the stokehole, and looking down at the stokers you find it easy to understand how the word " stoko " came to be offered as a rendering of the English word " hell " in some early efforts at translation by Dr. Laws. You may have imagined that Lake Nyasa being so very much smaller than the Atlantic will be as smooth as a duckpond. You soon learn better when you are aboard ; in fact in some states of the Lake your only chance of keeping dry will be to climb to the top of the mast.

The first call the steamer makes is probably in some small Loading up bay where there is a carefully arranged lot of firewood awaiting with firewood its arrival. The captain or the foreman of the native crew goes off in the dinghy and after measuring the firewood pays in cloth, and straightway his boys load the stuff on to the boat and carry it to the steamer. If the steamer is going a long trip in a hurry, and there is plenty of firewood on shore, several trips will be made till every available space of the *C.J.* is filled up and the wood begins to spread into places not intended for it. Very often these wooding stations are not in places where there is other work to be done, and so the priest on board is very likely waiting impatiently till this necessary work is done. Off she goes at last and presently comes to the first village at which one of the priests is to get off. He and his boys are put ashore in the dinghy with all that they need for the time of their absence. Johnson always had his goods packed in native baskets (*miseche*), a packing which was quite good enough for many things, but decidedly not good enough for the books that he carried with him, including dictionaries, concordances and such-like ponderous tomes. Bruder's *Concordance of the Greek Testament* gradually disintegrated under this treatment and became useless to Johnson or anyone else. Food such as cannot be bought ashore has to be taken from the steamer, together with a supply of salt, soap, beads, and especially cloth for buying food. One missionary found a magic lantern with some scriptural slides useful, not only for instructing the villagers, but also for securing a supply of eggs. The demand for seats was so great that a charge of one egg was absolutely necessary and sometimes the exhibition would yield eggs enough to last a week. When it was found that some of the eggs chirped, the plan was made of advance bookings, the eggs being brought along during the day, carefully tested and exchanged, if they were good enough, for a paper ticket admitting one person.

Johnson had sometimes lively experiences in getting ashore. The landing-places were not all good and the Lake, as has already been pointed out, was not often like a millpond. On one occasion at least, Johnson and Eyre were going ashore in the same dinghy at a bad place and there seemed danger of the boat being swamped. Eyre shouted out, " Jump out, Archdeacon, you're bound to get wet " ; and the Archdeacon jumped into water up to his waist and was pulled ashore by the ready hands of some natives who rushed in to seize him.

The steamer after disembarking its first passenger goes on probably to the next village but one and drops a second priest, who will minister to that village. Then it returns to a village in 1890 between where it casts anchor for the night and the remaining priest carries on in that village. Each priest ashore takes evensong and probably preaches, looks into registers, examines candidates for the catechumenate or for baptism, hears the confessions of those Christians who come to him, and very likely hears two or three cases, administering Church discipline or reconciling those at variance. He has a busy evening, and rising early celebrates, takes more classes and possibly, if time allows, looks into the school and sees that it is going well. Then he has to pack himself up and either wait for the steamer to call for him or possibly to go to some agreed point, there to embark again, and so off for another day and a like piece of village work. The steamer carries not only the priests who are doing this village work, but very likely some priest going to or returning from Likoma who is a passenger. There are always many petitions from natives for a passage from here to there or back again, and the captain has to decide whether such petitions can be granted.

When the steamer is moving, meals, for such as care about Food supplies meals on a moving steamer, are served in the small saloon or perhaps on the upper deck, where there is an awning that tries to keep off the rain, the sun or the sparks from the funnel. The African fowl, sung in verse by Chauncy Maples, forms the staple of the meat supply, while rice takes the place of potatoes and most vegetables, except at favoured spots along the Lake side where the Mission has a garden or where the natives have learnt to raise vegetables for their own use and for sale. Beans can always be relied on, not the succulent variety known as French beans and eaten green with the pod, but ordinary beans that have left their pods and are generally very dull stuff indeed.

A shortage of fowls can always be met by drawing on the tinned foods in the steamer store. But in the early days the steamer store was very often empty of even such things as flour, sugar and tea—to mention the chief things which we must look abroad to get. These shortages were not due to short sight, but to the incalculable delays on the river below the Shiré Highlands. Goods ordered long ago might be waiting still on the bank at Chinde or at Port Herald or some other point on the long line of river communications. Cloth in particular might be held up and without cloth for barter the resident on the Lake

G

shores was held up too. Ultimately, on most of its trips, the
C.J. would find its way to Fort Johnston and to Mponda's,
where the general Mission store was ; and there would be a busy
loading of the steamer with the various stores ordered by all the
different European stations on the Lake and, of course, stores
for the steamer itself. This work required sometimes several
days and as there was, in the days we are thinking of, a resident
priest at Mponda's, the Archdeacon and his assistant priests
generally avoided reaching that place but were thrown ashore
at villages north of this end of the Lake, and spent their week-
end or interval of two or three days in their customary ministra-
tions as described above. Kota Kota on the west side was
started as a U.M.C.A. station in 1894 and had always from that
time on a resident priest and staff of lay helpers, male and
female, and a developing work, of which we have not said much,
because it was always to all intents and purposes outside Johnson's sphere of interest even when he was Archdeacon.

On the return trip the C.J. would carry incoming mails, just
as it had picked up and carried outgoing mails on the way down,
and it can easily be imagined that the arrival of the steamer
with the monthly budget from home was a very great event, at
Likoma in particular. Kota Kota had a government post with
its magistrate or collector and other officials, and it was on the
Trans-Continental Telegraph Line ; moreover, the Government
steamer and the trading steamers all called at Kota Kota much
more frequently than they did at Likoma, away on the other
side of the Lake. Every trip of the steamer was more or less
like the one we have described, and you must think of Johnson
as living for years a life of just that sort. Subordinates came
and went, but Johnson and Eyre seemed to go on for ever in
that round. The engineers and captains changed, but for a very
long period the work remained the same, and the two friends
carried on through all other changes of staff. From time to time,
of course, it was the C.J.'s duty and pleasure to carry the
Bishop round the Lake on a tour of visitation and confirmations.
Sometimes Johnson or Eyre would leave the steamer for a while
and accompany the Bishop on a trip into the hills to Unangu or
to Mtonya, or in exploration of the possibilities of new developments in the hill country. But the steamer, first the C.J. and
later the much more roomy C.M., was always the base of their
operations.

# CHAPTER VII

## Training of Teachers

ONE of the special activities of Johnson from the first was the training, somehow or other, of native agents. That must always be the first concern of the pioneer missionary as soon as his field extends beyond the village where he makes his home. Even in the first days at Chiteji's, when Johnson was all alone with no fellow member of the Mission nearer than Masasi, he had to try to make use of his first converts to bring in and teach others. His own work was never for long based on a settled home, and that is one thing to be remembered all through his career. When he came in 1886 to take charge of the C.J. and was able to spread himself over a wider area, it became absolutely essential to have teachers, native teachers, who could live among the people and carry on in the absence of the missionary priest the teaching of those who were drawn into the influence of the Church. Johnson's letters to Maples when the latter was in England are full of details about the movement of teachers from one place to another, the supplying of a gap made by the lapse of one or the death or removal of another. As in other places many of the first teachers were necessarily very imperfectly trained. If a man was zealous and, as far as could be judged, of stable character, he could be tried as the leader of the growing band of adherents in his own village. Slowly but surely the work grows in this way, and there develops a band of people from whom the real teachers of the future can be chosen. At a very early stage the teacher has not to teach of secular subjects more than the ABC, and that chiefly in order that the learners may as soon as possible get the power of learning from a book themselves. But in the very early stages, through which Johnson, more than any other of the Nyasa missionaries, had to work his way, there were no books and hardly any written words. It must be remembered that the Bantu races of Africa had never, before their contact with the

1886

Europeans (and that meant in most cases, if not all, with the missionary), had the idea of using written symbols for the sounds they made. The European gave them, not the sounds, of course, but the first efforts at representing the sounds by the signs we call letters. Why should the missionary take the trouble to teach his people to read and write ? In the first place, it is the obvious means of extending his usefulness beyond the people actually in reach of his spoken words ; and the missionary, in the first days, had a very real need to spread himself as far as possible. In the second place, it very quickly becomes a thing very ardently desired by those who see others in possession of this wonderful new power. In the third place, the missionary needs the help of the written word to extend his own knowledge of the people and to store it up for others. So it may be taken for proved that there is an inevitable need for scholars who, as soon as they have climbed a few steps, shall become teachers to help those who are climbing behind them.

At first, teachers from Zanzibar

As soon as the *C.J.* was available Johnson began to want to take some of these very elementary teachers in the steamer, to go with him to the villages and help in the first work, and also to help him in his own studies of the language and the people. He had by now some Zanzibar-trained teachers, of whom Augustine Ambali was the senior and Eustace Malisawa was another, both later to become priests. The lame boy whom Johnson carried from Mataka's at the time of his being driven from there had been brought up at Masasi, and also became a teacher who served many years in the Lake Diocese. But the supply of teachers was always an anxiety very near to Johnson's heart, and on the *C.J.* he began a work which later was transferred to the *C.M.*, as we shall see. On the *C.J.* there was

Teacher training on the *C.J.*

positively no accommodation for this work of teacher training, and for teacher and taught the conditions were such as any other less persistent man than Johnson would frankly have described at once as impossible. Still something was done, and, even when what was done was insignificant in itself, at least Johnson was calling attention to a need and pointing the way.

1899 The " peripatetic " College ?

At one time (in 1899) it happened that the *C.J.* was laid up for the time, and the Archdeacon's " curate " (who did not re-gret the enforced absence of the steamer) happened also to be pretty keen on the training of teachers. A plan was formed which came to be called the " peripatetic College," and was

another of the devices Johnson used to supply teachers. The 1899
Archdeacon enrolled about a dozen boys, some of whom had
certainly been teachers already, and they travelled with him by
the Lake side, sometimes afoot, when they carried his loads and
were his porters between stations, sometimes in the steamer's
dinghy, which they learnt to row under the coaching of the old
oarsman of the Ouse and the Isis, and this they liked a good deal
better than walking, and, I think, better than the doubtful
happiness of being carried in the steamer. As with the *C.J.* the
two priests did their best to cover two villages at a time and yet
to meet together where the Archdeacon was with his boys for
school work for as much of the time as could be spared from
travelling, and from the regular work of visiting a village school
and its Christians. The boys were, of course, very useful when
the work was the visiting of the school and the inspection of its
registers and equipment. The duties were distributed among
them and each on arrival knew what he had to attend to and
each had to give a report on what he had done and seen. This
was a useful training for the budding teacher, and it was of real
assistance to the Archdeacon and to the school under visitation.
But this was not all that the students of the peripatetic College
learnt. The whole expedition moved at a leisurely rate down
the coast and stayed as long as seemed necessary at each
stopping-place, and when the inspectorial work was finished the
students went to school themselves, and learnt some English
from the " curate," or explored the mysteries of Arithmetic (at
which the Lake boys are naturally rather good), or took turns
to satisfy the Archdeacon's consuming thirst for help in the
the translation work of which he always had something on
hand. Several together would very often spend hours with him
thrashing out the finer points. It may be due to this sort of
work, in which the Archdeacon always called in Tom, Dick and
Harry to help, that the natives of Nyasaland have always been
conspicuously keen on arguing with one another on their own
speech. Then there were demonstration classes by one or other
of the priests in the village school, with the students attending
closely to learn what they could of method and matter. Drill
and physical exercises were for the most part entirely unknown
and the students were taught such things as these, and were
allowed to practise on the classes.

The " peripatetic College " came to a sudden end over a food

1899

dispute, the students not seeing eye to eye with the authorities on the working out of the agreement under which they had joined, but it was an interesting and useful experiment that, like everything else, showed the urgent need of a College with a settled home and its own buildings. It showed among other things how tremendously keen were the boys who would put up with such conditions for the sake of improving their education and fitting themselves for work as teachers. It was not that the teacher's calling was a highly paid prize for which hardships might well be undergone ; it was simply that the students did intensely wish to serve their Master.

1900

To carry on the story of teacher training to the end, it is necessary to add that the next step was the building of a very simple set of buildings, all scrupulously on the scale suitable to the Archdeacon's ideas as to cost and congruity with the native style in their own villages. The first buildings were planned and put up by the Rev. Caradoc Davies, who was working with the Archdeacon at the time, and the work began as a college for the work for which Archdeacon Johnson was re-

Diocesan Training College

sponsible on the mainland. In 1902 it became the Diocesan Training College for teachers from all over the diocese, from Kota Kota and Likoma, from Unangu and Monkey Bay, from every place where the education had reached the stage of enabling the boys to pass an entrance examination. All existing teachers were assisted to get a certificate from the College by a plan of short courses, and it was decreed that after a space of two years no teachers could be employed anywhere without the

St. Michael's College

Diocesan certificate to be obtained only at the College. This College, called from the beginning St. Michael's College as a link with St. Michael's College, Aberdare (now at Llandaff), of which Johnson's brother Harry was Warden and of which Caradoc Davies was an alumnus, has continued to produce all the

1932

teachers the Diocese has needed. Its Principals have been in order Padres Barnes, Marsh, Arthur Douglas, Dennis Victor, G. N. Bacon and P. H. Hill, and there has naturally been a steady growth in efficiency.

Early difficulties of teacher training

One of the consuming anxieties of Johnson in the days before the establishment of anything like a system of training on the spot was the necessity of sending boys to distant Zanzibar, as the nearest place where they could get anything more than the very elementary teaching given in the village schools. The

ARCHDEACON JOHNSON, 1900

*Reproduced from a photograph of a group of Missionaries*

terrible danger of this was that it took months for the poor boys to get from the Lake to Zanzibar and months for them to get back. Moreover, Zanzibar had, and deserved, the sort of reputation that rather undeservedly has attached itself to Johannesburg in these later days through the biting description of it by John X. Merriman as the " University of crime." At its best, going to Zanzibar meant transference into a totally new surrounding where old ties did not exist and new ones could not easily be formed through the medium of strange languages. The boys indeed fell into a Christian family at Kiungani, but it was a long time before they could get at home there. The language difficulty came in too to make more difficult the acquisition of the desired learning, and there was often a feeling that promising boys came back too much impregnated with Coast manners and possibly customs to be really useful teachers in the old conditions.

Here are some extracts from Johnson's letters to Maples during the latter's furlough of 1890 to 1891 :

I am glad to see that the Likoma boys are fairly up at Kiungani.
*November* 17, 1890.
I went with Barnaba (to his people) and he got leave to go. I was anxious about Msumba and Chia boys, I hope seven will be ready for baptism at Christmas and they cannot get to Zanzibar much before then, and when there must long feel strange and miss Chinyanja, so I spoke to them of waiting till after Christmas, and all are willing except one Chikokota ; he could hardly get leave alone, besides other reasons against his going.
*January* 19, 1891.
These long journeys and delays are a great feature in our teachers' trial, W. E. K. and D. S. with their three charges knocking about somewhere between here and Quilimane makes me sad when I think of it. I am sending a list as little misleading as may be of our coast schools, Richard the complete coast man [*i.e. of the Indian Ocean Coast where Islam is dominant*], makes me tremble, and So Songolo has made me nearly cry, but yet I hope it is not all paper work. We tried a " quiet day " with teachers at Likoma. I fell into Swahili " as it is spoke " by myself, I hope somewhat was understood. D. Benjamin has the *savoir faire* to look as if he understood all ; I was helped and we had no particular disagreeables. . . . The journey to Zanzibar is full of dangers and scandal and expense.

I received your letter as to W. E. K. and D. S. after writing to you and of course long after hearing from Jones Bateman (head of Kiungani) settling they were to return. Their wretched dawdling in steamers, etc. on the way to Zanzibar bore out my worst fears, they were a month at Vicente, happily with our party coming up.

Length of
journey to
Zanzibar

If one realizes that the distance from Likoma was as long as the journey from Birmingham to Constantinople, that it involved just as great changes of social environment and custom, and that at the date of these extracts it was almost as adventurous a journey as Gerard's Journey from Holland to Rome, it is easy to enter into the anxieties of the priest who sent them, and to admire the pluck of the lads who at his bidding faced the perils of the enterprise. Since 1902 it has happily been no longer necessary to run these complicated risks, and St. Michael's College has worthily done the work for Nyasaland that Kiungani at one time did for the whole diocese before there was any second Bishop.

W. P. J.'s
contribution

Johnson's particular contribution to the desired result was his steady insistence on giving the boys a training as little removed as possible from the ordinary conditions of native life. There may have been inconsistency in his way of working for this end, but there was never any doubt in his mind as to the end itself. And his insistence on it was not without its effect. It was impossible to work with Johnson and forget the immense importance of continuity in the development of the native people. It is so easy to think, and perhaps so natural to think, that all we have to give, exactly as we see it, is a tremendous boon to the native ; it is not so easy to keep in mind the point of view of our beneficiaries. Johnson never allowed himself or others to forget it.

Other
developments

During these years a good many other things had been happening in the diocese. In the first place Nyasaland had become a separate diocese with its own Bishop. Bishop Smythies had in 1891 been reluctantly obliged to admit that he could no longer perform adequately the difficult duties of Bishop over so very far-flung a diocese. He agreed to the division of the Diocese and went home to consult about it. It was a long time before the Home Committee found a man to take on the Lake diocese, but at last the Rev. Wilfrid Bird Hornby was consecrated on St. Thomas's Day, December 21st, 1892, and came out to the Lake as the first Bishop of Nyasaland. He travelled by way of Zanzibar and the Zambezi and a large band of new workers came with him. Unfortunately, not only the Bishop himself, but a large number of the new recruits, failed to stand the severities

1893
Bishop Hornby
first Bishop of
Nyasaland

of the climate, and were either dead or invalided in compara- 1893
tively a few months. The Bishop resigned in 1894 and afterwards occupied for some years the diocese of Nassau. Among Archd. A. G. B.
the recruits of that year 1893 one alone survives and still is at Glossop
work on the Lake that he loves, the veteran Archdeacon Glossop,
whose name is for ever associated with Likoma Island, where he
has spent most of his years.

The year 1893 saw another very interesting beginning in the The *Nyasa*
shape of what was called at first *Occasional Paper for Nyasa-* *News*
*land*; it was edited (and largely written, too) by Chauncy 1893 to 1895
Maples, and was printed at the Universities' Mission Press at
Likoma. It first appeared in February 1893, and subsequently
quarterly, with some slight irregularity until its last number in
December 1895, which was devoted to the sad news of the
drowning of Bishop Chauncy Maples and Joseph Williams, the
sinking of the *Sherriff*, and the murder of George Atlay by the
Magwangwara. No more issues of that paper were contemplated when the busy brain and the nimble, ready pen of its
founder were no more.

But in 1902 Bishop Trower started the *Diocesan Chronicle*, 1902
and succeeding Bishops have continued it as an indispensable *Diocesan*
record of diocesan happenings. *Chronicle*

The *Occasional Paper* changed its name after its second
number, and was henceforth known as the *Nyasa News*. This
change was dictated by the desire to give it a wider appeal, and
to interest all residents in Nyasaland in it both as readers and
as contributors. Johnson was a frequent contributor both of
articles and notes. Chauncy Maples reviewed Dr. D. C. Scott's
encyclopædic dictionary of Mang'anja. He also wrote for it the
celebrated " Plaint of an African Fowl," protesting against
the general abuse showered on that quite indispensable bird.
Johnson's articles range over such subjects as " the Facts as to W. P. J.'s
the sale of Children by their Parents," denying that this oc- articles in
curred except under stress of very special circumstances; *Nyasa News*
" Facts and Theories," from which it may be permitted to " Sale of
make a quotation in order to show what sort of facts and Children by
theories were in the writer's mind. parents "

" One soon learns that Africa herself is apparently, like her child
the chameleon, different to different observers. One says that
people are emotional, another that he has never seen a tear or " Facts and
excitement called up by any oratory. A Superior of the austere theories "

1902

Trappists speaks of the hopelessness of advance unless clothing comes first. One who lives delicately deprecates any change in outward dress, even of those with whom we live closely. . . . We can only help others by gradual study of the natives, the fauna, and the country. . . . We have to fear ourselves. It is so captivating to take wide views, to lump together people who seem all alike because they are black ; it is so captivating to draw either the black side or the light, instead of what we see ; it is so much easier to represent a man as doing everything, knowing everything, than to draw a character ; again, it is so much easier to belittle what he does, and pooh-pooh what he knows."

1893
Defence of the
Yaos

In another article (of November 1893) he makes a great defence of the Yao people against some severe criticisms of their character. As his heart was always more given to the Nyasas, this defence is a witness to the impartiality of his judgment. He maintained that the Yaos' faults were not so much the faults of the race as the evil effect on them of the Arabs and the Coast, to whose influence they were more liable because they were much more than most tribes a far-travelling tribe.

1894
" An Answer "
to a critic

In May 1894, he contributed " An Answer " to " one of the oldest and best informed " of the Mission, who said " You must accept your position as being not only messengers of the Gospel, but representatives of civilization." What did he find

The Gospel and
Civilization

in that opinion that required an answer ? It is a point so characteristic of Johnson's attitude that his answer must be examined briefly in order that we may understand what he was at, and what were some of the underlying principles of his action. He says :

" The Gospel might have come in on the crest of a wave of civilization, or on a crest of a love to the English, or as a process of imitation of our manners ; it may have been so elsewhere, but what I contend for is that it is not so in the sphere the s.s. *C.J.* visits at present. . . . I here wish to emphasize that we live amongst the natives in no sense as chiefs, or masters ; as far as we are masters, e.g. employers of labour, we lose at least as much as we gain personally ; we never hear any case of law at all, never arbitrate, in native parlance have no *bwalo* (court) at which native disputes can be

Missionaries
and the
natives

brought out. We have many palavers indeed in cases which the native Christians wish decided as to the right and wrong of some practice before God. We teach each man as an elementary duty to honour his chief. It is, we teach him, his duty to settle who that chief is, and the responsibility rests with him, only let him at his peril realize the importance of recognizing his rightful chief, not thinking that a mixture of missionary and self-will can take the chief's place, 1894 or save him from responsibility. Nor do we find the native, who is worth anything, at all inclined to substitute us for his own chief; we have often had to put up with petty tyranny in the past; from this we are to-day to a great extent saved by the respect felt for the gunboats, even at a distance, and we are thankful for it, but now if we begin to give ourselves airs, the native Christians would not be with us at all.

" I think that our work can only be understood rightly, from understanding this, viz. our fellow countrymen have had no influence, let alone authority, in the sphere in which our converts lived, whether Likoma or elsewhere, nor have we had any force to back our word. I believe we still wish to live with our converts on the same lines, and on the mainland we have no alternative. . . . Now, if you feel you can raise a standard amongst a people ' scattered and peeled,' as my correspondent put it, one's whole energies must be devoted to building up a quasi-English life, and grafting your convert into it, for a man cannot live *in vacuo*; on the other hand if you find yourself only a sojourner in Angoni land, at Msumba or Unangu, your whole energies must be devoted to renovate the native life around, until by your good, health-giving works which outsiders shall behold, they must learn to acknowledge God, when their very existence is called in question in some ' day of visitation.' Surely as missionaries who are called to work on our lines, we must beware of the state within the state, of putting our fittings first, and the natives second, of so conducting our embassy as to hinder communication with the court of native hearts to which we are sent. . . . Such work as turning out good workmen on English lines must be the exception with us, as sending a boy to the colonies is at home. Our main work is to train them to serve God in Church and State at home, remembering, as perhaps we see a kindly smile at these grand terms, that the Church came to the fore long before men learnt to know what the State was. Let our people come into Portuguese, German or British sphere, and take their place there; it must not be by individuals becoming Portuguese, German or English hybrids, but by a streamlet of tribal life being carried into the river of a wider sphere of humanity. We must lay aside all ideas of being mirrors of the world, and must be servants of those we are sent to serve, if we are to do our part side by side with Statesmen, and Warriors, who indeed are called to be mirrors, and to put themselves first in their spheres."

Johnson hated the idea of people coming out to the mission work with the idea that their part was to stand on a pedestal and have the native people bowing and bobbing round them. He had, as he suggests in the quotation just made, had bitter

experience of being despised and ill-treated among the natives
whom he came to help with a single eye to their good ; he certainly had learnt with St. Paul " how to be abased " and he felt
very strongly that he had in himself apart from his Master
nothing whatever in which to boast before anyone.

The use of
Swahili

One of the controversies debated in the *Nyasa News* was that
hardy perennial, the use of Swahili in place of the vernacular,
and on this naturally Johnson held strong views. The matter
was discussed in successive numbers by Mr. A. C. Madan, of
Zanzibar, a warm advocate of Swahili and a mere visitor for a
short time in Nyasaland ; by R. S. H., whom we may guess to
have been one of the Scotch Mission on the west side of the Lake
or at Blantyre, and lastly, by Johnson. The local champions,
both R. S. H. and W. P. J., firmly but courteously demolish
the case presented by Madan and are clear that there is practically no use for Swahili in Nyasaland, and on the other hand
many dangers. Johnson always feared the effect of Swahili as
giving a quite false importance to the Coast influence which he
regarded as not only foreign, as foreign as the missionaries and
their language and ways, but also as actually evil. There was no
surer way for a boy to rouse his ire at any time than by aping
the Coast men either in speech or dress or even in the style of
greeting. In translation there was often heard expressed the
view that a Swahili word was a better thing to introduce than
an English one where the vernacular was in want of a loan, on
the supposed ground that it was more native or more akin to
the native speech. Johnson always resisted this argument and
maintained that it was only to the European, to whom both
were unfamiliar, that the Swahili word looked and sounded
more native. When he carried his opposition to the point of
substituting " Flag " for " Bendera " in a hymn, reason may
have been on his side, but rhythm any way preferred three
syllables to one, other things being equal.

"Coast"
fashions

In other articles in *Nyasa News* Johnson occasionally di-
gressed into illuminating bits of personal experience in the very
early days, or into notes on Nyasa customs and ideas. There is
the less need to quote from these because he has collected his
very valuable notes on the people and life and customs of the
Lake in the little volume entitled *Nyasa : The Great Water*,
which ought to be read by every student of missions and
ethnography.

# CHAPTER VIII

## The Disasters of 1895

O N the resignation of Bishop Hornby, there could not be much hesitation as to his successor. Bishop Hornby himself said :

" There was only one man in all the earth of whom it could be said to be right that he should be put as Bishop over that heroic friend of his, Johnson, and that man was Chauncy Maples."

The Bishopric was accordingly offered to Archdeacon Maples, then in Nyasaland, by cable from the Archbishop of Canterbury, in whose hands appointment lies, as the Diocese was, and indeed is still, a missionary diocese under Canterbury. He would have refused at once, but he was persuaded by Johnson to postpone his decision till he had gone home and consulted chosen advisers. He went home and, after hesitation partly due to the fact that he had himself advised his predecessor to resign, he accepted and was consecrated in St. Paul's Cathedral on St. Peter's Day, 1895, as Bishop of Likoma, a title which remained the title of the See until 1908, when it was again changed to Nyasaland.

He left for the Lake on July 11, made a rapid journey, taking what was then the usual route via the Zambezi, and spent as little time as possible in getting to Fort Johnston at the south end of the Lake, where he found letters and the Mission sailing-boat, the *Sherriff* (named after the Brixham trawler who had died at Likoma in 1891). Steamers going to Likoma were not in sight, and it was uncertain when one would be available. The s.s. *C.J.* was at this time laid up for repair, and Johnson had arranged for an A.L.C. steamer to meet the Bishop at a port on the Portuguese side, as he had originally planned to come overland via his old station of Masasi, and his change of route had not become known to those who were anxiously awaiting his arrival at Likoma. The story of that fatal trip in the little steel sailing-boat is well known. The new Bishop and his companion, Joseph Williams, who had been with him when both started for Africa in 1876, were drowned in the capsizing of the boat, and the Bishop's body was recovered some days after, south of Kota Kota, and conveyed there for burial. Two days earlier George Atlay, the priest at Likoma, who had been in charge there in the absence of Maples, had been murdered by the Magwangwara. Only two months later Arthur Fraser Sim, who had in 1894 begun the work at Kota Kota and to whom it had fallen to bury the Bishop there, himself died of fever and was buried not far from his Bishop.

This series of disasters, robbing the little Mission band of four valuable members, of whom two were veterans and the other two very valuable recruits, caused not only grief and sympathy with the Mission among the other settlers in Nyasaland, but also provoked no little criticism. It seemed that someone ought to be blamed and the Mission with its supposed carelessness of the lives of its members was the only possible scapegoat. In the last number of the *Nyasa News*, published in December, and containing an unfinished article written by Maples before he left for England, Johnson wrote the plain facts of the deaths of the Bishop, Williams and Atlay. We cannot do better than give Johnson's words as they stand, as the best contemporary account.

" Weeks, and months, in passing make it easier for us to write of our Bishop's death, and of Mr. Atlay's murder, even to weigh the questions which rise as to the proportion of blame, if any, which attaches to those concerned.

" We can even be thankful for well-meant criticism as to our whole system, or parts of it, or the idiosyncrasies of individual members of our staff. For does it not show that we are ' Roman citizens.' We acknowledge that we have duties, as being individual members of the English Community, and we by no means wish to shun criticism.

" We can no longer claim forty years' experience in the country between two of us ; but one result remains, we have learnt to relate facts as we saw them, and we are in no hurry to draw morals from them. Morals are not the strong point of Africa.

" Let me lay before our fellow countrymen the simple narratives of Bishop Maples's death, and of Mr. Atlay's.

" The Universities' Mission had two barges, the *Sherriff*, without air-tight tanks, and the *Ousel*, originally fitted with them. These

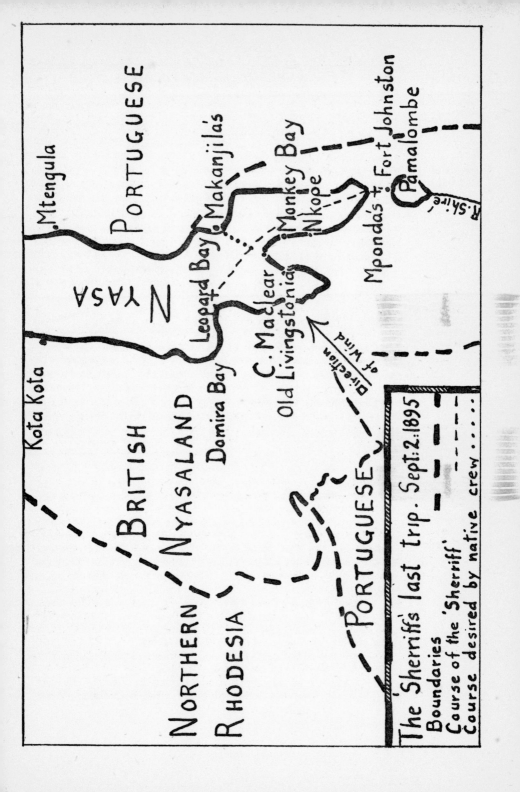

Mtengula

PORTUGUESE

NYASA

Makanjila's

Leopard Bay

Monkey Bay
Nkope

Mponda's ✝ Fort Johnston
Pamalombe

R. Shire

Kota Kota

BRITISH
NYASALAND

Domira Bay

C. Maclear
Old Livingstonia

Direction
of Wind

PORTUGUESE

NORTHERN
RHODESIA

The 'Sherriff's' last trip. Sept: 2. 1895
Boundaries — — —
Course of the 'Sherriff' — — —
Course desired by native crew .......

boats have made a round dozen trips to Matope and back to Likoma. In one of these Messrs. Crouch and Dutton of our Mission came up ; in another Messrs. Wimbush and Brooke. If it is asked, ' Can the native even sail the boats properly ? ' I answer ' Certainly not— they practically never sail on the wind. I have perfect confidence therefore that they will do nothing but what is safe.' If a European is on board, and sits still, the same would hold good ; but directly he takes the command they will look to him.

" We have only one *capitao* who had *any* idea of managing a boat, and he took the boat down on the trip, when they met Bishop Maples. We had certain information that he was coming overland, through the Yao country, and I had gone so far as to make arrangements that the A.L.C. steamer *Ilala* should lie at Mluluka on September 20 to meet him. We thus could not arrange for a special crew.

Was it safe ?

" Now one word as to the safety of these two barges. On this matter I must be pardoned if I prefer the opinion of a Brixham fisherman in our Mission to that of men with far wider but less special experience. Sherriff of our Mission held that these boats were perfectly safe in any part of the Lake. I have little knowledge of the art of sailing, and yet have been in all weathers by day and night, with any sort of crew in these boats, and never had cause to lie to or even shorten sail.

Bishop Maples's fatal haste

" What then really happened ? Bishop Maples was so bent on pushing on and completing the wonderfully short passage, which seemed to augur so well for our future hopes, that he was heard to declare that he would go overland, if no boat came to Fort Johnston before the steamers. Our boat reached there on Sunday, September 1, and they left on Monday. Then ran on to Nkope, where we have a school, and bought fowls, had food and prayers. The *capitao* and crew begged to sleep there, as the south wind was freshening.

Little ballast in boat

" I ought to state here, that the boat, which had been refitted for the trip, was very light, carrying less than thirty loads, whereas 130 is no large cargo. She had no stones aft, and the baggage seems to have been placed in the middle of the boat. Left to himself, the *capitao* would not have sailed thus, as so laded the boat would hardly steer at all.

" Thus they ran on. The crew wanted to go into Monkey Bay, and failing that, straight before the wind, which had some west in it, but the Bishop held on the course towards Leopard Bay. They had had all the sails boomed out. After Cape Maclear they shifted the main-sail over to the same side as mizen (starboard), the jib remaining boomed out on the port side (?). Still the men pressed to be permitted to run to Fort Maguire ; the *capitao* still at the helm.

" Then the main-sail was lowered—how strange it seems and how sad in the pitch darkness, though up on the hills north it was bright moonlight.[1] How could they have gone on at all with mizen and jib, and that as the men assure boomed out ? Then, as the boat shipped water, the Bishop bade them reef the mizen. The *capitao* gave another the tiller to do this, and the boat almost at once broached to.

" What can we say to all this and knowing, as I do, that the Bishop had had some little experience in sailing ? We can only lay our hand on our mouth ; but surely ought not to generalize in a panic.

" Mr. Joseph Williams was asleep in the house of boughs made over the stern, and sank with the boat.

*Williams goes down sleeping*

" The *capitao* and another stuck to the Bishop, using an empty iron box, and a wooden one of clothes, to support him. The latter soon sank. The Bishop had on his cassock, and refused their entreaties to allow them to tear it. The waves broke over them. The boxes sank lower. The cassock soon filled with water, like the leaden ones of the ' Inferno.'

*The Bishop's struggle*

" ' Can you see land near ? ' ' No, not near, but we can see it.' Broken prayers and groanings too : ' Save yourselves! Save yourselves! ' ' I am a miserable sinner! ' And prayers again. Another wave broke—bigger than its fellows—and our brother had sunk in the pitchy darkness. Can we blame those who struck out wildly for dear light and dearer life ?

" I need not enlarge on the *capitao's* imprisonment, that was soon ended by the kindness of Mr. Taylor at Fort Maguire ; the weary trudge up to Kota Kota and back again ; the finding our Father's remains in the water ; the wearier return, and the burial. Mr. Swann's sympathetic activity relieves the dark picture. And the grave (now no longer alone) seems to beckon us onward."

*The capitao imprisoned and soon released*

This most tragic death left the Mission without a Bishop for another long spell, till, exactly a year after the consecration of Maples, Dr. Hine was consecrated on St. Peter's Day, 1896.

The death of Mr. Atlay was in a different category from this so terrible accident by sea, because it was murder, however the circumstances explain or mitigate it. It was, of course, another case for criticism of the Mission and its methods, and it bears on our story as illustrating the dangers through which Johnson

*Mr. Atlay's hunting trip*

[1] There seems some discrepancy here about the light. In September a storm such as this would be merely a windstorm and the clouds would hardly make a pitchy darkness if there was a moon. In fact, the moon was full on September 3 that year, and so it seems that this last phase must have taken place in the short hour or so of darkness between the setting of the moon and the rising of the sun.

H

at all times passed unscathed. What were the relations of the Mission with the tribes among whom it worked when such a thing as this murder could take place ? As, in the absence of the Bishop, his old friend Johnson was the senior priest in the Diocese, the responsibility of all these sad events fell on him, if on anyone, and it concerns us to see what account he gave of it at the time. As regards Atlay, Johnson is not in any sense on his defence, nor could he at any time have been blamed. In the same *Nyasa News* from which we have quoted already he writes as follows :

The Angoni and their general relations with the Mission

" As a Mission we ought to point out, that the Angoni or Mag-wangwara have not as a whole simply cast off their former friendly attitude. And that those who have, can plead a reason, though a wholly insufficient one, for their conduct.

" The Angoni are, broadly speaking, in three divisions under Zimchaya (alias Haruli). His share of the lakeside villages was nearly coextensive with the German sphere. This is equivalent to saying that he has been deprived of his subject villages by white men ; in other words the Germans have stopped Haruli's raids. How far their other relations with this chief have been friendly or otherwise I cannot say.

" Haruli has one village under him farther south, viz. Ngofi, north of the Unga River (the south side is under Mlamilo). And there the very *Nduna* (head man) who brought the Mission a tusk last year, lately threatened me while preaching. But this I put down to drink.

Their power decreasing

" The other two Angoni chiefs, Mlamilo and Songela, have the Nyasa villages in the Portuguese sphere more or less subject to them. Their power has decreased rapidly, partly owing to their fighting with the Yaos, partly owing to the Nyasas' growth in unity, hardly at all directly to our action. So that, from north of Likoma down to Mluluka, we have from time to time met the Angoni, of Mlamilo and Songela, on a friendly footing.

" On the Sunday before Mr. Atlay's death I had received two letters from Mlamilo, asking me to encourage the Wanyanja to help him to attack Mlinganile, the Yao robber-chief, who had burnt the village of Chisanga. I refused to be mixed up formally in the matter, or to write, but I thought the Wanyanja might well help in this war. After seeing Ngongani, Mlamilo's envoy, at Msumba, I came north and met the ill-starred boat *Sherriff* at Chisanga, going south, and on Wednesday, heard of Mr. Atlay's disappearance.

His body found

" The following Tuesday we found his body in the stream, by his little encampment ; our faint hopes that he was alive were thus terminated. His Winchester repeater was in the water with him, loaded. The lives of those who took his life—not more than ten— had been in his hand.

" The question might naturally be raised, ' Was Mr. Atlay rash in going where he did ? '

" Weary, after many months of close work and never-ceasing responsibility in the absence of the Bishop, he was hunting rather a few days' rest than game. He was a sportsman and took his guns with him, but he was bent on rest. He had often expressed a longing for it in talking with me.

" He only went one day's march from Chiteji's village, along a route which Bishop Smythies and Bishop, then Archdeacon, Maples had followed from the coast and in returning to the coast. The same route we had all repeatedly traversed lately in going to and from Unangu. It is true the attitude of Mlinganile, mentioned above, had made it unadvisable to send caravans through his village, but this would not apply to a place forty miles north of his hill.

" Here the Angoni (Magwangwara) alone were to be feared, and after their friendly overtures, Mr. Atlay would see little cause to fear treachery. Nor can we blame him for not realizing that but one day's march had brought him to the main Angoni path, which runs down to the south end of the Lake. His encampment was in fact rather short of this road, but his camp smoke would not escape the attention of any party traversing it.

" Captain Berndt (a German official) kindly furnished us with a letter to the Arab Rashid, who lives with Mlamilo, and I at last secured trustworthy messengers, to take my own letter, and Captain Berndt's, to Mlamilo himself. A party of Achikunda hunters went. They were all received by Mlamilo, and delivered Captain Berndt's letters and my own to Mlamilo and Rashid. (I have known the Arab Rashid for a long time, and have been able to do him some service.) Mlamilo at once bestirred himself to recover two Nyasa youths, who had disappeared when Mr. Atlay was killed. It had been reported that such were in Haruli's country. Mlamilo went to him in person and insisted on sending for these two youths, who were in two villages of Haruli's, with the men who took them. Haruli did not oppose and Mlamilo wished to send these two youths, and some guns and property taken with them, direct to Likoma by the Achikunda. Rashid demurred and took Mlamilo aside, and so he only sent a revolver and letter by the Achikunda. Rashid sent the rest of the property, and the two men, to Langenberg for examination. And now by Captain Berndt's kindness and justice, we have received these two last back again, and the missing property.

" Their account is that some ten Angoni rushed upon them and Mr. Atlay, while resting at midday. They seem to have hustled him with their shields, until one threw a club hitting him in the

1895

back, when he half stumbled, half ran, into the water. It is doubtful whether he then argued with the Angoni, or if the witness only reproduces the subsequent camp-fire talk of the Angoni. But one witness represents the Angoni as answering an appeal of Atlay's by saying, ' We have found you here, an *Mzungu* whom none of us know, and heavily armed. *Wazungu* have taken our villages—so we mean to kill you.' Both witnesses say they followed him to the water and speared him there in the leg, then in the right side, and then thrust him under with a pointed bamboo.

Haruli only to be held responsible

" Should we not in very horror of the crime, distinguish Haruli and Mlamilo ? The party were all Haruli's men, and are well known by name and by sight to the two survivors. Mlamilo has helped us all he could, while Songela is not implicated. Rashid writes, saying the actual perpetrators will be given up to the German Government."

Atlay's body taken to Likoma for burial

Atlay's body was taken down to the shore by the care of So, the teacher who had been with him, and who, along with George Chande, Mr. Atlay's boy, had escaped and brought to Likoma the news of the attack, but without that of the actual killing, which they did not see. The body was conveyed to Likoma and buried there at midnight by the bright light of the nearly full moon.

A. F. Sim dies of fever

The death from fever of Mr. Sim in October of the same year completed 1895's tale of disasters, and left Kota Kota without a priest just when the new work had reached an interesting stage.

Difficulty of filling up gaps

It has to be remembered in estimating mission losses that a vacant place cannot be filled at a day's notice by the first comer. There is the language difficulty to be surmounted, and it is the general experience of Africa that the younger a man begins to learn African languages the better chance he has of getting to know them well. No difficulty or disillusionment is so heart-breaking as to find, after having given up useful pastoral work in one's own country in answer to a missionary call, that there remains an insuperable, intangible barrier between one and the very people one longs to know and help, this barrier of

Youth an asset

language. Therefore, let the young man debating within himself a call to service among the natives of Africa, remember that his youth is a priceless asset and that he has a far better chance of

Need of reserves

useful service *now* than if he should wait till he is forty. Consequently, a Mission needs a reserve of men so that, in the event of such a gap as Sim left, there may be on the spot a man to put in his place while the new recruit comes out to join the

available reserve. No wonder missionary Bishops grow old and
wear out, when they live in perpetual anxiety just for lack of
this available reserve of man-power, hard put to it to keep existing work going and hindered from desirable extension.

Johnson carried on through the anxious months that followed, doing his own work on the mainland and taking refuge
for rest and refreshment at Likoma from time to time, but missing sadly there the bracing comradeship of Chauncy Maples. W. P. J. and
Of these two Johnson was undoubtedly the stronger, harder C. M. contrasted
character, and Maples in his letters often shows his appreciation of this, but Johnson was only strong and hard by virtue of
his indomitable will. In himself he was most sensitive and
loving and he had always found great help and support in the
happy family life of Likoma under Maples. It is idle to specu- Their
late as to what might have been done if that old partnership had partnership
continued with Chauncy as Bishop and Will Johnson as his
Archdeacon. We may be permitted here to digress briefly to
consider Johnson's relations with the six Bishops under whom
he served. For Bishops Steere and Smythies, he had always the W. P. J. and his
greatest veneration and admiration ; in the case of the former bishops
there seems never to have been any difference of opinion and it 1. Bp. Steere
is probable that the two understood one another far better than
was the case with Bishop Smythies and Johnson. It is said that
Bishop Smythies admitted that he never understood Johnson,
and constantly, loyal as he was, Johnson was conscious that 2. Bp. Smythies
Bishop Smythies rather half-heartedly supported his plans. In
one letter, referring to some " kind letters " from the Bishop
about his work, he says, " Is it quite wrong to whisper to you
(C. M.) how sometimes it seems *carte blanche* to go out into the
wilderness, etc. ? I cannot profess to judge of these things, nor,
believe me, do I think it quite wrong, if I was not so hideously
disloyal at times." His self-accusation of disloyalty must be
understood as referring only to those innermost feelings which
he could only reveal to his most intimate friend. In practice,
no one could have been more loyal than he was to Bishop after
Bishop. With Bishop Hine there was always on both sides a 3. Bp. Hine
very great respect, admiration and affection. No less different
from one another than Maples and Johnson they yet seemed to
understand one another and their loyalty to one another was
wonderful. In 1900 there was a real but trifling difference of
opinion between them on a language point, Bishop Hine

1895    favouring Swahili loans against Johnson's preference for English loans. A similar difference arose when Archdeacon Johnson began to introduce "Yahveh" for "Lord" in place of the native word

1900    "Ambuye," which was of too wide a connotation, for it covered also not only grandfather but even grandmother. The Bishop[1] felt that the name Yahveh was one too sacred to trip constantly and lightly off the tongues of native teachers and preachers and wished "Ambuye" to be retained. In the midst of the controversy the Archdeacon became seriously ill and had eventually to go away for over a year visiting his brother in New Zealand and

1901    recuperating there. All the time that the Archdeacon was away, Bishop Hine, against his own feeling and wish, insisted on the use of the Archdeacon's word in place of his own. The Archdeacon returned from New Zealand, ready to yield to the wishes of the Bishop on this point, but by that time Bishop Hine had been translated to Zanzibar and Bishop Trower was appointed in his stead.

This mutual loyalty and real effort to understand one another's points of view was characteristic of all the relations of

4. Bp. Trower    these two. With Bishop Trower the task of getting to understand one another was very much more difficult. Johnson was steeped in Nyasa ways of thinking and working, desperately anxious to catch the native point of view and from long experience painfully aware of the difficulty of doing so. Bishop Trower's mental atmosphere was that of Australia, where he had been at Sydney protagonist in the struggle of Catholic churchmen for recognition and freedom. It was remarked of him that he came to Likoma with his fists up ready for a fight against a supposedly disloyal staff; and he never attained to any considerable knowledge of the natives or their language. He was one of those who started too late, and never could understand the subtleties of the situation as they struggled to find utterance through Johnson. It may be that Bishop Trower had heard, after his appointment, of a cable from Nyasaland to the Home Committee sent by all the priests of the Diocese (except one who could not be reached, but who said afterwards that he would *not* have signed it, and, of course, except Johnson

[1] The S.P.C.K. refused to print the Prayer Book with this form of the word which W.P.J. had introduced in his tentative translations. The Archbishop of Canterbury held it important, and as he took a personal interest in S.P.C.K. a committee was appointed to consider the point. Result was it was refused, and we had to go back to "Ambuye."—J. E. H.

himself) asking that Archdeacon Johnson's name might be submitted to the Archbishop. This cable arrived too late, for the appointment was made as soon as Bishop Hine's acceptance of Zanzibar was received, but if it came to the knowledge of the new Bishop it may account for his quite unjustified idea that he had to reduce a disloyal diocese to order and it may have made a little difficult his first relations with Archdeacon Johnson. It is very pleasing to be able to record that Johnson and Bishop Trower won through the first difficulties to a real esteem and mutual affection, and a good deal of understanding, though generally their points of view remained poles asunder.

To finish this digression it must just be said that with Bishop Fisher the initial difficulties were as great as with Bishop Trower, and that unfortunately, though both tried hard, they never succeeded in understanding one another. This did not impair Johnson's continuous loyalty, but it did make things difficult. It must be remembered that Archdeacon Johnson, in 1911, when Bishop Fisher came, was already close on sixty years old and that it is very hard to shift from a rut of thought or action in which one has been moving over forty years. A great deal of the difficulty in working together came from the Archdeacon's constant desire to present a case for the inarticulate native and to secure the development of the Church among them on lines as little foreign as possible.

Bishop Hine arrived at Likoma in March 1897, and one of his first acts was to make Johnson Archdeacon of Nyasa, an office which he held for thirty-one years.

1901

5. Bp. Fisher

# CHAPTER IX

# In Perils Oft

THERE are two isolated episodes of Johnson's life in his early days on the s.s. *C.J.* which are so contrary to his ordinary experience and so unlike what is expected in a missionary's life that they must be looked into a little in detail. One is the outrage of 1888 at Makanjila's village ; the other a somewhat similar one at Mkalawili's village in March 1890, in which Johnson's cook Stefano was killed. A full account of the first is contained in Archdeacon Johnson's *My Reminiscences* ; there is a contemporary account of it in *Central Africa* by the same hand ; and there is no doubt an official account of it buried in a Blue-book, for H.B.M. Vice-Consul Mr. Buchanan was involved in it.

1888

The steamer early in 1888 was lent to the Vice-Consul for a journey up the Lake to settle some troubles at the north end and when this business was over Johnson, who had accompanied Mr. Buchanan to the north end, conveyed him south again and on the way took him to visit Makanjila, a Yao slaving chief whose village was on the east side close to the narrowest part of the Lake and just south of what was shortly after marked off as the southern boundary between Portuguese and British territory. Johnson had known this Makanjila and his predecessor, and the earlier Makanjila had been quite friendly with him and favourable to his work. The Makanjila of 1888 was a very different man, little better than a madman, responsible three years later for killing certainly two Europeans who went ashore from the A.L.C. steamer *Domira* under a flag of truce and, possibly, of killing Captain Maguire at the same time. In

The point of view of the slaving chiefs

extenuation of the behaviour of these slaving chiefs it must be remembered that what seemed to them a quite legitimate trade in slaves, a trade which they had been induced to take part in by the Arabs at the Coast, who seemed to them a quite superior race of people, that this trade was being relentlessly suppressed,

both on the Lake and on the Indian Ocean, by those inter-
fering Europeans, who weren't being captured themselves and
weren't the relatives or even the owners of those who were
captured. Johnson's way was to enter into friendly relations
with these people and get from them permission to carry on
evangelistic work among their people, and so gradually to
acquire an influence, direct and indirect, which would put an
end to slave-raiding. On this trip he was acting as host to Mr.
Buchanan on the *C.J.* and the visit to Makanjila was the official
visit of the Vice-Consul, who asked Johnson to accompany him
ashore. Johnson had a bad leg and could only get to the village
in a *machila*, a mode of conveyance he never used except when
compelled. An assembly of hundreds of natives was waiting
in the open meeting-place in the centre of the village, and not
only the chief but the people seem to have expected from the
show of pomp on this visit that something special was to happen. They seem to have expected to be given the British flag
as a sign of their being taken under protection by the British,
and from Johnson's presence and the use of the well-known
*C.J.* they expected negotiations for opening a station there.

To their surprise and puzzlement, Mr. Buchanan's address
was more like a threatening lecture, and the prospect of a hand-
some present became more and more distant. Mr. Buchanan
spoke Yao fluently, but that by no means implies that he was
understood as fluently as he spoke. A great deal of nonsense is
talked about Europeans speaking a language " like a native,"
but in fact this is an extremely rare accomplishment. It may
be attained by some who have grown up as children among
natives and most exceptionally by one or two who learn the
language by constant association with natives in their work
and in their play. Mr. Shannon, captain of the *C.M.* for many
years, who saw a great deal of his hands on board and who
hunted with a boy or two whenever he could find time, was one
of those rare people of whom it is credible that they speak " like
a native." Mr. Johnson never did with all his experience and
study of native languages, and Mr. Buchanan did not either.
He aimed at conciliation, and his object was to assure Makanjila
that he and his people would not suffer from any strained relations that might exist between British and Portuguese. In
fact, his message was practically " Codlin's the friend, not
Short," but he no doubt coupled it with warnings that they

must be on their best behaviour. As a dog who understands not a word of his master is moved by tone and manner, so apparently in this case the undertone of threat drowned the main message of conciliation and friendliness. Certain it is that the Vice-Consul was misunderstood and the crowd, doubtless knowing full well what their chief wanted, began to stampede

A stampede

the white men. The crowd hustled them and began to tear their clothes off them. Johnson showed no fight and they were rather nonplussed by this, and simply led him off a prisoner to a hut in the village. Mr. Buchanan resisted and tried to get out a revolver, but happily failed. Johnson says, " I advised him to

The Europeans arrested

come along, as the thing we had most to fear was the frightening them." It seems odd for the victims of such an attack to have been afraid of frightening their assailants, but Johnson's knowledge of the native no doubt guided him aright in this fix. Their retinue (except one native soldier killed) managed to escape by swimming to the *C.J.*, which remained in the offing, unable to help. Late in the afternoon the *C.J.*

The *C.J.* ransoms them next morning

went off to get firewood, without which she couldn't keep steam up, but she returned next morning and carried on negotiations with Makanjila, resulting at last in the release first of Mr. Buchanan and, after a little more haggling as to terms, of Mr. Johnson, too. They were ransomed with kegs of red paint, which Makanjila coveted for the adornment of his dhows (slaving vessels), and by the time the official report reached England and a Blue-book, the dhows, written in Swahili *daus*, had become " daughters " by the simple process of mistaking *daus* for the customary legal abbreviation of that word.

The end of this Makanjila

The worthlessness of this Makanjila is shown by the fact that not long afterwards he was shot by his own people.

To us who have been brought up on the tradition that the appearance of a white man is enough to strike awe into the wildest savage, this incident teaches the falsity of that tradition, and throws a great light on the hardihood of Johnson, who had since 1881 been accustomed to travel alone among hostile tribes where at every step his life was in his hand. In extenuation of the disregard at Makanjila's village of the majesty of the British flag which the Vice-Consul displayed, it must be noted that as yet the boundaries were not delimited, and that in any case Makanjila had not, up to that time, placed himself under that flag, and could only recognize it as the great hindrance for him 1888 to a free trade in slaves.

Round this incident many absurd and unlikely details have been embroidered by those who prefer legend to history. This sober account is based entirely on the evidence of one of the principals, Johnson himself, and may be relied on.

In 1890 in a village of Mkalawili, the village known as Chilowelo, some forty miles north of Makanjila's, Mr. Johnson was once more in danger. There is a full account of this affair in *My Reminiscences*, which agrees in all essentials with the letter Johnson wrote at the time to Mr. Buchanan, making formal report of it to the proper authority, not as seeking redress, but to secure that such reception should not become a habit.

The letter to Mr. Buchanan runs as follows :

DEAR MR. BUCHANAN,

It seems natural to write promptly to you after our joint experi- March 1890 ence, and wise to do so from your official position. I shall write to Mr. Johnston,[1] of course, only I take it for granted that he has left the Blantyre neighbourhood.

I do not write so much to seek any immediate redress as in the hope that some step may be found to avert an evil that threatens to spread and affect so many besides myself, perhaps even all the English residents.

I need not recall our experience at Makanjila's except to remind you that there the flag offered some plausible excuse, and to tell you that we were treated in much the same way at Mkalawili's yesterday, an envoy from Makanjila's being the principal actor in the scene. It was a regular plot and a complete change of front on Mkalawili's part. Unlike Makanjila's, at Mkalawili's I have had formal leave to teach, and only the visit before last the chief promised more help, and was very gratified by my bringing over letters from Kachulu's (Kazembe's), whither we had gone hoping to meet the s.s. *Domira* coming down the west side.

Only yesterday some of Mkalawili's people told me at Losefa that their chief had come down to the village on the Chilowelo on purpose to await our coming, and to send letters across to Kachulu.

We landed about 5 p.m. and I found the chief at once and firewood was brought for sale as usual. I noticed that a canoe with perhaps seven persons went straight off to the steamer when Mr. Mills, who was in charge, was very busy finding a place to anchor, as the water is so very deep. He warned off this canoe and one or two more ; it wouldn't be safe to let these Ajaas (Yaos) crowd round,

[1] Afterwards Sir H. H. Johnston.

and he threw half an Indian corn cob at one of the canoes ; they came off at once, laughing apparently, to where I was sitting with Mkalawili, they all went towards the boat and soon we saw the people with firewood going off, and the salt was upset over the wood. (N.B.—Salt is used for buying firewood and takes the place of beads and even calico sometimes.) The chief, when I asked him what was the matter, said, " Let us go and see," and he asked calmly enough and kept his man back, wishing a man to go off (to the *C.J.*) and ask why a man, and he a sick man, had been struck, and meanwhile detaining the rest of us. I tried to argue the case that we could not allow strangers with no note from the chief on board, but to no purpose, and at last I sent the boatswain (Stefano) off. Meanwhile the men, led by a man in white with a sword, became more cheeky, plucking at the teacher's jacket who was with me and even pulling some brass rings off his arms, but with thirty men round what could one do ? The chief still kept cool and mildly reproved these sallies, but when the boatswain came back with a bar of soap and some four to five fathoms of striped cloth, he laughed at it, and harped on the man (who had been struck by the half mealie cob) being sick, etc. There he was, however, nothing the worse, no mark and smiling. All was, I am persuaded, a plot.

*A trumped-up case* (margin)

Since we were at Kazembe's, Makanjila's dhow has been again, and they had brought back men from Kachulu to Makanjila's and so round to Mkalawili's, where we saw them yesterday. Probably then Makanjila is getting the confidence of Mkalawili and Kazembe, who would not trust him before, and one of the conditions has been, " Turn out the *Mzungu*" (white man).

*Influence of Makanjila* (margin)

The young fellow in white with a sword told me afterwards that he was from Makanjila's and recounted our abuse there. He alone at Mkalawili's spoke against me as a teacher. I saw matters were getting more serious, and, after claims for several kegs of powder, three pieces of cloth, etc., none of which we had on board (we are in fact out of everything), the chief ceased to restrain his men, they ran our boat up and soon tore off our clothes, knocked me over, with knives in my face, pieces of firewood waved close to me and the man with the sword moving actively quite close. I hardly saw any hope of getting off in their excitement.

*W. P. J. attacked* (margin)

Two men were kept, one got off swimming. I was left in my shirt and boots ; a good deal of the excitement went off in running the boat up. Messages and counter messages came from the chief, one with the teacher, whom they ill-treated, that he was to go off and get clothes for me. I was thankful to get him off, I did not know how many were left in their hands. The sun had just set and from then till about 9 p.m. I was the centre of a scoffing group with one or two very mild friends.

The most trying thing of all was a man with a beard, so much I 1890 could see in the dusk, who came from the houses in an awful excitement when the steamer had come in nearer. He swore a party had landed and gone round inside, and he came and stood close over me with his knife, declaiming and making as if he would cut my throat ; but some expostulated and backed me up in swearing that no one had left the steamer.

So wearily they demanded and taunted till at last they let me off on my promising to send the remains of a keg of powder I had. I think *The boatswain* some did it hoping to bring the steamer in nearer, and then a *Stefano* friendly hand or two really got me off in a little canoe. Alas! when *Rehani missing* I got to the steamer I found our boatswain and late cook at Likoma, Stefano Rehani, had not reached the steamer. We yelled and yelled and asked about him, but they did not know where he was or would not say, so I threw the half-keg to them as I had pledged, since they would not send for it, anyway.

Our boat is in their hands. It seems an unprovoked attack and *Boat detained* may so easily act as an example up the coast. Personally, I, as a teacher, what can I expect ? or what ought I to expect ? but I feel I ought not to involve others who have a different line.

I have ceased to visit Makanjila, as I have plenty of spheres elsewhere, but Mkalawili invited me up to him this time, so I cannot feel guilty of rashness.

From the *Reminiscences* we learn further that the unfriendly attitude of these villages was not wholly due to the malign influence of Makanjila, but was mainly caused by troubles between the Portuguese and the Yaos inland at Mwembe, Mataka's village.

It is a regular custom of native law that, if a man wrongs you and you cannot get hold of him to pay him out, you may justifiably seize anyone of his relations or of his village, and either hold him as hostage or work your retribution on him. Any white man was thus liable to be held to account for the ill-doings of any other white man, the white men being all of one stock in native eyes.

Poor Stefano Rehani, the boatswain, who was killed at Chilo- *The story of* welo, had had an unusual history. Johnson had found him *Stefano Rehani* attached to a shooting-gallery in Wales. Someone had brought him to England and either lost him or cast him off. He came back to Africa with Johnson and settled at Likoma, where he married happily. He was usually cook at Likoma, but at this time had been dismissed from that work for getting drunk and sent to work on the steamer as a means of getting straight again.

1890

He was killed before his penance was completed, poor fellow. They did not leave till they had done all they could to find him or ransom him, and at last they were told plainly that he had been drowned in the deep pool which gives Chilowelo its name. The boat that had been seized was not recovered till a year later.

Mission work started later at this place

Mission work was eventually started at Chilowelo, but not till some years later.

These troubles were by no means normal, even in the early years to which they belong, and Johnson's relations with the outsiders, the " *Wa-pa-bwalo*," were generally friendly.

Islam

The strip of coast under Yao chiefs from Mluluka southwards was always less amenable, partly because a considerable Muhammadan influence brought in by slave-trading Arabs was stronger there than elsewhere. At one time, it looked as if this Muhammadanism was creeping northwards along the Lake side, but it was always checked at Msumba, under God, by the great personal influence of Augustine Ambali, who made that large town a stronghold of Christian teaching, and who worked there for many years, a bulwark against Islam.

A British official coquetting with Islam

There was at one time a mistaken notion among the powers that be in Nyasaland that Muhammadanism was a faith to encourage as being better than heathenism and more suited to the native than Christianity with its heavy demands. Indeed, it is on record that one British official, presumably himself a Christian, solemnly presented native chiefs with copies of the Koran and his blessing. The possession of a Koran couldn't harm the chiefs much, because it was very much a sealed book to them, and in fact, to quite a number even of Muhammadan teachers. Archdeacon Johnson, who himself read Arabic and carried a Koran with him, seldom found a Muhammadan " *mwalimu* " (teacher) who could read it or who knew more of it than a few formulæ learnt by heart. This so-called Muhammadanism was truly but a bastard form of the faith that worked such wonders in Arabia and Northern Africa and at one time threatened to overrun Europe, and had none of such virtues as may be allowed to exist in the genuine faith of Islam. The measure of countenance and encouragement it has received from some British officials in Africa has been enough, we may think, to make Queen Victoria—the Victoria of tradition—turn in her grave. Tolerance is one thing, such encouragement as the presentation of the Koran as a valued gift from a Christian official to a heathen chief is as mischievous as it is absurd and uncalled for.

Johnson, of course, came up against this bastard Islam of Central Africa from the beginning and he met it with real knowledge of the Koran on his own part and a constant readiness to discuss it with its proselytes and its teachers. These teachers were generally natives, slaves or men more or less detribalised, who took up with Muhammadanism and were sent, often as far as Cairo, to be taught the observances and such texts from the Koran as they could learn by heart. They generally learnt to write in Arabic letters but did not learn Arabic. On returning to a village their knowledge of writing made them useful clerks or secretaries to native chiefs, who sent formal letters to one another in their vernacular, but written in Arabic characters. Johnson, on one occasion—the occasion of the murder of his boatswain, Stefano, at Mkalawili's—went to Kazembe, a chief just across the Lake, to get him to use his influence with Mkalawili for the release of Stefano (whose fate was as yet unknown). Kazembe set two scribes at work who produced neat and formal letters, but Kazembe spoilt the effect of their performance by saying : " We had better send someone to tell Mkalawili what the letters mean " ; and it was so.

On another occasion, Johnson was walking along between two villages when three lions crossed his path, turned and for a while stood at gaze. He felt " uncomfortable " and so did the boys who were with him, but they stood their ground without showing the fear they felt and the lions turned and slowly went their way. It is well known among natives that at such a time to run away would be fatal.

Under this heading of " Perils " there may be told here one of the more remarkable of Johnson's lion adventures. It is interesting also as showing the growth of legend, not only among natives, but also among white people. Moreover, the actual lion of this story has involuntarily lent his mighty jawbones to provide the U.M.C.A. office in London with a notable inkstand ; his mouth stands dumbly open and from it issue now the peaceful messages and business communications of the Secretary—unless in these later days he has condescended to a typewriter or a fountain pen. Still, the inkstand is there.

## THE LION STORY

*I. Told in* 1932 *by Mr. De la Pryme.*

One day a boy arrived with a lion's skin, and a note from W. P. J. asking me to get it cured. " How did it happen ? " said I, and the staggering answer came, " Oh, the Archdeacon, as he was walking along a footpath in the bush, sort of felt something sniffing at his heels, turned round and found a lion following him at close quarters, he just gave a backward kick with his foot, stunned the king of the forest and finished it off with a knobkerrie." " You're a first-class liar," was my remark on the subject. Later, with great difficulty, one was able to extract the story which can be found on pages 52, 53 of *A Hero Man* with the addition that he was praying aloud all the time.

*II. As told in " A Hero Man."*

The version in *A Hero Man,* published 1931

Archdeacon Johnson arrived one evening at Mbweka, and as the heat was oppressive had his bedspread put out on the verandah of his hut. Something brushed against it in the night and awoke him. A few moments after he heard loud cries in the village. A lioness had seized a man who had gone outside for a moment ; his brother rushed to his rescue, and the lioness, dropping the first man, seized the second. W. P. J. ran to the spot and pulling a large handful of straw from the thatch of one of the houses thrust it into a fire and held the lighted end against the lioness's mouth while some men held on to her tail, and others killed her with the heavy poles the women use for pounding corn.

*III. As told by a native from Mponda's to Mrs. Swale on the Zambezi.*

A native version told in 1911

Our little cook from Mponda's hearing us mention Archdeacon Johnson, grew very excited and exclaimed, " You know Archdeacon Johnson ? He can never die—all the natives say so. Nothing can hurt him, no beasts. One day he was sleeping in a village, and a lion came and took the cattle. He got up and said, ' You no go and kill that lion ; I go and speak to him,' and he went down and met the lion ; and he put out his hand with a stick and said, ' You no kill any man any more,' and the lion lay down and died." All this told with much gesture and rolling of the eyes.

*IV. As told by W. P. J. to Mrs. Swale, long before, in* 1901.

From W. P. J. via Mrs. Swale

Mrs. Swale said : " I should have taken all this for legend but oddly enough I knew the true version, for when the Archdeacon was with us (in N.Z.), I once asked him if he had met with lions. He said only once [*the Archdeacon must have forgotten*] when he was visiting in one of the Lake villages and was disturbed at night by an uproar amongst the natives. He said he got up, snatched a bamboo from the hut-roof and ran down to the cattle kraal. There he came face to face with a lion, and thought the end had come for him. He stretched out his hand with the stick in it, with some idea of thrusting it down the lion's throat, when to his amazement the beast fell

at his feet and died. It appeared that the native guarding the cattle
was seized by the lion, and his brother came to the rescue and with
other villagers beat it off. On examination the spine of the lion was
found to have been broken by the blows, and it died just as the
Archdeacon met it."

*V. As told by W. P. J. in an address to boys.*

Our Lord wants us to act as the headman did at one village.
We heard a weird sound, half shriek, in the still night about 11.30
p.m. We turned out but were behindhand. The chief's brother had
rushed out at once, and, finding his brother under the lion, threw
himself on the brute, utterly unarmed, others rushed out, no spears,
no guns, only the heavy pounding-sticks of very hard wood, *and*
grass torn from the roofs and lighted. The lion seemed afraid to
break through the fire and some caught him by the tail, while the
heavy sticks crashed on his head. Anyhow, we carried the beast in
triumph to our hut on a pole.

The man first caught by him died the same night. He had been
under instruction and was baptized before he died. The brother
gave me an idea of self-sacrifice. He had been badly though not
deeply torn. I saw him twice, the agony was great until his wives
threw water on him; then feeling relief he demanded how his
brother was and tried to go to him, then the pain prevailed, so again
water and again he forgot himself crying out for his brother. Dr.
Howard, for whom I sent, kindly came down from Likoma, arriving
early next day, too late to help the chief but able to help the
brother[1] and to examine the lion. We need our Lord to give us the
right line at a pinch.

[1] The brother ultimately recovered, after months in Likoma Hospital.

1900

As told by
W. P. J. in his
own notes for
an address to
boys
1921

I

## CHAPTER X

# Mission Methods

A T this point, the writer may be allowed to be a little reminiscent. In 1898, when I joined the Mission, it was very largely due to the influence of Archdeacon Johnson, whom I met at Aberdare and who visited me in Cardiff. One little incident in this connexion is worth relating, as it is very characteristic of Johnson. I had, at the time of his visit to me, already joined the Mission and passed the medical examination, etc., but my vicar had asked me to remain until he had found my successor or at any rate till the next Confirmation classes were over. When Archdeacon Johnson learnt that, though promised to the Mission, I was still tied to my curacy by a rather indefinite promise he made no attempt to " direct " me otherwise. It was not his way to make up a man's mind for him ; he would put the facts before him and leave the decision to him. This was sometimes rather tantalizing to one who simply wanted to be *told* what to do and who was quite ready to obey but not quite clear enough to *choose* his own line. Many people are like that. We went together to evensong in the Mission Church for which I was responsible, and the Archdeacon read the Lessons, standing up close under a gas-bracket, and keeping the excess of light from his eye by two of his fingers, through which he peered at the

brightly lighted book. It was the fifteenth evening, with Psalm 78, and after the service, as we walked home, the Archdeacon said to me, " Did you notice how helpful the Psalm was to you in your indecision ? " " No, what was there to help ? " " Well," said the Archdeacon, " you see that when David was called he wasn't allowed to wait till the lambing season was over ! "

> Verse 71 : " He chose David also his servant : and took him away from the sheep folds."
>
> Verse 72 : " As he was following the ewes great with young ones he took him ; that he might feed Jacob his people and Israel his inheritance."

I gave my vicar my ultimatum on the following Monday morn- 1898 ing at our usual meeting, and fixed a date for leaving.

On arrival at Lake Nyasa, it was my happiness to find myself 1899 allotted to the work on the mainland under Archdeacon Johnson for the first eight months. Normally, we were the *C.J.* Working with flying squad going up and down the Lake side from Ngofi to W. P. J. Losefa and as far as the south end and the villages on the south-west shore, but, to my great relief, the *C.J.* was laid up for repairs almost immediately and other ways had to be found. The Archdeacon and I were made responsible for the line of villages from Ngofi (north of Likoma) to Losefa, and the Archdeacon had the steamer's dinghy while I relied on Shanks's pony. The Archdeacon was fonder of being on the Lake than I was. This was the time of the " peripatetic College " already described. To a new-comer it seemed very important to have full information about the methods and principles on which the Archdeacon worked. A certain amount could best be learnt by watching, and by taking such part as was possible to a novice. But we were often separated, and it was clearly desirable that the Archdeacon's helper should as quickly as possible understand these principles and methods. Accordingly, I begged the Archdeacon to put something in writing for my instruction and guidance ; and he most kindly wrote out a great deal and not only gave it me but also sent a copy to Bishop Hine. Both A precious Bishop Hine and I have treasured these documents as a valuable document account of Archdeacon Johnson's fundamental ideas of Mission work, and they can now be put on record here to help the reader to understand the man and his work. I have added here and there an explanatory note in smaller type.

### NOTES ON MISSION METHOD
#### By W. P. J. (1899)

" MY DEAR LORD BISHOP,

Barnes asks me to write out some heads of our system in mainland villages. I have done so hurriedly, and, as it seems at the same time a sketch of what we are doing, it seems only honest to shew it to you.

Yours ever obediently,<br>W. P. JOHNSON."

AXIOMS

1. No system any good without Our Lord, the flesh profiteth nothing. When ye are weak then are ye strong. Not by might nor by power, but by my Spirit saith the Lord of Hosts.

2. Consistency better *ceteris paribus* than inconsistency.

3. Better to act as if one believed the Christian teaching in the Church to be true.

4. The proclamation of the Kingdom is in general quite a different object from the instruction of catechumens ; it must *precede* in theory, and, in general, actually and in time, though it may be renewed with good effect.

5. One cannot safely ignore a man's connexions, especially his family and bringing up, in considering how we ought to approach him.

6. To use native agents and native elements of life as far as possible with a view to growth of native character.

IN APPROACHING NEW VILLAGE
Most important to realize you are regarded
    (*a*) as an outcast, or
    (*b*) as the member of a society, tribe, etc.
So your object (1) to proclaim our Lord's Kingdom.

This primarily, as in His sight, any intellectual effect on people very subordinate, so particular form of words a subordinate consideration, if we really speak of Him and as sent under Him.

2. To endeavour in all things to act consistently with claim to be of His Church, not only in personal action but in all connected with one.

Probably in most villages much has already been learnt correctly or incorrectly of your society, family, etc.

If wise you do not shirk this consideration of your tribe and company, you rather emphasize it as the instrument of the Lord.

Note.—*It has sometimes been thought that W. P. J. would have the missionary lay aside his racial advantage in order to approach the native as nearly as possible as one just like himself. These words dispose of that erroneous idea.*

Those then who are drawn towards you and yours through the Word are invited to come for regular *instruction*, to learn who the Lord is and, a great part of that knowledge, what His Church was and is.

As our natural origin becomes more and more known so this instruction and, what is its essential accompaniment, the life must have in part a negative side. An *Mzungu's* Lord is supposed to be an *Mzungu* ; the tribe of which we speak an *Mzungu* tribe. Later an Englishman's Lord is supposed to be the Queen, the tribe of which we speak an English tribe.

Note.—*Mzungu*=European.

No lie is so dangerous as a half-truth and so here we need the greatest circumspection if we are to teach men to bring their family life to God ; we must be true Englishmen and loyal subjects but this

must not dim the reality of our tribe the Church, and our Lord the 1899
Christ.

From O.T. times we can teach that people ought first to rest in the
gate of the Church and not to enter hurriedly.

When a teacher first goes to a place, very much, if not all, for good
and bad depends on the knot gathering round him.

Surely if he and his companion, possibly his wife, and a few others
who have come from elsewhere worship, it is good for those who have
been admitted to the gate as catechumens *after more than a year's
instruction as to the nature and origin and moral law of the Church* to
share in worship as far as they may.

Hence they have been admitted to matins and evensong (and the
*Missa Catechumenorum*) under certain important limitations.

1. Youths and grown-up people who ought to be working are not
called to matins (nor to the *Missa Catechumenorum* except on Sundays or after a long absence of the priest) ;

2. Schoolboys or others working close to the church so that they
can attend without breaking up their work are invited to attend.

It seems most important not to interfere with the duties of life,
most important for all to pray as near sunrise as possible, as all the
elder people go to hoe *before* sunrise.

*Objection.* Matins and evensong are meant for Christians only.
This met (1) by saying the Absolution and Lord's Prayer in a low
voice clearly meant to reach the Christians only—and the Glorias
the same, or if sung then sung in Swahili or English.

(2) By the catechumens going out before the Creed.

It is not meant that intelligent catechumens cannot hear or follow
these parts so said, but they are reminded in this way of what they
are told elsewhere, that they are still only in the gate, not yet
admitted to the Church.

Further, the objection has been yielded in theory by the late adop-
tion *on the part of the objectors themselves* of a short form of the
present Litany for the use of catechumens with Christians, where the
petitions are offered to our Lord as God and so, in a great part of
them at any rate, assume the Mystery of the Incarnation.

Note.—*This argument is part of a controversy raging in* 1899 *and long since
decided in the direction of the liberty the Archdeacon pleads for.*

The catechumens are admitted to the *Missa Catechumenorum*, in
which it is proposed to insert the Litany as above. We have not
had an Introit, as we long to have words that *the people can follow*
but this ought to be.

The Lord's Prayer ought to be said in a low voice as above.

It is a grave question how far the catechumens can find benefit
from prayers *together* apart from the Church ; their sharing as far as

possible in the blessing around the worship of the Church seems equally to be desired and appreciated by them.

(*N.B.*—In any big mainland station duplicate services for catechumens alone would be practically difficult and often lead to more instead of less of the whipper-snapper class making others pray ["*kusalika*," as they say].)

Note.—*The Archdeacon had a great horror of any system that produced too large a percentage of smart young schoolboys unblushingly setting themselves up as teachers to lead the Christian congregation in a village. He wished to have elder men who carried weight by their age and position and not merely by book-learning.*

If we now look at a developed station we should find :

1. Communicants' Register carefully kept. If possible priest to go through it after any feast day, and note more or less cause of absence (e.g. at Msumba this has been done for six to seven years, and also at Chia, but there the book has been lost by the teacher).

(*N.B.*—Sad need of further instruction of Christians. Most important to utilize every opportunity for instruction in points of the Faith, until we have some more organized classes.)

In view of the scattering of the population and the consequent

Note.—*The scattering referred to was a result of the peace from raiding enjoyed by the lakeside people after the establishment of British power on the Lake. Formerly every village was a crowded collection of huts inside a stockade, the* linga. *In 1899 these were beginning to disappear and by now nothing is left in most villages but the name* linga, *referring to the line of the vanished stockade. The crowded village or town became a widely separated group of tiny hamlets planted in every suitable bay.*

infrequency of all assembling together we try and impress on Christians the importance of coming to church on *Saturday evening*, so as

(1) to prepare for Holy Communion, if possible
(2) for some course of regular instruction.

*Unconfirmed.*

(1) those lately baptized ;
(2) those who have not, owing to absence or misconduct, been confirmed before.

Note.—*The problem of the children baptized as infants was not yet insistent in 1899. These children make a very large third class at this time.*

Teacher takes these twice a week in historical part, and in Catechism of Confirmation ; the priest three or more times on spiritual side, besides treating the subject in addresses in church.

(*N.B.*—Old Catechism very disjointed and obscure, now I hope better adapted to purpose. So also Catechism for Eucharist.)

Note.—*The Archdeacon at or near the time of writing these notes had been busy revising the old Catechisms, which were based in the main on the writings of Preb. Sadler. I have a vivid recollection of the confused pages of his copy, annotated to distraction with corrections in the Archdeacon's none too easy hand. In pity for the printers as well as the Archdeacon I undertook to make a fair copy and did so*

*Catechumens.*

(1) From admission to season immediately before baptism (as Advent before Christmas, Lent before Easter, forty days before Pentecost).

(2) During season before baptism after they have been separated for that purpose.

1. (*a*)  To be tested in life as catechumens.

(*b*)  To be taught Gospel for the Sundays.

(a) At *Missa Catechumenorum* on Sundays.

(b) *One* other day in week.

(*N.B.*—At Msumba and elsewhere the teacher takes them in the Gospel after the Ante-Communion Office.)

2. To be taught in questions on the Creed, leading up to the mystery of the Trinity.

(*N.B.*—Evening before Baptism on proper use of Baptismal Office ; at Eucharist before Baptism explicitly on the Blessed Trinity and Trine Immersion.)

(*N.B.*—Office for admitting catechumens to be used at general outdoor preaching on Sunday [or other day if necessary] as below. MAIN points of the Office of Admission. The Promises expected.)

We make a great point of five points they are to observe :

(1) Prayer morning and evening.  They are taught and have to recite *such prayers.*

(2) Honouring of marriage, this explained at length in instruction both to married and unmarried.

(3) *Work six days a week* as matter of obligation.

(4) Worship together with Church on the Lord's Day.

(5) Coming one other day to the Mission for instruction.

(*N.B.*—All this proves *possible* under our new circumstances, now that the people are scattered, as well as at Blantyre, etc., to a great extent.)

*Hearers.* This includes those who have come forward to be *written down.*

They ought to come to the outdoor meeting on Sunday, and to go through its teaching afterwards, also one other day in the week, when the Sunday lesson should be taken again.

N.B.—*W. P. J.'s idea always was that the First Lessons for the Sunday given us by the Church and showing the preparation in history through which the children of Israel went constituted an ideal course of instruction for the Hearers. Most of us found it difficult to share his enthusiasm for this idea.*

As a year draws to an end if they have proved fairly keen (as proved by attendances relatively) they are taught the prayers referred to above for catechumens ; also the Ten Commandments in a form suggested by Mr. Dale's book on the Ten Commandments as bringing out their application here—this as subordinate and preparative to use of *the* Commandments in the *Missa Catechumenorum*.

They are also taught explicitly that the Old Testament lessons lead up to our Lord and centre in Him, so they answer the first question (in the Office for Admission of Catechumens) " I wish to be taught all the words of Jesus Christ, and to receive Holy Baptism," that is, full admission to His Society.

It is to be hoped that all this is more or less a body *in evidence* before the heathen world, so again we aim at having a thoroughly *outside preaching* on Sunday. Too often this is in Mission buildings which is to be deprecated, as the outside world do not like to be " run in " as it seems to them. Let us try to find a suitable shady tree, common ground for all, and to this lately we have invited Christians as well as catechumens, hearers and all in the village some time after the early service (Eucharist or in absence of priest Ante-Communion service taken by teacher). We have sung the *Venite* (Christians and Catechumens only standing, omitting the *Gloria*), then the First Sunday Lesson, omitting heads of chapters, etc., as far as possible making it intelligible to the people and reading " Lord " for the Divine Name.

Then exposition of the O.T. lesson (given us, observe, by the Church).

(*a*) on the lines of tracing the origin, history, moral laws and customs of the Church.

(*b*) endeavouring to teach the history of individuals, etc., as the Holy Scriptures do, not to drive out these lessons by drawing morals.

(*c*) the application to a great extent to rest in the fact that we Christians and catechumens are speaking of our fathers, our tribe, our God; and pressing those around to agree to the conditions for joining us. Then Christians and catechumens form two and two and sing a *well-known hymn*, " The Lord is my Shepherd," and so move off to the church for matins.

(*N.B.*—One teacher remains writing down any new candidates to be hearers, and then takes the hearers in the same subject asking questions on it.)

The Christians and catechumens enter the church and have portion of Litany as approved by the Bishop; then the Second Lesson with or without address; then *Benedictus*, catechumens going out at the *Gloria*, then as on other days, only saying (in addition) the prayer for All Sorts and Conditions of Men and the Thanksgiving.

(*N.B.*—The people seem willing to stop for this and it makes a more adequate provision for worship on Sundays than the Celebration alone.)

In the afternoon the teacher takes a children's service ; the diffi-  1899
culty has been in the varied elements : (1) a few Christians, (2) a few
catechumens, (3) a heathen.  Sometimes the Scripture taught in the
week has been taken.  Sometimes Miss W.'s Catechism (?) [probably
Miss M. E. Woodward].  (Some catechisms are open to grave objection.)  Often hymns are sung.

We always aim at visiting some little gathering-place in the
village to reach the elders who, alas, do not generally come to the
organized preaching, and in these meetings one must speak as one
finds opportunity.

Their own boys, singing hymns which they cannot understand
a bit, will soften the hearts of these elders, who may resent the over-
dress of these youngsters.  It may help *qua* Proclamation of Kingdom.

Note.—*The Archdeacon had always a great feeling for the old men and was
quick to object to such behaviour on the part of the smart youngsters of no village
importance as had the least savour of disrespect for the primitive elders.  With him
fine feathers did not make fine birds.*

SUMMARY OF SUNDAY WORK

   1. Eucharist (or Ante-Communion in priest's absence).

      7 a.m.    Late on Sunday on purpose.
                (Catechumens taken afterwards in the Gospel. *Better
                not* so, but it is a common custom.)
      9 a.m.    " *Mzungu's* " breakfast.  The bell should be sent out
                to call villagers to next service.
                (In some places the bell was a drum.)
   9.30-10.    Sunday preaching under tree as above.  Procession
                to church.  Matins and Litany.  Hearers' Class
                finished.
                Lunch according to means and fancy.
      3-4.    Catechizing.  (If all or most are Christians it is best
                to take the Church Catechism.)
                Outside preaching.
      7 p.m.    Evensong—preaching.
                (Catechumens dismissed as usual.)

Every day it is well to return to church after evensong for any who
wish to see you.  *All* who do so must sit down in orderly manner at
end of church and *keep still* till their turn comes.

SUMMARY OF WEEK CLASSES (any amount of local variation)

*Hearers.*  On Sunday and one other day at least, men and women
to be taken together.  When the year is up some are separated off
and form another class often taken frequently for instruction in Ten
Commandments, Prayers, and Answers to Admission Office.

These should at end of year have *some* ideas of the history of the
Chosen People down to our Lord's Coming ; should be more or less

familiar with their worship of One God, their Ten Commandments, the Old Covenant, and with the fact that Abraham, Moses, etc., were not simply *Wazungu*.

The Church begins to loom out a very little, even possibly our Lord is not quite an empty name, nor a " *boma* "[1] official.

Behind all this outward routine the pith of the matter is in the lives of the teachers, the Christians and Catechumens—hence the reality of the work of shepherding.

*Catechumens.* Class once a week as above.

Another class at special times for those immediately under instruction for baptism ; the Questions then taught aim at bringing out the true issues involved in this declaration of a new Faith.

All boys in school are taught Genesis, Samuel or other simple historical book as translated ; the very difficulties of the system seem to me advantages over the fatal facility of teaching Catechisms to the uninitiated.

Christians and catechumens should be taught one of the Gospels, the Acts and I Corinthians at the same time separately.

Great care ought to be taken in admitting schoolboys as catechumens or for Baptism. At Likoma, at least formerly, no boy was made a catechumen till he had been resident two years ; elsewhere while the ιattraction was less, the discipline was less, a year's attendance has been a minimum.

*Note.—One of W. P. J.'s ruling ideas was that a busy European centre like a Mission station was a tremendous disturbance of the natural conditions and he was constantly on guard against the danger of mistaking the pull of self-interest for the real desire to learn about our Lord. Consequently, he wished to keep all Mission stations down to the minimum and as far as possible to avoid making them great centres for employment of natives and for buying their produce. Latterly, I think he came to see that his ideal was not practical and was indeed a little Partingtonian.*

### Considerations on admitting

(1) a Hearer ; anyone who offers is written down as a hearer.
(2) a Catechumen. After a year, sometimes two years or three years, and due instruction as above.

We consider

(a) if candidate is a schoolboy, has he been regular for a year ; and we ascertain if he is engaged.
(b) if he is adult, is his or her position as to marriage known. If married, to whom ?

If he is married to more than one wife since he has been accessible to Mission teaching, then certainly he is not admitted ; if polygamist from old times and otherwise earnest, the case is referred to the Bishop.

[1] Government.

If the candidate is single, why? especially in case of a woman 1899 who may be living in the greatest temptation owing to claims, etc., on her ; she ought to be helped to face these questions before binding herself with new promises.

Again, as to work, have they work?

(a) if schoolboys are they regular?
(b) if adults how many fields have they, etc.?

What is their general character with the elders of the Church?
*Baptism* (a) Infants.

Boys, if their father and mother are Christians and heartily wish it, as they generally do. Witnesses as in Prayer Book preferably Communicants. They arrange *all this* with the teacher ; if it is not properly done, the baptism is deferred, but this is *rarely* necessary.

Girls, as these have been habitually taken off to the initiation dances without any consultation of priest or teacher and often against their wish, we have been afraid to baptize girl infants.

Note.—*The initiation dances form a series beginning in childhood, culminating at puberty and ending with the first pregnancy. The chiefs have a vested interest in their continuance as each involves a payment to the chief of the village. This is referred to below and a way of meeting their claims is shown.*

(*N.B.*—Boys were not initiated at Msumba, and it was given up at Pachia, Chisanga and more or less north of those places.)

Note.—*In my experience, beginning in* 1899, *I do not remember meeting anywhere a case of a Nyanja boy, not Muhammadan, who had been initiated.*—B. H. B.

Some teachers' girl infants have been baptized on the maternal uncle's[1] agreeing to promise that she should not be initiated, as the father's position and the uncle's consent seemed some guarantee.

Now we seem to be making some advance, as these Christian parents and the maternal uncles who agree that their girls should not take part in the initiation dance of their village at all, but should pay the *mat*, etc., customarily paid to the chief of the village, have at Chisanga entered their names and if we can get five or six in a village so to agree we can trust them to support each other and so keep their children from sharing in the predominantly heathen rite. If we have five or six such entries we can baptize the girls.

Note.—*It will be observed that the Archdeacon does not give any countenance to the idea of attempting to Christianize the heathen ceremonies. This is not because the idea had not yet been put forward but because where it had been suggested the native clergy and teachers were dead against it for the most part.*

### POINTS TO LOOK TO ON VISITING A STATION

From the above it is of the greatest importance as well to prevent hasty admission as to do justice to regular attendance, that

[1] The maternal uncle in native custom among these people has real authority, the father practically none.

1899

A. (1) Hearers' register should be kept properly, names clearly written, date at top of column, month, year, etc., and class, whether men's, women's, etc.

(2) Catechumens' Register, with date of admission, name of wife or husband, etc.

(3) Communicants' Registers.

(4) School Registers.

B. Service Books, especially

O.T. Lessons for Sundays, for teaching the hearers and reading in Church.

Lessons for the Day and Calendar of year.

Hymn Books, Psalms, Prayer Book.

* Other parts of Bible.

*Note.—At this date the whole Bible had not been translated and even for the N.T. we were largely dependent on locally printed copies of single books. Now the whole Bible is bound together in one volume printed by B.F.B.S. and mainly translated by Archdeacon Johnson himself.*

The teachers should be encouraged to buy these books, but gradually as wanted with a view to reading them, and so getting another and so on. The teacher should always be encouraged if possible to read the Lessons in the presence of the priest in church and be encouraged if possible to look them through beforehand.

*Variations.* Sometimes only one Lesson is read. Sometimes owing to having few psalm books the psalms are not said. Hymns are sung in place of psalms, Te Deum, etc. The *Gloria* of the *Benedictus* is said in Chinyanja aloud as the catechumens are supposed to have gone or to be going. The Litany is said at Msumba on Wednesdays and Fridays.

W. P. J.'s fundamentals

To make a selection among the principles laid down here it may be said that the fundamentals, the key-notes of Johnson's message, were :

(a) The Proclamation of the Kingdom is the first duty of the Missionary.

(b) The family life is the deepest and dearest element in native social life and thought. No one is anything apart from some family to which he belongs. The Church is the great Family, not abolishing other ties but transcending them. So admission to the Family is the aim to keep before every adherent from the start.

(c) The Church among the Nyasas (or any other race) is a true native development and not a foreign intrusion. This must be insisted on by keeping its thought, its agents, its appointments as entirely native as possible. The

Church-builders must always be coming back to the 1899
question " How does this proposed step help on the
development of a truly native Church in this country ? "

(d) As the Jewish race and the world were prepared for the
Christ-to-come by the discipline of their history, so, as far
may be, these people must have their Christianity firmly
based on that history as given to us by the Church in the
Old Testament.

Minor points that constantly occurred in Johnson's lines of
teaching were his insistence on the value of work ; his clinging
to the practice of " reserve " in Church Services by dismissing
the Catechumens before the Creeds and by using a foreign
tongue for such parts of the Services as involved specifically
Christian Mysteries, to which they had not yet been introduced
in their teaching ; and his constant regard for the old men for
whom long tradition and the entanglement in heathen ways
made the acceptance of new teaching very hard.

When he insisted on the value of work, he did by no means
intend to approve the growing practice, so dangerous to social
life and so detribalising, of going far afield for the sake of money
or from mere love of change and adventure, to seek employment
among Europeans. No, he thought first and last of the normal
round of work in the native villages, and he had no patience
with the idea that, unless a man is cooking, washing plates or
doing field work or mine work for the European, he is idle and
lazy. He knew well how much work was involved in keeping the
home fires burning and the home pot filled. Certainly, he would
have commended the man who, in order to ransom relatives,
went to the ends of the earth in search of the necessary higher-
paid work, and he would have regarded a man who carried such
a scheme through as a hero ; but his absence from the life of his
home and tribe he would have counted a most disagreeable
necessity.

*What W. P. J
meant by
" work "*

Johnson himself led a most hard, lonely and adventurous
life ; but he didn't do it for fun, and he had scant sympathy
with those whom mere love of adventure called to missionary
work.

It is clear that his ideals were high, and their attainment hard.
Nothing braced him to the endeavour but the absolute certainty
that he was doing the will of his Lord, and that in all things his
Lord was actually with him.

# CHAPTER XI

## Rival Policies

WE have seen how high were Johnson's ideals and what a tremendous demand they made on all who would follow them. It is easy to understand that there were few to follow where Johnson led. That is not strange at all; what is positively amazing is that Johnson himself followed this hard path without wavering and that for fifty-two years. He had received his commission, and it simply never occurred to him that any hardship in the appointed path was an excuse or a reason for taking another path, still less for turning back. For himself the way was clear and there was only one thing to be done. As to others it was for them to judge what our Lord required of them. He expected of others the same unwavering perseverance in the path, and if he didn't find it in them he was simply puzzled; " I can't understand X," he would say, " I can't see what he would be at." He is described by men who worked with him on the steamers as the hardest taskmaster they ever knew, but everyone knew that he was harder on himself than on any other, and that while he would " heartily sympathize " (a favourite phrase of his when perhaps he couldn't really understand some fellow worker) with the other's difficulties or hesitations, he never complained himself of any hardship and gave himself none of that facile pity which we lesser beings keep in stock for ourselves. He yearned for sympathy, but the real sympathy of understanding was what he yearned for, not the enervating sympathy of compassion or pity.

His inability to realize the limitations of men of weaker will and less heroic mould did not so much hinder him in individual dealings, but was certainly a great handicap to him in framing a general policy to be worked out by all sorts. For this reason it is probably true that he would not have made a good Bishop, though there were not a few who would, not only in 1902, but in 1910 also, have rejoiced if the Archbishop and the Home

Would he have been a good bishop?

Committee who advised him had had the courage to make the bold experiment of appointing as Bishop a man who was undoubtedly a prophet and a saint but who might well have been an indifferent administrator. There was never the slightest indication that Johnson for himself ever desired the great responsibility and it is quite possible that he would have declined it. But it is more probable that he would have regarded it as a God-given order to try out his policy in full, and as an endorsement of his constant stand against those features of Mission policy which, in his view, did not make for the building up of a purely native Church in Central Africa. Certainly, he accepted the Bishops whom God set over him in all loyalty, and went his lonely way under whatever conditions were imposed. The boulders in a river bed disturb the current, but cannot divert it from its constant search for the sea for whose bosom its waters yearn. Johnson's pertinacity was of the same kind with that of the fluid but irresistible current ; and naturally there was often some disturbance of the surface though the depths were calm and constant.

What, then, were the points on which Johnson's policy found itself in conflict with that of others ?

Johnson had definitely a " pioneer " mind, and his early experience and training were not only in close harmony with the dauntless courage natural to him and necessary for a pioneer, but they also thrust him deeper into what he himself recognized as his rut! He was willing to recognize that he was in a rut, but he also wanted others to perceive that they, too, were equally in ruts, though doubtless other ruts than his. Sympathy meant with him trying to peep over the edge of the rut and, if possible, to reach a hand to help the fellow in the other rut. Back in 1891, writing to Maples of one of his fellow workers, he said, " That you cannot make some one out often means that it would help him *to be made out.*"

We shall not be far wrong if we see the beginnings of a clea- Maples and vage in the very different characters of Maples and Johnson, Johnson, two from the beginning of their association. At Masasi it was the types work of Maples—as later at Likoma—to build up the centre, a most valuable work which Johnson freely recognized and admired. But even then, Johnson's place was not at the centre, but somewhere away on the vague circumference, the growing point, and Maples was filled with admiration for his friend.

Their ways were different and in a larger view it seems clear that they were complementary the one to the other.

Moreover, in those earlier years, the centre and the circumference were not far apart. At the cross-roads the path to the north-east is not far from the path to the north-west, and travellers on either can still call to one another. But later it becomes more difficult and the difference begins to look like irreconcilable opposition, and the greater grace is required to keep the two extremes from flying altogether apart. It was easy for Johnson to " heartily sympathize " with his friend Chauncy, when the one returned from his Gospel raids to the comparative ease of Likoma, which was a hard enough life for ninety-nine men out of a hundred. It was far harder for the venerable pioneer in the war days to understand or sympathize with Bishop Fisher's point of view, and a degree of settled comfort about Likoma which reminded him of a splendidly ordered hotel with its efficient running, its large numbers catered for (e.g. at a Synod), and its grand Cathedral, so far beyond what undirected and unsubsidized native work could compass.

One can imagine the beginnings of this immense disparity. Johnson arguing strenuously with Maples as to the ultimate issue of a trend only just making itself felt.

**W. P. J. not consistent**

It may be allowed that Johnson was not always consistent. The steamer *Chauncy Maples* was as alien as Likoma Cathedral and probably as costly—but while the Cathedral was pegged down solidly to one place, the steamer was at least floating hither and thither and justifying its existence in many places.

**Nor indifferent to creature comforts**

Nor was Johnson, as he has sometimes been painted, indifferent to creature comforts ; he revelled in the annual box of Christmas cheer that an Aberdare friend used to send him ; brandied cherries were hailed with enthusiasm and eaten, at any rate tasted ; but there would quickly come the reflection, " If these are so jolly for me, what about these my native friends with their monotonous diet of porridge and relish." And half at least (unless he had some greedy European with him who had no scruples about taking more than his share) of the cherries or what not would go to the nearest of those native friends. In his latter years his letters contain many expressions of gratitude for these comforts. Here, for instance, is one passage out of many taken from a letter to his brother Harry in 1918 :

" Here is a cup of tea and some home-made gingerbread from

dear Miss Armstrong. It is very good of her to send them as they are short at Likoma, but the thought plus the food gives me much pleasure. Some of these ladies simply live to help, in trust on our Lord. Miss A. wouldn't mention this last truth often, if at all, but *does* it, while I *talk* and eat her gingerbread."

Johnson was at any time quite capable of arguing over gingerbread regarded as a symptom, partly because his vision was preternaturally acute for anything that could conceivably get in the way of developing a thoroughly native church, partly because he dearly loved arguing for arguing's sake. Not once nor twice, he has been known to argue keenly with another eager disputant over some perhaps trivial matter—the source of a quotation, the meaning of a word, some hypothesis of natural science—and, if the dispute has had to be broken off for a time, to come back to it again with equal keenness until the discovery that the disputants have unconsciously changed sides in the matter brings the whole discussion to its proper end in laughter. *His love of argument*

He was not unaware of his own imperfections as a leader. Writing in 1911 to Chauncy's sister, he said :

" It is natural to feel that the days of the Mission are, if not in the past, certainly not confined to the present. New men and new ways —we laugh and half see the fallacy of our reasoning, half believe that we see farther. Yet it is easy to criticize and I do feel that Chauncy, Bishop Trower and our present Cantab (Bishop Fisher, consecrated in 1910) are alike in that they make a helpful centre to all around, which I certainly do not do ; to do that you must make a centre for yourself, no wiggle-waggling, no dreams, no sense of failure. We have just come south with Bishop Cathrew (Fisher) and seen much of the good and of the weak points ; I only wish I could help him more. *Chauncy took me by storm first, was not above stooping to conquer, and then I felt at ease.* Perhaps years and years of living with ' natives and languages ' make me not melt or trust easily, and yet continual aspirations after a real love and understanding make the common camaraderie of the world more impossible still."

Some words of Bishop Fisher's, written after the Arch-deacon's death, not only illustrate this passage, but also show a remarkable insight into the Archdeacon's character. Writing to Johnson's brother he says : *W. P. J.'s humility*

" One main difficulty was his humility. I don't think he ever realized how exceptional he was and that the sacrifices he could and did make in life and work were simply impossible for smaller folk."

K

The statement of Archdeacon Johnson's principles quoted in full in the last chapter shows that his aim was always to interfere as little as possible with the normal social life of the tribes.

The evil of a large station

One of his fixed ideas was that a large European station such as Likoma did inevitably interfere far too much, however pious the intentions of those who made and believed in them. There was a very great deal of truth in his contention which one could admit, without doing more than take such care as was possible to minimize the recognized evil. Johnson was impatient with those who not only took no pains to minimize the evil but did not even recognize the presence of any evil and who frankly gloried in these big stations, seeing no other possible course.

Bp. Fisher's very different view

Bishop Fisher, who inherited Likoma and its Cathedral and had no real experience of any other conditions, not unnaturally had as profound a distrust of Johnson's primitive ways as Johnson had of anything like costly elaboration. He couldn't see any reason for not having things as well and neatly ordered as he had been used to having them in England.

Large station causes an upheaval

Undoubtedly, if you should place a large settlement, such as the Mission station at Likoma, in the middle of a wilderness, there would in a very short time be paths leading to it from every village or hamlet within twenty miles, and there would at once be set up a regular traffic of people to and fro, bringing merchandise (fowls, eggs, milk, mats, fish, rope, wooden bedsteads, anything that could be exchanged for cloth or salt or soap or beads, or at a later date for money). There would be a stream also of people looking to the European for work and the resultant pay. The advocate for big stations would see in all this perhaps a natural and pleasing witness to his importance, perhaps a way of helping the natives, perhaps he might value it specially as bringing people within reach of evangelization.

Johnson would admit the last two as real gains, but he would certainly feel that one could have no certainty that the best people, the ones most worth getting hold of, were attracted at all by these considerations, and those who did come would very often be the least satisfactory members of a tribe or village, the seekers after gain, after new things, after the outward shows (fine dress, etc.), of an importance they could never get in their own villages. The fear of these mixed motives for listening to the foreigner had a great share in causing Johnson's distrust of the big station method.

Another objection to them was the greater cost of such work, not only because it meant the spending of more money, but also because of the impression it gave the natives of the Mission as a milch cow with an inexhaustible flow. Johnson, who had lived at Mataka's in famine time on the memory of the last meal (a day or two ago), and the hope of the next one, knew at first hand the grinding poverty of native life, the living from hand to mouth. No one else had such intimate knowledge, and everyone was easily led to suppose that, as we had our regular meals, so our native neighbours had their regular meals, or that if they hadn't it was their own feckless fault. The native was so familiar with real hunger that he just drew his belt a bit tighter, and bore it with a grin that gave no sign of what he endured. The Spartan boy with the fox at his vitals was an everyday performance with many. Of course, if the European was responsible for finding food, he would hear of any shortage soon enough from those he fed, and he might easily fail to discover how frequently his independent neighbours were hungry from necessity.

*and is too costly*

A bunch of missionaries, inwardly thinking what fine fellows they were, and how bravely they endured real hardships, often presented to the natives around them a very different picture of men living in riotous luxury, impatient if breakfast was five minutes behind time and quite unable to stand up to real hunger. " Did such a picture help to build up a native Church ? " was Johnson's continual question to himself and those who lived with him. He bore constant witness to this native view of the Mission and its missionaries and was, perhaps, morbidly anxious to make people bear it in mind. Undoubtedly this very strong feeling of his made him always unready to throw on the natives even their due and proper share of the inevitable church expenses, though he always encouraged them to give of their labours to build schools and churches in their own primitive style. He always feared to set up a big station of Europeans. He definitely objected to the building on so grand a scale of the Cathedral at Likoma. For years he made a tiny vestry or school serve him on his journeys for his quarters in every village, till consideration for a colleague, at a time when the *C.J.* was laid up for repair, led him to give orders for the building of a priest's hut in each village as near the school and church as might be.

*Native view of Mission and missionaries*

*W. P. J.'s way*

Did he " pig "
it ?

What moderns took sometimes for a depraved preference for " pigging it " was really due to a conscience morbidly sensitive on these points, a conscience that could hardly allow him to take a step without asking what would be its influence on the building up of the native Church.

Thus it must be remembered that the ways of working which were peculiar to Johnson were not the result of casualness or carelessness, nor were they due to a preference for conditions too hard for most men ; they were part of a whole, a carefully considered whole, that had for its aim and end the good of the native and of the native Church.

The rival
policy

The rival policy of the big stations, etc., does not need so much exposition because it is just exactly what English people, fresh from their own ordered life at home, would naturally devise.

It is the easiest line to take. It may be the best line. It was widely different from Johnson's line, and that line must not be dismissed lightly as foolish, unimportant, mistaken.

The golden
mean

As so often the best is probably the golden mean—in this case the carrying out of a " big station " policy, not in blind confidence that it is the only conceivable one, but in full awareness of all those fine shades of feeling which determined Johnson's policy.

W. P. J. as
pastor

We have said that Johnson had above all a " pioneer " mind, but this must not be taken to mean that he lacked the pastoral instinct. He was a pastor all the time, but he was always drawn to the sheep that were outside the fold, and it is probably true that he underestimated the importance of shepherding the sheep safely inside the fold. He did not see that both the seeking of the lost sheep and the feeding of the home sheep were works of *equal* importance, and he never was so keen-sighted in respect to the dangers and needs of the rapidly growing Christian family as he was to the necessity of going after the outsiders. The newcomers, like Bishop Fisher, saw first the immense numbers of Christians, young and old, to the exclusion of the people in the darkness outside. Naturally, they paid attention to what they saw, and failed, in Johnson's view, to understand the more hidden things or even to be aware of them. Johnson was always fighting for this unconsidered remnant—no *remnant* indeed, but the solid mass of heathendom outside the Mission influence, and

As an advocate he tried hard to get others to feel as he did. Unfortunately, he was not at all good at presenting a case and his advocacy was frequently misunderstood. One early friend of his recalls the phrase " subtle transitions of thought " as a happy description of his style in conversation and in writing. It required a mental acrobat with unusual insight into Johnson's mind to follow his reasoning. Probably Maples, who had known him from Oxford days, was able to do this ; probably no one else in later days, certainly no man.

The result—an amount of misunderstanding and friction in his later years, which might have been tragic to think of, were it not that, through all difficulties, Johnson persevered in striving for loyal co-operation. It was not only in Africa that Johnson's " pioneer " mind showed itself. Wherever he was, his concern, his deepest concern, was for the people on the fringe and beyond it. We have seen that he picked up Stefano Rehani from a shooting-gallery in Wales and brought him back to his native Africa, to be murdered in the end at Mkalawili's. In later years he stayed with his brother Harry at St. Mary's, Cardiff, where he found the amazing cosmopolitan population of that dockside parish. Writing from there in 1920 to Miss Nixon Smith, he said : *Width of his sympathies* *In Cardiff in 1920*

" I am now stung by the thought of how *chaje* (useless) I am *qua* these blacks here, as many *wamuna* (men) as on Likoma, all English, work, work in every sense except that they are out of work! I hark back and think of getting in touch, not by learning Sierra Leone dialect (singular or plural) but by playing with some of them over their tongue. . . . I want to hear of a vast dictionary (no mere vocabulary) of ' Chi—Sierra Leone.' "

Again from St. Mary's, Cardiff, he wrote in 1921 to Mrs. Cook, sister of Chauncy Maples : " O Lady, here in this parish more than 1,000 Arabs from Aden, fifty Egyptians, five hundred West Indians, three hundred West Coast blacks, plus Chinese and Japanese, not counting Portuguese, Greeks, Maltese, etc., etc., etc." He had evidently got much more in touch since the letter first quoted and had made some census of the aliens in the parish. His " urge " to proclaim the Kingdom spurred him on to do something ; the smallness of what he could do made him feel that he was an idle and faithless herald, and, in the end, always drove him back to the Africa that he knew and where he could feel that he was not a mere passenger but could " pull his weight."

## EXTRACTS FROM LETTERS BEARING ON MISSION METHODS AND POLICIES

*Bedford.*

To Mr Wm. C. Toll

It is very lonely here, we can venture to lie off nearly any village now in this larger boat (the *C.M.*) ; the Lake is quite calm to-night, the moon brilliant and there are a few shooting stars—the frogs keep up a distant roll, and the native tom-tom tries to, but cannot, upset the calm. It is not half such an easy problem as it seems, "how to really let the tribes hear about our Lord." Friends realize that we must learn the language, but that is hardly any way at all. It is grand work to try and live with one mind ὁμοθυμαδον on board and then to send out roots on shore. One so often comes across an old man obviously and often consciously going downhill to a grave not very far off, oh, to give him the help we have inherited!

*1902.*

To the Rev. Duncan Travers

Women for the *C.M.*

Shortly after the completion of the s.s. *C.M.* Oliver asks for more —I, in moments of wild rashness, ask for women on the steamer. The Bishop (Trower) can't see it, but is very good. Between ourselves he does not tumble to our rough work where no clean garments shine, no people welcome us as givers of large amount of work. This is inevitable. One cannot see more than a certain distance into people even when they do not wear shirts—and a *bango* (reed) church is not to the human eye a slap-up church, and untrained teachers will howl rather than sing, let alone breaking of Commandments. . . .

Giving the franchise to a school-mistress

I say our women in the villages need a boss like Miss X to pay them, mother them, rate them and defend them, as I do with the men ; and, as no schoolmaster will come, I want to give a schoolmistress the franchise ; she will be able to look over essays, notes, etc., *ad lib.* with these teachers, who are writing notes by the ream on this *C.M.* Why do we four whites (on *C.M.*) need no nurses, though the stokers will get themselves involved in the machinery, and the deck hands run awful risks with the anchor. We are often having all manner of cases on shore, e.g. a wounded Portuguese soldier (a native), a Christian, who was shot and dragged himself thirteen days at night to the Fort. New hands would be no use, they must know the language and not be sea-sick, must keep off the upper deck in the gloaming, not mind boy waiters or noise round their cabins or people looking in at the top, or going ashore in boats, or obeying orders generally or putting up with a bathe when they can get it ; they or one of them must know German as we invaded German territory last week ; one must be able to cook and start a school of cooking which shall be famous, C.M.M.C. or school of

C.M. Mission Cooking ; oh, what a future would be before such a 1902 teacher and such a nurse!

Steamer work represents visiting versus residence, but why does this exclude women's education, or care of the sick, carpentering, etc. ?

(It may be added here that Archdeacon Johnson never got his hoped-for ladies for steamer work. As a sober judge, Dr. Howard, wrote about the same matter about the same date :

" The Archdeacon is very keen on having two ladies, a nurse and a teacher, on the steamer ; the Bishop is keen on not having them. Well, I don't really know ; there is a good deal of work that they might do, but accommodation is limited and it is a rough-and-tumble life. I see many pros and cons, and I don't know how it will be settled."

As the calls on the *C.M.* for serving the general purposes of the Mission increased, the provision of permanent accommodation on board for two ladies in addition to the fairly frequent passengers became more and more impossible, and indeed was never attempted.)

*July* 30, 1928.

Root objection to station life is expense of system ; there must To Bishop be three whites plus white food plus white houses. These are the Hine things that take money hand over hand ; so it must be but to what degree ?

*October* 9, 1896.

Do pray for our real union in heart ; I think it is very difficult To Miss for some to realize our union in life and soul, amidst such differences Woodward of disposition.

Bishop Hine writes very kindly. [*This was between Bishop Hine's* Dr. Hine's *consecration and his return to the Lake as Bishop.*] I could have appointment wished for a triumph of Liberty, Equality, Fraternity or Death, as Bishop Rights of the people—subsidizing their work, keeping Europeans in their sphere as helpers in this grace, etc., etc., but the current is too strong or perhaps our Lord Himself does not wish it. Yet it may be Bishop Hine will enter into the real meaning of Africa for the African Church better than I could have done, and on any other ground I should dread and shrink from the work, as indeed I do (shrink) too much now, therefore pray for me.

*February* 9, 1897 (*Baptisms*).

We used the boat again and set young Indian corn plants just To Miss forming their first tassels to hide the ends that were too obviously Woodward

1897

boat, very pretty the little screens looked, young Indian corn is very graceful. We tried processions again but with very partial success; like all else in England it comes so natural to do these things that it all seems natural—but it is only second nature, if not more remote. After all such processions, rivet-driving, bread-making, are simpler affairs than what it means " to believe," etc. Truly we seem at times like children playing with bits of human nature, a rather dangerous game, and so I beg all good Christians to pray for us.

*From New Zealand in* 1901, *when the Diocese of Zanzibar had been vacant rather long.*

It does seem a scandal that there is no power in the Church at home either to recall her soldiers from Zanzibar or to send a captain. No men come, the work dwindles and becomes insignificant and then it is said no good men ought to be wasted. "A demmed vicious circle" as Mr. Mantalini might have said, and it seems to stick to the whole history of the Church in our colonies. Why is a Mr. Rhodes one of the best-known names in the Empire? He was nothing before he came to South Africa. It seems to me that we do harm at the Universities, they have no idea that any sphere or vocation exists in the Church in the Empire; they are all little Englanders.

Yours antipodally,

W. P. J.

*April* 10, 1918.

To his brother    It is difficult to be kind AND to teach the natives to realize that the Mission is not the goose that lays the golden eggs, or like a milch cow; the idea is not confined to natives—robbers of temples all of a sudden leap right out of the Acts of the Apostles and " pass one the time of day," as dear old Sherriff used to say, in broad daylight here in this year of grace.

*March* 12, 1922.

I still feel deeply, why a white layman of no definite trade at Liuli, why two nurses where only work for one, when each white man or woman costs six times any native? and money is short! The Bishop (Fisher) says if we add on to number of schools and teachers, i.e. a new circuit, it will fall through if no priest, whereas a local white man (i.e. a white layman on the spot) can be removed and no vital blow—but this is a very two-edged argument. Anyhow, I seem to need to help both white and native life, e.g. the huts I find so helpful cost a lot (one at each village, whereas I used to sleep in the church, often the school too); doubtless my way of

life has raised a prejudice against me [*i.e. among his European* 1922
*colleagues*], each fears he may be compelled to do the same ; might
I not help to remove the prejudice, e.g. help (out of private funds)
with better furniture, mosquito-proof houses, hire of cows to give
milk (there is none at Liuli) ; this last item the Mission may pay if
it can, but that is doubtful, our longing for milk is not.

So again schools are good and need help now and again ; yet they
put pressure on one side of native life and do not help to get food.

(*In this same letter he goes on to outline other help both for
natives and for the Europeans associated with him, ploughs, canoes
and fishing nets so that schoolboys could secure at once exercise and
food, printing press, magazines and a library—all to be provided
out of private funds.*)

1923.
X is able, keen, sees clearly, critical, and has little idea that he
may fall into some of the same pits that I have explored. He has
his own way in most things but even so I fear he won't stop. Pray
for us both. [*X didn't stop*]. . . . The Treasurer sent me a paper
called Budget. Oh, my stars, here is office in uniform!

*July* 15, 1922.
I don't think our station life is a success, it means living apart
from the natives—and the latter do not rise morally, nor physically
come up the hill. [*Most stations are on the higher ground while the
native villages are near the shore below.*] I always feel my " table "
when alone makes any progress round me a miracle of grace—and
this was magnified a hundred times at Likoma in retreat, all was as
in a good hotel, most helpful to us all, but the contrast!

*May* 8, 1926.
Heaps of work given, heaps of Confirmees, thank God, thank God,
but how great the need of more trust in proportion, more grace!
I expect I did not feel this as I ought to have done when the Steamer
was in my hands. Now the R.C.'s work the coast north of here in
canoes only, while we with two steamers leave it! ! !

*November* 29, 1926.
Dr. Wigan is a carpenter and a devoted worker wherever he can
help, and he has been carpentering here, as no arrangements had
been made, or few, for the ladies' comfort. It is all instructive to me.
You have ladies, then you must have endless things, where, if
anywhere, can you draw the line ? Teachers and eke printers, used
to seem to me to get a rough bed-rock idea of vocation or at least
of duty—now cooks (and probably soldiers) get the latter, fancy a

cook who did not produce breakfast! The teachers, not so much, though some few even more, and dispensary boys will outdo us even in duty.

*December 2, 1926.*

May I venture to plead that I have generally been in a comfortable back seat and not much tempted to wish to supersede the elders? Is this true? I recall vividly being in opposition to J. Bond Lee [*at Bedford School?*] and you may laugh as you recall later and more underlined cases, " Time would fail you to tell of " Bellingham, Belcher [*both laymen on* C.J. *in early days*], Penney [*at one time General Secretary, U.M.C.A.*], Bishop Smythies—and now alas, alas, C. N. (Bishop Fisher). Yet I *feel* (oh, these feelings!) that I have rarely wanted to oust, though often too much of the shoving one's own view. . . . I feel as if I always prefer elder men, not least you who if younger " in a manner of speaking " were and are the elder brother facing this naughty world.

*May 7, 1927.*

I am having to face the question, " *Can I, or can I not hope to realize my plans of developing with only native help?* " and it seems very doubtful—not only is very much jungly, but immorality is rampant ; but I have to remember very great mercies and certainly advantages of exceptional kind in grasping facts. I ask myself what is the background of I and II Corinthians.

To H. A. M.
Cox

(Who took over the Msumba part of W. P. J.'s work and carried it on even to W. P. J.'s satisfaction.) 1921 or 1923.

I can see much to admire and be thankful for in the present system, but cannot ignore how it is the *Europeans that eat up the money* ; each priest we have always (hitherto) assumed was necessary *mpaka kufa kwake* (*till death*) ; but not so laymen or women, it used to be felt that we ought not to ask them to come unless absolutely necessary to the evangelistic and pastoral work ; and now over and above that question of risking life is the question of funds. . . . The question of *donnas* [*ladies*] and of laymen is very difficult ; sometimes they are so very much the heart of things, sometimes! ! ! and each of us eats up three native priests.

*October 6, 1919.*

I yearn for some common heart of things, some common heart of men. A jolly good thing if it leads (or rather pulls, shoves, kicks) my heavy heart to look beyond the usual mill to Him. . . .

I often feel we have lost the steamer because we did not rise to

such an opening, such a sphere. I don't think you even guess what 1919
it might have been. No better than you are, true, too true, but you
and yours all round the Lake, why not ? [*sic*].

(The reference here in " losing the steamer " is to its gradual
withdrawal from mainly evangelistic work under Archdeacon
Johnson to the work of carrying mails and stores and Mission
passengers under the direction of the Bishop. Mr. Cox started
at Msumba a European station of a kind almost approved even
by an extremist like Johnson—but Johnson would have liked to
see Mr. Cox spreading himself by means of the steamer and so
serving a much wider area, however admirably he might have
been able to work a single district. The Archdeacon had no
doubt but that the first plan was preferable.)

*February* 10, 1922.
Again I am sadly puzzled with these young laymen not called to To B. H. B.
carry out their specific calling (as e.g. our fitters are and the doctor),
but raw youths, united in the shortness of shorts and amount of
body showing, they may have reserves but it is difficult to know
where. . . . How can three *donnas*, one layman and one old fogey
(a priest) mix up ? True it would be a great triumph of grace but
each costs as much as four natives.

*July* 20, 1919.
I feel you started with the people at Likoma as a learner, a To Miss
privileged person who was given an entrée—you not only *said* Nixon Smith
they were brothers and sisters but treated them as such, and, if
it would not work, blamed yourself. How convey this to dear
Miss X—who stands on the firm rock of white supremacy and sees
many seamy things in the sea of life around. You would help her
with less strain than Miss Z gave you—for you would treat her as
you treat them, find (or make) all manner of starting-points and then
work from that base to victory. . . .
How long these places (Likoma, etc.) can wag, left to an *Mzungu*
[*European*] over-man is a question—we *Wazungu* are very foreign,
very, very—just as I find the Jews would call all and several of us
" Edom," definite enough for the likes of us. I hope you will not be
offended if I say I think our daily life requires a miracle of grace
not to offend our native brethren, I mean *qua* believers. You a
Christian, I a Christian.

So ho! together we *don't* go!

I should say that they are well and fairly treated by the *Boma*
(Government) *qua* men, if it were not for one or two big blots.

# CHAPTER XII

# The s.s. " Chauncy Maples "

1899

W̶E have seen how the *C.J.* began and the modest ends it was used to meet, and we have seen that about fourteen years later Johnson, in the part of Oliver Twist, was asking for more in the shape of another steamer. The work had already grown so considerably that the calls on the *C.J.* for general Diocesan errands had come to interfere too much with the special work of carrying the missionaries from village to village

Transport work of *C.J.*

along the Lake shore. As a matter of fact it never did seriously hold up the evangelistic work, because Johnson never allowed it to do so, but the two kinds of call on its help did clash with one another and produce some difficulties. Mails reached Likoma not oftener than once a month and that quite irregularly. Stores urgently needed—have you ever been three months without flour, or sugar, or tea?—might be waiting at the south end of the Lake for the steamer to bring them up. More often in the earlier days they were liable to be stranded for many months on the shores at Chinde or Port Herald or on some sandbank of the Shiré or the Zambezi, because the rivers were low. Whatever the cause of delay, the *C.J.*, pottering (as it seemed to impatient people at Likoma) from village to village,

becomes too much as the Mission grows

was pretty sure to get most of the blame. On the other side, you may be sure that ministering to the native congregations always seemed to Johnson and his colleagues on the *C.J.* a work far more important than supplying the mere physical needs of a bunch of greedy Europeans. To each his view. The " greedy Europeans " tried to be as patient as they could, and the *C.J.* always did its level best, but it simply couldn't do all the work to the satisfaction of all. The work was too big.

Moreover, we have seen that Johnson, even on the *C.J.*, with its very limited accommodation, tried to carry with him three or four teachers for training, for translation work, for "refresher courses " in theology and pastoralia. As the need of a

Another boat needed

second steamer became more and more pressing, he began to 1899
dream of one which should be specially designed for the two
ends of (1) the village work, releasing from that the *C.J.* to
become the errand-boat of the Diocese, and (2) of a floating
college for the training of teachers and ordinands. After more
than a dozen years of unremitting service and of minor accidents on Lake and river, the *C.J.* was in urgent need of a good
overhaul. When the *C.J.* was laid up by an accident or for repair or overhaul, there was no Mission boat to take its place,
and it was at such times the indispensability of the steamer was
most felt. Everyone agreed in longing for a new and larger
boat. When Archdeacon Johnson went home towards the end 1897
of 1897, he had a clear notion in general of what he wanted, and W. P. J.'s new appeal
was again to plead his cause here and there over England, where
the glamour of his name and the known story of his thirteen
years of service unbroken by a furlough gave him a tremendous
appeal. He had pleaded successfully for the *C.J.* in 1884, he had
gone out with it that year and had been struck down by blindness ; he had been brought home and surgical skill had restored to him, as already related, the power of seeing (with difficulty) with about a third of one eye ; he had returned to the
Lake thus handicapped, and England and home had known him
no more for thirteen years. He deserved, and was given, a great
reception wherever he went, and very soon after he left again The *C.M*
for Africa there was enough money raised to build the steamer,
and by October 1899 the building was finished and 3,500
packages were on their way from Glasgow to Chinde. Its plan
and the necessary technical specifications were drawn out by
Mr. J. E. Crouch, who had for some years captained the *C.J.* as a
member of the Mission, so as to provide what Archdeacon Johnson desired for the work he had in mind. Two great engineers, Its designers
Sir John Wolfe Barry, who built the Tower Bridge, and Mr.
Henry Brunel, superintended the building, and brought
Johnson's dreams and hopes into relation to the solid facts of
steel and other necessary materials. Is not the full detail of its
building written by the historian of the Mission, Miss Anderson-
Morshead, in her little book, *The Building of the 'Chauncy
Maples'* ? Our concern here is with the special features included in the ship to make it serve Johnson's purpose as a floating college. To this end the chief thing is the schoolroom, the Its accommo- dation
greater part of the deck-house, giving desks and seats for thirty

1899

scholars, and capable of quick conversion into a chapel by folding back the doors at one end that screen the altar. The saloon at the opposite end of the schoolroom is divided from it by folding doors and can thus on occasion be thrown into the chapel. Amidships, on the next deck below, are four cabins for Europeans *and* a bathroom ; aft of these and separated from them by a watertight bulkhead, are the students' quarters, and right at the back, close to the foot of the companion ladder, a tiny cabin made for the Archdeacon himself, and near it a corner for a small printing press. The stokehold and quarters for men and officers of the ship run forward of the house amidships ; the roof of the deck-house, with a sick bay projecting through it as an upper storey, makes a convenient promenade deck the whole width of the ship. The total length is 127 feet as against the 65 feet of the *C.J.* ; its greatest breadth is 20 feet and the depth of water required to float it 5 feet 11 inches.

By an extraordinary coincidence, Johnson was again withheld by sickness from taking part in the first work of the new steamer, just as his blindness had prevented his being at the birth of the *C.J.* He left England after his second visit home (in twenty-two years) on November 5, 1898, and spent 1899 and most of 1900 in regular work, but in October 1900 he was down with blackwater fever and after a slow recovery he was ordered —definite orders were needed—to go away from Africa for some months in order to regain his strength. He refused to go to England, but was induced to go and visit his elder brother in New Zealand. He got back from New Zealand nine days after the dedication of the *Chauncy Maples* on St. George's Day (April 23), 1902. In a letter to the Rev. Duncan Travers (Gen. Sec., U.M.C.A.) on May 3, he told something of what he felt on coming to the Lake to find his new Bishop and his new steamer. His words, jumping from one cause of thankfulness to another, intentionally, remind one of Shylock divided between concern for his ducats and his daughter.

"I am quite unable to express what I feel. You will find this little more than a series of exclamations. Oh, my Bishop! Oh, my Steamer! Only in my case, they are both found, not lost. How can I express his sympathy, or what it is to have a proper washing-basin and water laid on. My soul is full of praise for mingled visions of a crowd of cheering blacks, and an altar and all that appertains to it that more than realized what I could dream of in worthy

---

*Marginal notes:*

Its size

W. P. J. again cut off from its start

Dedicated April 23, 1902

W. P. J.'s gratitude

1902

fitness, yet with nothing to jar in unnecessary ornament ; for old friends and such men as Glossop, Howard, Davies, etc., with a background of health, Indian clubs, boxing gloves, etc., of really comfortable wire beds, and then, right up in heaven, such a wealth of witness to those who have evolved this steamer and built it of steel, pine and teak, but none the less of devotion to our Lord and science and skill of sympathy and prayer which can look and aim beyond the earthen vessels who may use the sacrifice—so I must apologize to you and Mr. Brunel—and you will allow me to add to Crouch, to C. J. Viner, and all at the Office, too, howbeit they ' attain not to the first three,' and I must draw in my Lord of St. Albans too (Bishop Festing). I say I must apologize to you all and several, for mixing you up in my mind in a general thanksgiving not only with your peers, our dear Bishop, etc., but with the stately outline of the *Chauncy Maples*, the ' wide room ' of the upper deck, the sick bay, the wheel-house or palace, davits and dinghies, old friends in stokehold and on deck.

Bucknall Smith has come down and is telling me of teachers who have distinguished themselves in one way or another (probably by getting into trouble), so I will only remember the *Sanctus, Sanctus, Sanctus*, and the one consecrated part of our new home, the altar with the mother-of-pearl cross.

I can only pray that it may become the local habitation of an African home and that all who have joined in this overflowing of liberality may feel our Lord's presence more and more fully. . . . Howard tells us casually that Mr. I. Brunel is called home and this when our hearts at last begin to feel what his life's sympathy meant at home ; only the same morning the Bishop (Trower) had been telling me of his coming to the last Committee and supporting our work. *Requiescat in pace* and may he have taught me at least to feel more worthy gratitude to those who remain. In truth life moves on different planes, as I feel of the natives here, and often help and sympathy is on too high a plane for common or garden gratitude. Some crisis, some call is needed to raise one to appreciate what is really being done by others to help us."

The *C.M.* added immensely to the joys of the steamer work—perhaps it would be truer to say that it reduced enormously the horrors of a life on the Lake and it did provide quite admirable accommodation not only for the occasional passenger, but for the steamer staff. It even made possible part of what Archdeacon Johnson had desired in the way of a college. As his letter shows it was a tremendous joy to Johnson, but it must be admitted that it by no means succeeded in supplying fully the need of a training college.

1902
Augustine
Ambali on the
C.M. as a
College

A few heartfelt words from dear old Augustine Ambali (*Thirty Years in Nyasaland*, p. 59) will give some idea of the difficulty—" And for eight years I was deacon under Archdeacon Johnson working under him, and I never saw in all my life a man like him ; he is wonderful man and very keen on his work. And after eight years Archdeacon asked me to educate on board the *C.M.* for one year to read there. But we could not educate there well, and the reason it is this that we are not seamen ; the Lake it is very rough and there are motions every day. And there is no private place on the *C.M.* for our meditations and prayers, but too much noise of people and too much waves and rolling, rolling always ; and we were ill very often because it is rough Lake. And we could not do anything on board, but we spend time for nothing, roused and routed by the waves." Poor Augustine! He was by no means the only

Lake Nyasa
can be rough

sufferer. Many may suppose that because Lake Nyasa is inland and quite small compared with the mighty ocean, its roughness must be very trifling. *Experto crede!* One who has gone round Africa, crossed the Mediterranean and the Channel, and each of these several times, assures us that by far his most trying hours have been on such narrow waters as Lake Nyasa and the Bristol Channel.

Johnson himself had been upset by the choppy waters of Lake Nyasa, though he was quite a good sailor, and in any case his indomitable will would not allow internal qualms to interfere seriously with work ; but not even that will could control the qualms of other people. Some people—and Johnson was pre-eminently such a one—can work steadily amid whatever distractions. No one who knew him would have been surprised to see him in the middle of a busy railway station, working away at a piece of translation with a note-book and two or three books of reference strewn round him. He might disturb Paddington, but Paddington and all its bustle wouldn't disturb him.

Too rough for
a floating
College

But such detachment is very rare and it was on the rock of this difficulty that the *C.M.*, as a floating college, came to grief. That is not by any means to say that it failed altogether to satisfy the high hopes of Johnson and those who planned and built it. It only means that it failed as a means for carrying out

The *C.M.* in
the war years

one of the uses for which Archdeacon Johnson desired it. Apart from that, it has abundantly justified its existence. The dreadful years 1914 to 1918 put it to a new use. One may rejoice that

ARCHDEACON JOHNSON AND STUDENTS ON THE S.S. " CHAUNCY MAPLES "

the Mission steamers were allowed to help Britannia rule the 1914-18 waves in one remote corner, while one deplores the sad necessity which turned messengers of peace into handmaids of war.

But there is more to deplore than the fact that our *C.M.* had to be at the disposal of the Government during the war years. Commandeered for war work All the available craft on the Lake, steamers, and smaller boats, were commandeered for the same service. There was fetching and carrying of all sorts to be done, an army to be fed and supplied, and it was fortunate that the Lake was there with its 300 miles of length to lighten the task of transport in a country where as yet roads were quite rudimentary. But all this inevitable work, for much of which the *C.M.* was the best boat on the Lake—she carried more passengers than her designers ever dreamt of providing for—had its effect on Mission policy. Think of it ; for over four years the Mission steamers were at the disposal of the Government, and how was the Mission work, built up on the use of steamers, to be carried on ? The Government, of course, allowed the steamers to carry the necessary Mission stores, mails and also passengers where it was possible, but the old programme of visiting all the mainland villages and going hither and thither, one step forward and, maybe, two steps back, was naturally impossible. The frenzy of European The effect of the war on Mission policy and work nations in far-off Europe compelled a change of Mission methods in this heart of Africa. Alas, that it could be so! And, oh, that it may never be again!

In the old days of one steamer, as we have seen already, if that steamer were under repair the work had to be done other ways, but from 1902 until 1914 no such necessity had arisen, for the *C.J.* and the *C.M.* never went on strike together. From 1914 to 1919 both were engaged primarily on other work. It was not until 1921 that the *C.M.* was released in good repair. After the strenuous war years the Government had to overhaul her thoroughly and renew her boilers. Mr. Crouch, who had had so much to do with her designing and with her putting together on the Lake in 1901, was brought out by the Government to do the necessary work. All the time that the repairing was being done the stout old *C.J.* carried on alone the necessary work of the diocesan transport. It must be remembered that, as the Mission work grew, the inevitable transport of mails, stores, passengers grew, till such transport became a whole-time job for one steamer.

L

1902

Before the war, the *C.J.* had done this while the *C.M.* did the " mission " work proper, and even then it was as much as the *C.J.* could get through. The war changed the old Mission policy of providing for nearly all the mainland work by putting it under the floating centre, and made necessary a subdivision of that district, which was far too large for two or even three men to work without a steamer. In December 1906 the two native deacons, Augustine Ambali and Eustace Malisawa, were ordained priests and were given parishes which they worked under Archdeacon Johnson. During the war the mainland villages had to be divided up still further under European and native priests. Likoma undertook the strip of coast nearest to the island. The station of Malindi at the south end was responsible for another strip. The villages on the south-western shore were put under Mponda's, the mission station close to Fort Johnson. The Portuguese section south of Likoma Island had to be worked on foot by men who would formerly have been attached to the steamer. Up to 1914, the Mission stations were only Likoma, Kota Kota, Mponda's, Malindi with Unangu in Yaoland, Msumba and Lungwena on the Lake side, of which the last three were under the care of native priests, Yohana Abdallah, Augustine Ambali and Eustace Malisawa. Besides these there was a very large *C.M.* area consisting of a strip of coast of over 300 miles in length and a number of places which could be reached in a day's journey from the Lake. This large *C.M.* area or station under Archdeacon Johnson had no European stations in it except St. Michael's College (up to the lamented shooting of Arthur Douglas in 1911), and this, of course, was not an ordinary Mission Station but a Diocesan Institution to which the two nearest villages were attached to provide some training in pastoral work. It was this large *C.M.* area which, during the war, was subdivided into parishes. To-day this area includes seven central stations, each with its resident priest and its larger or smaller district. Be it understood that when we say seven resident priests, we mean places for seven resident priests when the Bishop has priests to put there. Furloughs, sickness, deaths, resignations are constantly making it hard to keep the stations staffed and the Bishop really needs, as we have already said, a reserve of young men getting qualified to fill vacancies as they occur.

This explanation of the changed policy leads us up to what is

1906
Augustine
Ambali and
Eustace
Malisawa
ordained
priests

" Steamer "
villages divided
up

Where is the
reserve of
young men ?

almost a tragedy, quite a tragedy from the point of view of
Archdeacon Johnson. He carried on all through the steamerless
period, and went to England for furlough in 1920, returning in
October 1921 full of plans for resuming his old pre-war work on
and with the steamer, which was by that time repaired and once
more running. It was not to be. The Bishop had other plans.
He placed Johnson in the north, the quondam German territory,
with a vague and large parish, and the beloved *C.M.* was re-
served for its necessary but humdrum task of general transport
boat for the Diocese. This may have been necessary, even with
the *C.J.* still going strong, but it was none the less hard for the
Archdeacon.

He accepted loyally the decision and worked under it to the
end, but he was never reconciled to this appropriation of the
*C.M.* for donkey work, however much it might be needed. He
would gladly have confined himself to a parish on land in the
Mandated Territory, if he had seen the old *C.M.* still carrying
on under another something of its old work as a " missionary "
steamer. He continued to the end to feel that a far wider area
could have been served on the old *C.M.* lines ; witness his words
to his brother quoted above (p. 153) where he noted that Roman
Catholics were working a district by canoes, while the U.M.C.A.
with two steamers left it untouched. It is possible that Archdeacon Johnson never fully realized that after all a steamer
could only visit effectively stations along the Lake side, and that
in the new days of peace from raiders and slave-traders, even
the lakeside dwellers were tending more and more to move their
villages into the hills. Even in 1900 this movement had begun
and it is possible that it was accelerated by troubles with the
Portuguese, which drove a large number of people not merely
into the less accessible hills, but even over the northern or
southern borders into the lands of the Germans or the British.
The abandonment of the old methods was bound to come, and
the war merely hastened an inevitable development, but the
change was none the less hard for the old pioneer to accept.

The *C.M.* has not ceased to be an invaluable aid to the work
of the Mission on the Lake, even though its work has changed.
It now runs to a printed time-table, published for some months
ahead and priests-in-charge and housekeepers have full warning
as to the days when they may send their orders for stores, etc.,
to the south, where the Diocesan distributing centre is, and

1920
1921
W. P. J. has to
" lose " the
steamer
He loyally
accepts this
loss
The *C.M.'s*
time-table

when they may hope to see their stores arrive. In an organization on such a scale as the Mission in Nyasaland such a regular service is of great value to the work on all its sides, and if the *C.M.* did not exist, it would be necessary, as used to be said of the Austro-Hungarian State, to call it into being. One round trip of the *C.M.* takes normally nineteen or twenty days and an interval between trips of ten days or a fortnight is needed for collecting stores and mails and for minor repairs.

The *C.J.* in its old age is kept at the workshop end of the Lake for emergency use and either boat may have its programme interfered with by urgent Diocesan needs.

# CHAPTER XIII

# Archdeacon Johnson in New Zealand

1900-1
W. P. J.
seriously ill

WE have already noticed that in 1900 Johnson was dangerously ill of that malignant disease known as blackwater fever, and that for his convalescence he was ordered to New Zealand, where his elder brother Jack had settled, married and had a family of sons and daughters.

Dr. Howard, who attended him through this illness, says that the Archdeacon himself was quite certain that in all his twenty-three years of hard pioneer conditions he had never before had this sort of attack, a thing which is surprising because all the general conditions had constantly been present, and it is usual for those who are predisposed at all to the sickness to have it in the first few years. Anyway, there is no doubt that he had a very severe attack in October 1901 and that Bishop Hine, himself an M.D., fully expected that he would die. The trouble with blackwater fever is that it drains the patient of all his strength and leaves him so weak that without the most careful nursing he is hardly likely to pull through. The heavy percentage of fatal cases is doubtless due to the difficulty of getting the patient quickly to a hospital where he can get that skilled nursing. In this case, Johnson was doubly fortunate in being brought at once to Likoma, where Dr. Howard attended him, and Nurse Minter (now Mrs. Howard) nursed him, a combination of skill and devoted care which could not be bettered. His life was granted to the constant prayers which went up for him from all around the Lake, and in December he was well enough to go away for a complete change. It will easily be imagined that the Archdeacon had positively to be coerced into taking this holiday. The doctor and nurse both testify to his model behaviour when he was really ill. " So as to get back to work as soon as possible "—that was the motive of the Archdeacon's passive obedience ; but once he felt he was well he chafed and fumed if he was not allowed at once to return to his work. In

His character
as a patient

1900–1

1900 he could see no difference between his case then and in numberless other illnesses which he had had, and after which he had lost no time in getting into harness. The Bishop, backed up

Ordered to take a rest

by the Doctor, insisted on a complete change and it was no use for Johnson to be fractious.

Goes to New Zealand

Ultimately he refused to go to England, but yielded so far as to go to New Zealand, where he could see his elder brother and make the acquaintance of his hitherto unknown nephews and nieces. Dr. Howard and Nurse Minter accompanied him as far as Aden, and took care, as far as they could, that he did nothing rash, but he was occasionally " fractious " and submitted to this mild tyranny with something less than his usual courteous grace. He was being driven and he did not like being driven, even when he knew how good it was for him. He wouldn't allow the Doctor to send a cable to New Zealand so that his brother might meet him, but in this the Doctor dared to disobey without telling his patient ; and the patient was very glad indeed when he reached Auckland to find Mr. J. C. Johnson waiting for him on the quay.

From Auckland, he was taken northward by steamer to Whangerei, and thence by rail and buggy (sixteen miles over a bad road with his brother and Mrs. Johnson) to the farm home

Welcomed to " Willow Bank "

at Whananaki. He was delighted to find the home named " Willow Bank " after the house of an aunt in the Isle of Wight. Here, as he descended from the buggy, a frail figure in grey suit and grey hat, he was set upon by the swarm of five children and at first hardly knew what to make of them, as they greeted the uncle whom they had only known of as a sort of hero of fable. " My dear Emily," he said to his sister, " are these all yours ? How jolly! "

Memories of his niece Phyllis

We might quote here the memories of him, still vivid to-day, of his niece Phyllis, one of the five children of that first meeting.

" He was ill and lay in bed for weeks, and we crept in to kiss him ' good night '—I've an impression of a knight on a tomb. I want you to catch a glimpse of the way the dear bachelor thing, all unused to children (at any rate to white ones), fell into our lives and loved and was loved. He wrote years afterwards, ' The family at Willow Bank taught me the practice of love, I only knew the theory.' I don't think he needed much teaching. Long before Uncle Will was really well, he was up and learning to ride under our tuition. I can hear him saying on some matter of holding the reins, ' There is a wrong way and a *right* way, I want the right way.'

" First he celebrated on Sunday mornings in the drawing room (our nearest church was sixteen miles away) ; I can remember—as I passed the open verandah door—seeing him kneeling before his makeshift altar, and being awestruck by the devotion of his almost prone figure. Later I attended his Confirmation Classes, though I was considered too young to be confirmed, but no instruction that he ever gave had half the effect of the glimpse of that prone figure. I fancy he was never a good instructor, but no one could be near him without learning something from him. He soon began Sunday morning services in the village schoolroom, giving way once at least to a visiting Wesleyan minister ; he attended the Wesleyan service (somewhat to the young minister's anguish, I believe) and after the service I remember him, waiting to speak and shake hands with the young man. He prepared six candidates for Confirmation, one an adult ; he visited the Maoris, and was always very warm towards them—he baptized several of their children. I remember his coming home laughing from a christening, when the baby was named ' Porter,' because the aged Maori grandfather had once been given a bottle of port wine and wished to perpetuate the pleasant memory.

*Getting to work at once*

*The Maoris*

" He rode about to settlements within a radius of fourteen miles, visited the people and took services ; and what with bad roads, indifferent horsemanship, his blind eye, and dauntless courage, his life was in danger a good many times. He was generally mounted on a well-mannered old horse who could be trusted to bring him home safely. He once forced the poor old horse, much bewildered, to swim our tidal river, to the danger of both their lives, because he hadn't realized that one must wait for the tides. He was very keen to do everything that the people round him did, and was very anxious to help. I remember him chopping firewood. Once he was asked to ride to the Post Office and store for the mail and to bring back 3 lbs. of rice ; we had instructed him the day before as to the way one strapped a coat on to a saddle, so he strapped the paper bag of rice to the saddle and rode home, to arrive with an empty bag and a trail of rice behind him, we laughed at him and he, to our surprise, was very cross. I remember him sitting for hours on the wide verandah, with a huge Hebrew book held up to his eyes, he had, too, an unsociable habit, which vexed mother, of bringing his huge book into tea with him. He read all sorts of lighter things, he said wholesome novels were good, for they introduced you to various sides of life you might never meet for yourself. I remember how he chuckled over *Great Expectations* (not for the first time), loved G. W. E. Russell's *Collections and Recollections*, read Kipling

*Making himself useful*

*His reading*

*grave and gay*

(his favourite quotation to us was the lines from *Barrack-room Ballads*, beginning ' Gettin' clear o' dirtiness, gettin' done with mess '); he was very fond of the Jungle Books and gave us a copy of *Captains Courageous* with the inscription ' That you may grow to be " Captains Courageous " for Christ.' For amusements, he translated and studied, told mother once that he would like nothing better than to go in for a stiff exam. ; he learnt a little Maori ; followed my father about the farm when he could, rowed on the river, went long walks with all of us. . . . On Christmas Eve he supplied funds for a Christmas tree for the village children and dressed a Maori boy up as an Arab to give away the presents from the tree. The ' Arab ' wore one of Uncle Will's white cassocks and was a great success."

**His amusements**

There is abundant evidence in his letters to his niece Phyllis that the visit to that happy family in New Zealand did really teach him a great deal, and made him think as he had never thought before of the vocation to marriage and family life as something not less sacred than his own vocation to lonely service amongst alien peoples.

**What he learnt from this family life**

One friend whom he made during this visit really wonders whether he did not begin to doubt his own vocation. No one who knew him in Nyasaland could ever entertain that idea, but its occurring to anyone shows how much the family life of his brother meant to him and how intensely he entered into it by sympathy.

Here is another interesting impression that he made on a lady (an old friend of Chauncy Maples's), whom he met in Auckland, and on her friends :

**His impression on Mrs. Swale and others**

" There was an atmosphere of holiness about him which lifted one into another world, and the impression he made on everyone he met was remarkable. A doctor we knew travelled to Auckland with him, and said to my husband afterwards, ' What a saint he is ! ' My husband asked if he had had much talk with him, and he replied, ' No, it wasn't his *talk*.' He was not a good preacher, his sermons being as disconnected in thought and hard to follow as his talk. He preached one Sunday when with us and on coming out of church one lady said to her friend, ' Could you make anything of that sermon ? ' The other replied, ' No, but what did it matter ? You had only to look at his face.' Indeed, it was holy.

" He was a delightful companion, full of fun and of anecdotes of Chauncy Maples, and College life and old Mission days. He made very light of his loss of sight, noticing with pleasure the books in his bedroom, and saying, ' Isn't it delightful that I can read so much,' and yet one had felt so sad to see how great an effort it was and the

ARCHDEACON JOHNSON IN NEW ZEALAND

sightless look of his face. He made rather a pathetic remark to me apropos of preaching, saying, ' Chauncy never would preach when on furlough, except for the Mission ; now I would preach wherever and whenever I am asked, for I love preaching.' "

It is not part of our task to relate in any detail the life in New Zealand of Archdeacon Johnson. It is enough to mark it as an interlude of over a year in his labours in Nyasaland, an interlude which left him with dear memories and links which he kept up by correspondence with his nieces.

## EXTRACTS FROM LETTERS TO HIS NIECE IN NEW ZEALAND

*At school in Auckland, written from her home, November 18, 1901.*

Tell the little Brownie that he is a member of the one universal Catholic Church. The only question is of using the means our Lord has left, and the bondservants He commissions, and the marriage robe he provides. I want you to find out for me (1) the best place for large cakes suitable for a school treat, say for thirty children ; don't jump to the idea that I am going to get such a cake, but I do want to know ; like Miss Dartle, " I only just asked to know " ; (2) who keeps magic lanterns, slides, etc., in Auckland ; can you get me a catalogue ? ; (3) what can I get for mummy and daddy at Christmas, and do you want anything special ? you have young eyes and do not need spectacles, so help your bedridden uncle.

*On her preparing for an examination.*

Only two more months, fancy! It is wonderful how a little success will make the schoolroom, and even the companions who seemed so uninviting, seem so genial and pleasant. They used to encourage the athletes with rattles and other raucous noises, but I am afraid this letter will fall flat as you sit despondingly on the horsehair sofa. Think of the young baboos from some distant village in India who have just scraped together (or their parents have) enough to club together and hire a common-room and books, and then they lie on their backs and read, read, read. Surely, a New Zealander is equal to two and a half baboos at the least computation. . . . As to the exam. go in and win, but anyhow we are looking out for you, passed or not passed will not make much difference in that.

*Hokerangi Hotel, November 23, 1901.*

It was very jolly to find your father in this place when I came in on Valma. Valma was a bit lazy or tired or both and I went to two or three settlers' houses on my way up and only left home after 4 p.m., so I was too late for the regular tea, but Mrs. K. did well by me. Indeed, I needed some broad hints from my elder brother before I felt that I had done justice to the beef, onions, pickles, etc. Since tea I have made the acquaintance of old Mr. X, who talked affably and not like a man with whom one can have little sympathy —yet he is said to have strange beliefs or disbeliefs, perhaps he has not had much opportunity of learning of God's love and majesty. . . .

We all felt awfully sympathetic with you on that Saturday when you went on a lone hand—dear Phyllis, one's great comfort is to feel that we are not left alone even when we feel quite deserted—I have felt it so often that it is common honesty to tell you how I have found our Lord, and often when one is too feeble for that He raises up some chum to do the cheering business.

*From Nyasaland, April 9, 1910.*

My dear Phyllis,—I believe I answered the scrawl I have fished out of a drawer but it will serve me as a text, you dear old young thing. God gave us all this young glow and energy, and it is right and honouring Him to value it and even in a way long for it till one longs for Him, and that one is such a duffer at. It is something even to feel that I remember *the* House-father explaining to me how weird it was in the Colonies, people would get up and sing a song or recite and not know that they couldn't. That was beaten into us

at School, part of our creed for good and ill. I admit there are both sides, if you do a thing you can't, and know you can't, and know you make an ass of yourself, just to help others, that's grand, but not to feel anything is mostly brutish. So of our knowing of God, I have been very brutish ; I don't mean this as an introduction to my present state of enlightenment, but that, as one feels that one is brutish, there are hopes, unless one wallows and wallows and wallows and chuckles—but alas! one does sometimes. You do not, I dare say, certainly not in all the old ways, so God be with you. . . . My goodness, your letter is of November, a fearful time ago. Bishop Hine used to condemn self-pity and introspection in the strongest terms, and yet he had strong drawings that way and so saw it was

evil. One cannot cast it off altogether, it is this individuality through which we can help others, and hurt them too, and so hurt and help ourselves, we can't make up someone else. We must realize ourselves and that is just the way so many find the need of our Lord. Not how hard it is to hang oneself on a hook, or go out to a Mission in China—that may seem grotesque, impossible—but how hard to do what one is already madly trying to do, realize oneself, this may need the sacrifice of your pink parasol down the well. I believe our Lord is willing and able to come right into you, we draw the line, not He, till the time comes. Of course this doesn't mean that when I jaw, I am pleasing Him and drawing Him, but it is true,

true, true, truer than any of these truths that are fragments. You
see a bit and then all dies away, and you only " hear a faint noise
of Him," Him in your school and bedroom, and here in a boat.
Who set all this going ? You know all the beauty and life is there
and yet that you are not it, and He says, " Come," what He will
show you only He knows.

*No date.*

Somehow your letter, though vilely written, has pulled away at
my heart-strings, and produced some sort of noise like a rat in a
harmonium. You seem a better edition of my young life, only keep
straighter, and don't be a fool and try to get on without our Lord,
make Him yours till you feel like Olga [*youngest sister*] with the
old House-father and feel that he is yours more than anybody else's.
. . . Yes, I have read *Harrow on the Hill*, it was most interesting.
I think it had a preface by G. W. E. Russell, he was a contemporary
of mine at College and I saw a good deal of him but not in a wholly
satisfactory way ; he was admirable company but never in the least
took me into his own life, only brought himself into my rooms. I
often meditate on these things now and see them differently, I often
think that I was farther from many of those men than from a deck-
hand here now. I have no life or hope apart from what our Lord
gives, and that seems so overwhelming, the dangers, the hopes, the
brotherhood, this doesn't work out in a hurry, of course, still there
is an endless vista in the future and much points along it.

*Off Candia, First Sunday in Advent*, 1910, *s.s.* **Guelf.**

I feel rather a shirk running away from Nyasa and my people,
sitting on cushioned divans, regular meals, to say nothing of casual
white men all round. The latter are a very decent lot, ever so much
better than my remembrance of ten years ago. In going to New
Zealand, I had a good lot, but earlier—Yah! I have always funked
the repetition of the experience, but this trip nothing trying in that
way—one hardly ever hears an oath, and is not meant to hear it at
all, and no attempt at evil talk. True, I don't mix much, I wish I
could—a little too much of the hermit-crab, and yet not for lack of
sympathy with them all. They have rum ideas of prayers, e.g. that
a sweepstake on our run is evil. I can't say that I have gone deeply
into it, but it is not that sort of thing taints men, and the run is a
bit dull to most of these fellows who have been used to a busy
life. . . . Last Sunday, I explored among the fifty-odd third-class
passengers, and chummed up with a man reading stories in Arabic
about animals and suchlike to an older man ; the latter was
delighted at finding I knew how to read Arabic and offered me a
cigarette, and then a quarter of an orange ; he turned out to be

a Maronite from Mt. Lebanon. Most of the rest were Greek Uniates i.e. Greek Orthodox who have united with the Roman Catholics, or Italians, mostly from Johannesburg. They were said to have much money though little soap amongst them ; there were only three or four English at all, whereas this is an English boat and few of the other classes are not English. . . .

I am swotting away at three " nigger " dialects till I may become black. That is all bosh really as I dote on them and yet feel the danger ; it is just there that you come in, you all are alive more than I am, and so I must look up and try to enter more into the life around me.

*From England, January 3, 1911.*

No, dear, you were very good to me, an old fossil from Africa, only *I* was so seedy that I couldn't respond much to hearty love and funked a bit. I am a happy man, Harry, that is your Uncle Harry, here and your father there in New Zealand both comfort my a bit lonely heart. Yet, dear, let us try and find the Lord Jesus whenever we retire into our own room, or alone anywhere, you can't tell how great the need is, try, try, try to do it *now* and at all times. You see we can't measure how much other people do it, hardly how much we do it ourselves. I often find my thoughts wool-gathering in the midst of public worship.

*No date.*

To Mrs. Swale
New Zealand

If my niece (M. P. J.) taught me nothing else, she taught me to think of New Zealand as a living being to be wooed and won, and if we can't do that, still I hope that you and Mr. B. will help to build up some links.

*From Eastbourne, May 28, 1911.*

To M. P. J.
Travelling in
England

. . . I don't at all appreciate railway travelling, rushing from one end of England to the other—yet people are very kind, and there again if one looks simply to our Lord it is all right, but leave Him out and it is like a kaleidoscope or dream, but then I don't mean to leave Him out. . . .

Do write and tell me all about everything from the kiddies [*Miss J.'s pupils*] to the last dress, from your pony to the knight that comes or comes not ; believe me our Lord is the centre of everything except sin, and that would destroy all we love best, and lastly ourselves.

*From the C.M., September 11, 1911.*

A Retreat

. . . I expect you would find a Retreat (like our yearly one) rather weird ; our young engineer had never seen anything of the

sort, so the Bishop (Fisher) told him if he felt he would burst if he 1911
did not talk, he had better go and talk with some native in a remote
spot. You see we keep silence for two days and a bittock, but we
don't starve. We try to look up to God in our Lord and see where
we are. Our Bishop gave us some addresses which seemed very Confession
good this time ; if you like and feel moved you can go to some
clergyman for confession, but of course, you need not. I have no
idea how many go. I do. I find it helpful, but we can abuse any
mortal thing if it comes to that, can't we, dear ?

Our Cathedral is helpful and yet it is too dark for the likes of me, Likoma
one-eyed and purblind, and I should never have evolved any such Cathedral
idea or plan myself, but it is wonderful as it is. . . .

. . . Mind what you say when you pity Mr. J. for finding that
nobody cares for what he thinks so much of. Your New Zealand
will go off in dust and ashes if you run it without God and religion—
is that what he cares for ? Don't be cross, New Zealand and old
England are all one as regards this, and we must each try and call
God into our country, and to clear out the heart, just as they clear
out this old Chapel every Saturday, and make me sit up upon the
seat. Mr. Jenkin told me of a school church of his the people here
made themselves, they made a Bishop's throne and a parson's and
a small do. for the teacher. He said he asked no questions as to
the bricks, but they do say that many of the congregation are
working for a white man near in a brickfield ! Did they bring them
home by ones in their pockets ? He is going to tell Mr. F., that is
the white man's name, all about it some day and hopes he will be mild.

*In Portuguese Territory, February* 21, 1915.

Your last letter ought to be framed and kept. But I have no store
cupboards—I am the proverbial rolling stone plus a very dear niece,
if she would only write. Unsuccessful, indeed I am unsuccessful, Success is
most people after fifty have a saving inkling that they are not a comparative
success. But I would rather be your father than the most " rather
well-to-do " man in the world. Success is all comparative, often it
means a certain relation of your feet to other people's heads, you
tread on them and appear to mount. No one could think of me as
successful, at least I hope not, it would mean that he did not know
me at all, and his opinion could be neglected. Your father is not
successful either, in the sense of money making, but he is an elder
brother to make one try and follow him *up*. Is it love ? I take off
my hat to him. Is it being a quiet gentleman, a natural gentleman ?
he teaches me to realize what it means. . . . Successful, indeed!
Whoever asked if a hero was successful ? If one did, I answer
successful in mastering himself, and then in bowing the hearts of
those around him to love. He is just the example we need in our

work here, we whites and the natives, and I expect I should feel the same if I was in any other calling, but " I ain't and I speaks according."

*Easter Day*, 1915.

. . . Yes, dear, I can see you all have good points, but why not write to an ancient uncle among the blackamoors? If I turn black and come to see you as your long-lost uncle it will serve you right, for you do nothing to keep me white. What does it mean to-day, " His hair white as wool, like snow? " May He keep us white but nothing of the woolly bear about us. . . .

I like to tell the people of my two nephews gone to the war. The said war certainly helps the boys at least to understand a lot more about Europe and the white people, indeed, it must teach all of us a lot. Any roughing I have falls into the shade, or seems like the Cecil Hotel, or the Louvre where I and some Bedford boys made a small sensation by going there in boating things. It does seem terribly solemnizing, I received the last news as Miss N. S. often sends me a summary from Likoma if they get anything fresh, and my heart went into my boots as I saw something about the " Blockade of England," but it was only that the Blockade of England is acknowledged a failure (I don't understand even that, what blockade?), then it went on " Famine in Germany an acknowledged fact! " I realized how German hearts must go into their boots, what agony and misery—*Miserere Domine!* But our Lord can and will roll away the stone, for each heart.

*From the* **C.J.** *when the Archdeacon during the war years had a chance of a passage on her, October* 24, 1916.

. . . Last night I made Miss A.'s acquaintance, a nurse from Bedford St. Paul's, who came out two years ago. Hers struck me as a solitary life ; of course, our Mission life ought to make it a real home and there is a lot of real sympathy about ; still the place there half Muhammadan, an old slave centre, is an odd setting for a lady's life. A lot of men (and women?) must find it very hard to keep their bearings in foreign parts as home life gets farther off ; often, for long the home life seems as real or more real and they more or less arrange their life round the mail, but this can't go on for ever.

*June* 8, 1917.

. . . Let me tell you a bit how I stand. First I feel I have unique mercies at this time, in the borders of it are some sharpish thorns and I cannot tell how long it will last ; philosophers say the old must give way and old ways are obsolete, this is often true and yet sometimes false, and my defects and failings are at least in part owing to my not having been put, not to lead absolutely, but

Roughing it and the war

Blockade of England

Keeping your bearings in foreign parts

His loneliness

relatively, so that I get more and more isolated and, as often 1917 happens, get, in a way, to like it, i.e. as one likes something one is accustomed to. I have the deep sympathy of a few and really not of any of the men. So I may appear to declare myself condemned, but there is much one cannot picture on one sheet of paper.

(NOTE.—At this time the Archdeacon was feeling acutely the failure of understanding between him and his Bishop (Fisher) and, though it is true that he always had more sympathy from women, for whom he was ever a hero, a *preux chevalier* who not only did heroic things, but was always moved by the most gentle and perfect courtesy for women, whether white or black, yet he undoubtedly *He had more* had far more unspoken sympathy than he ever knew or guessed *sympathy than* from the men of the Mission, even when they differed from him on *he knew* policy. He considered the advisability of leaving Nyasaland and its people, notwithstanding their claims " on my care and knowledge," but he could never feel that God was leading him to that step so, despite all, he stayed.)

*October 28, 1917.*

Oh, you dear people of work, conservating work! I often wish I could help my people more by example. Alas, we often exhibit to them the standard of an easy-going Oxford undergraduate and they take enormously to it till hit over the head for not doing the grind, then they think how inconsistent we are, or that heaven is not yet. . . . The worst of your real worker is he is often so hard on those *The hard* who have not been brought up to it, e.g. a German who had been *workers often* through the mill laughed at the idea of a thin native finding his *hard* marching kit heavy. It is phenomenal how Europeans here don't understand how their people are starving plus working while they are doing no graft except eating ; this is often not hard-heartedness or lack of sympathy but of imagination.

*October 28, 1918.*

Do you ever suffer from ennui ? This is not directly in the course of my remarks, but just what one wants to know to be able to share in your burden. I don't think I ever have nor do I now—sometimes *His privileges* I wonder if I am not extraordinarily blest—to see realities is a very rare gift, and one does not claim it off one's own bat, but ? I sometimes think this daily worship, not the only way, but a wonderfully privileged way, if we do not actually tread it underfoot like pigs.

*November 13, 1918.*

Yes, there is all that you say about these great, simple and *Great causes* glorious causes—North and South—yes and Britisher and Hun, many sides, new lights, undreamed-of worlds. . . . To-day I have been reading an article by a Frenchman on England's starving of

Germany, strictly correct in tone but suggestive—and yet, dear, don't let us lose faith in these causes, rather learn that there are more than we know of. . . . Oh, Stow it! Yes, Miss, I stow it. . . .

**Look up, not down**

Don't look down, dear, look up. Do you remember Perseus and the Gorgon? He held up his shield and only saw the Gorgon in its brightness, and smote. If he had seen Mrs. G. he would have been paralysed. . . .

How could He say, Come unto me—an awful bore that soon palls—never mind, Come; a very vulgar person—never mind, Come; only poor So-and-So—never mind, Come;—nay, compel them to come in—and somehow, you find yourself, the highly respectable messenger, coming in—it seems so " comfortable like."

*Songea District, March* 6, 1919.

**A retort from *Punch***

When you say it is long since I wrote, I wish to quote *in extenso* from a picture in *Punch*. Editor of Local Paper interviews a Mr. B. Mr. B.: " I wish to correct something in your report of A.'s speech." E.L.P.: " Do you represent Mr. A.?" Mr. B.: " No, but you report a voice saying, ' That's a lie!' What *I* said was, ' You're a liar!'"

Not a word, my dear niece, not a word.

*From England during* 1921.

I note what you say about the nearness of the departed. I am very vague, any experience seems real only in our Lord, though alas, not so hopefully to others as many feel. Yesterday a good man but very intellectual came and talked mildly, most things seemed fixed and immutable to him except our Lord; he seemed to think they had a mechanical process to test children, brain, heart, morality, it's an appalling materialism.

All is so mysterious, is it not, and our only hope—a glorious one—to find Him near. He can take care of all.

*From Manda, apologizing for forgetting to write, April* 28, 1927.

I am sorry, but then muck along again and—do not remember my sorrow at the right time. That is the dark side, but our Lord is very merciful and calls to me as in the Angelus, and in all manner of ways, and won't let me wander far—but there is no mistake about darkness round. So it is as I write this close to the lamp on my verandah, the night looks pitchy outside, yet if I went out and looked up there are grand stars. I have been reading some Tennyson to-day and been much moved, yet somehow rather depressed; there may be a danger, I suppose, in finding too much need of the bracing Bible air when one comes up against some of the realities of life. Tennyson calls out these realities with unique power, but not the medicine as the Bible does, the real presence of the personal love.

**Darkness round**

**but stars above**

**Tennyson**

## CHAPTER XIV

# The War Years

ONE of the saddest features of the Great War was that it inevitably dragged into its grip nearly every corner of the wide world. One might have hoped that the out-of-the-way places of " Darkest Africa " would have been untouched, but it was far otherwise. That wide region, in which Johnson, from 1877 to 1884, travelled about, was at that date an unknown land, unknown at least to geographies and atlases. A quite up-to-date wall atlas of 1887 marked the shores of Lake Nyasa vaguely by dotted lines, though already Johnson's work on the east side had made possible something more definite and more accurate than the map-makers had yet been bold enough to record and publish. 1914 Nyasaland caught into the war

In 1918, that same area had been traversed in every direction by soldiers of Germany, Britain and Portugal ; motor transport was calling for roads everywhere and the amazing aeroplane came flying like a strange bird over lands still almost unknown. Natives from every part of Central Africa had been called in to help with transport, and the tribes which had been comparatively lately taught peace by the might of Britain and Germany now saw these rulers of their world flying at one another's throats.

True to his own aim, Archdeacon Johnson would have carried on his work without paying any attention to the storms around him, but he wasn't allowed to. He had already been working in the German territory, and had developed on his own lines between twenty and thirty village stations on the Lake side worked entirely by the steamer *C.M.* His mission was never in the least political, though it may easily be imagined that the foreign authorities could not quite believe that. Even the natives recognized in him one of the English tribe, bound to link on with his fellow subjects somewhere. But he had so maintained happy W. P. J.'s attitude

M

relations with both the Portuguese and the Germans that those nations did undoubtedly put him in a class by himself.

However, the relations between the powers at war issued very promptly in orders from both sides that practically put a stop to Johnson's work in the German area. The British authorities forbade their subjects to enter the enemy territory and the Bishop (Fisher) enforced obedience to their decrees. Johnson wished to go himself and obtain from the Germans permission for himself to remain at work in their territory on parole and to keep with him, under his guarantee of loyalty, such teachers as he needed, whether British or Portuguese subjects. This permission he never had, and was not able to return to the territory till it was in British occupation. Even then at first he was very much alone and was rather thrown back on to the single-handed work of the early days, with this difference, that whereas in those early days he had moved among people who knew nothing of his message, he was now shepherding a scattered flock that knew and loved him.

The Archdeacon's persistent efforts to get back into the German territory formed one of the occasions of difference between him and his Bishop, and one can sympathize with both. The Bishop was the one who would be held responsible for any unpleasant consequences to the Archdeacon, or any of the people, native or European, who were under him in his diocese. If the presence of a member of the Mission had made any international difficulties, again the Bishop would have been held responsible. On the other hand, it had never been Johnson's way to allow considerations of personal safety to sway him at all.

There were his people and, moreover, inevitably in distress, cut off from teaching, from Sacraments and from the guidance and comfort of their friend. The fact that there might be danger not only would not deter Johnson but would probably to him make the way the plainer. " Here's something I naturally shrink from, though it is my duty. Therefore, I must make myself do it." Such reasoning was not explicit, for that attitude had become an instinct with him. As a matter of fact the Archdeacon was on the whole tolerated by the Germans whether official or missionary, and generally he was allowed to move freely about. Once or twice they had to request him to go and

even provided an escort to take him over the border. His fellow Archdeacon Eyre at Mtonya was, of course, in the terri-

BISHOP FISHER (*centre*) WITH ARCHDEACONS JOHNSON, GLOSSOP, WILSON, AND EYRE

tory of our ally, the Portuguese, but he also was visited by the 1914
Germans once or twice and remained to await them, while encouraging his native people to flee, and he also was put over the
border at least once. The question of a priest's duty in such
cases seems hardly open to debate—his first duty is to God and
his Mission and his people, come what may. If his continued
presence is a danger to his people or is hindered by force, he
must at any rate, for the time, recognize the necessity and bow
to it.

Archdeacon Johnson was well known to the Germans, with
whom he came in contact before the war, and his heroic simplicity won their admiration and respect. This view of his
character stood him in good stead during the war. One war
incident may be allowed to illustrate the dangers of unhindered
movement in an enemy's country.

A native agent, a Muhammadan, was sent into the Portu- A diabolical
guese territory armed with an auger and some sticks of dyna- plot
mite. Someone, possibly some quite subordinate person, had
had the idea of sending him down to the wooding-stations of the
Lake steamers, all of which were in British hands, to bore holes
in a few stacked-up logs and insert the dynamite well in. The
steamers, it was hoped, would stoke up with this firewood and
explosions would follow, an ingenious and rather diabolical plan
which helps one to realize how diabolical war really is. Fortunately, the agent sent talked rashly of his plan in a village in the
Portuguese territory (Portugal was at that time neutral) and frustrated
his plans were defeated ; he himself was handed over by the
courtesy of the Portuguese officer to the British and met his
fate.

Suppose that such a plan had come to the ears of a missionary If W. P. J. had
in German territory on parole, suppose that missionary our friend been involved
Will Johnson and two of the steamers imperilled, the *C.M.* and
the *C.J.*, it is obvious that a very difficult situation would have
resulted. As a matter of fact, this particular affair was dealt
with by native agents and the British authorities, and even so
it produced some awkward relations between the Portuguese,
in whose area the man was taken, and the British, who took
action on it.

When the British came into control of what had been German A Berlin
territory, some German missionaries near the Lake were in- Mission closed
terned and it is evidence of their regard for Johnson that they down

told their converts to attach themselves to the " Archidiki
Mission," i.e. the Mission of the Archdeacon Johnson. And they
did so, Archdeacon Johnson doing all he could for them, giving
them the opportunity of being prepared for Confirmation and
admission to the Sacraments, but in loyalty to their pastors of
the Berlin Mission not putting constraint on them. He " played
the game " with them honourably, as one would expect ; and
he did also what he could to protect their buildings from the
accidents of war.

Some extracts that follow from his letters will show that there
was no doubt in his thoroughly English mind as to the rights
The base camp and wrongs of the war, and he took great interest and pleasure
at Ilela in mixing at the Base Camp of Manda with all sorts of soldiers
(Manda) who at different times were to be met there. It was an entirely
new experience for him to act as chaplain on occasion for this
crowd of people of his own race. As usual, he tried to make contact with them and to find out what interested them. Some of
these men were astonished to find in this aged-looking ascetic
priest in the wilds a man of the widest interests, including even
rowing, boxing and fencing. There is a story that on one occasion a friendly officer put on the gloves with some of the natives
A boxing bout to give them a lesson. After looking on for some time the
Archdeacon, much to the officer's surprise, offered to have a little
bout with him. Still more to the officer's surprise, he found that
this tough old man with one eye was no mean boxer and knew
well how to defend himself and to give as good as he got. One
cannot imagine that the officer received any unpleasant shock,
or that he dealt hardly with his opponent, but it amazed him to
receive such a challenge at all.
Standing up for   Writing to his brother Harry about a gift from Bedford
Bedford School Grammar School (£2 15s. from the Lower Fourth), he says, referring to a conversation in camp, " I felt quite hurt when a *Boma*
man (i.e. a Government official) said, ' Bedford is *now* a very big
Army school—second only to Cheltenham.' The ' *now* ' and
' second ' got a rise out of the old missionary."


### EXTRACTS FROM LETTERS

1914.
To B. H. B.   One expects some effects even in these parts from the war ; a
writer in the *Nineteenth Century* notes how the English name stands
out most effectively across the future. Well, I have found some

telling effects external and internal. Our Bishop was very sympathetic at first when I was hoping to be interned, helped to send
funds, supplies, etc., and incidentally (as he explained) made
Glossop his Vicar-General up here. He is nothing if not methodical.

(NOTE.—The war dislocated the Mission work by the com-
mandeering of steamers, etc., and the Bishop felt that he ought to
be at the south end in touch with Zomba, the seat of Government,
and on a telegraph wire. Communications with Likoma and the
northern part of the diocese being irregular and uncertain, he
thought it best to appoint a Vicar-General. As at that time Archdeacon Johnson was hoping to be allowed to stay in German
Territory on parole and on condition of not going to and fro between
the German and other territories, he appointed Archdeacon Glossop.)

Alas! I was told I must go or be made prisoner and put over the
border. So I went. You will realize that to get a letter to the Boss
in D.O.A. [*German East Africa, probably to the Governor of Songea,*
*in whose district the U.M.C.A. work lay*] and back takes seven days
from any point of this littoral along which we ran you in the *C.M.*
[*in July* 1914]. I wrote twice and got two answers to make sure
that he had received my first, asking if Portuguese teachers could
stay. When I got to Likoma, I found the Bishop had gone south,
and it suited me to run across in *C.J.* to go to Glossop's work on the
west side [*Archdeacon Glossop or another priest from Likoma went*
*over to the West side, in what was normally the area of the Free Church*
*of Scotland, to minister to a colony of Likoma people who had moved*
*over there.*] I hoped to get a canoe across or the *C.J.* to drop me in a
canoe on the D.O.A. coast. I could not leave the people like this,
though I had removed our teachers as positively ordered. There
were Government orders (British), no boat or steamer to go to
east side, north of Ngofi.

I proposed to E. [*the* C.J. *engineer-captain*] to run me across to
Wiedhafen (i.e. Manda) and drop me at night, not sleeping. He
refused.

I considered that the Germans would not object to my going to
take leave as I had promptly removed our teachers submissively ;
the natives wrote that the Germans gave orders that no alarm was
to be raised unless a steamer, painted as the Government steamer
*Gwendolen* is painted, came in ; they contemplated my going a
farewell trip round in the *C.M.*, at least so I believe. I wrote to this
effect to the Bishop, who answered cordially, but almost directly
afterwards I got a wholly different letter. E., the *C.J.* engineer,
had given him his account of my proposition to run me over " contrary to his, the Bishop's, orders," etc., etc., rubbing it in strong.
Next trip of *C.J.* the Bishop wrote again saying he had omitted to
explain that he had taken both the steamers into his hands! Now

1914

the *C.M.* was commandeered willy-nilly and I can approve and did from the first ; and the *C.J.* simply runs as suits the engineer, the Bishop has been most of the time at Blantyre and Zomba, and has not come back yet (December 21). He wrote, " I leave you and Winspear the Portuguese territory," and no help of any steamer of any kind ; it is true the *C.J.* gave us two lifts down the coast, but the engineer had *carte blanche* as to times and management, the V.-G. says he has no check on him ; no services or prayers with the

No steamer or men, so I thought it best not to use the trifling help offered. You
boat for may imagine that from Likoma to Losefa and back gives one time
Portuguese to think of good times coming when one will co-operate with
strip *Wazungu.* If our dear Bishop does not mean to give up Portuguese work, he is a very deep horse indeed, and he wrote in the above letter, the only one I have had, " The German work does not exist." He had not asked my opinion on any point. Now, I get an invitation to go up to German territory, in writing and a messenger, and so I need much prayer and guidance and am consulting Winspear and Glossop. My sexagenarian legs seem quite antiquated, can you get me any others, only not made in Germany ? I fully expect that our Bishop has had no end of bother, but he does not make it clear sailing for yours truly W. P. J.

Oh, the horrors of this war! Three months' fighting day and night, butchery, temptations as of old. " Who will show us any good ? " One looks in doubt to the Brotherhood and on beyond to the Resurrection.

(NOTE.—This letter illustrates sharply the difference in outlook of the Bishop and his Archdeacon. The Bishop hurried off to Blantyre and Zomba to be in close touch with developments everywhere, having the interests of the Mission as a whole weighing heavily on him. The Archdeacon's one idea was to carry on with the minimum of disturbance as much as possible of the work of the Mission among the natives whether in enemy territory, Portuguese territory or our own. Both extremes were needed but it was a pity that there was no one to hold them together better.)

*Base Camp, February* 21, 1918.

To K. H. N. S.    On Sunday I had a little feel of a " vacuum," when a man came to tell me only he and another had come to service in Camp, and the other one had " dispersed." I really fell to prayer and, thank God, quite a number did come. Perhaps vanity comes in in such an experience, it is hard to say. Bishop Hine used to use the word " futile " pretty often, and sometimes one feels, is it not so, that failure is often a move forward, but then it is hardly futility.

*April* 10, 1918.

To his brother    I see General Smuts is down and rightly on the black armies levied by Germans in Africa and few whites, but what can we say? The K.A.R. (King's African Rifles) have saved us, but what about the future? And why are more and more enlisting, it is a big question.

*October 11, 1918.*

The Germans are "here, there and where not," like a conjurer's half-crown in a lady's handkerchief—it gives one prickles down the back, but, of course, nothing to what millions are feeling. The Mbamba Camp is in full swing again—but mum is the word— censors behind every bush—the men there were kind and I enjoyed seeing them. . . . Please send another list of St. Michael's men at front, also if possible Bedford and Univ. list, the last I had is worn out. . . .

The natives do suffer in this war out here, nothing to the Belgians, etc., but these negative comparisons help no one. It strikes me all in a heap when St. Paul says, "I know how to be hungry"—I don't, but the natives do. Natives one up!

*November 14, 1918.*

I have heard of Armistice and surrender. *Te Deum laudamus.*

*November 1918.*

I value very much "The League of Nations," and the photo of Bishop Gore outside. I feel him agonizing as never before, and yet how can it effectualize itself (i.e. the League), it needs the Church to effectualize itself and it does not seem to do so in the court of the Gentiles. . . .

Ten days since I heard of Armistice and no other word, or sign; is it all a dream? No more shutting up of chinks and light-holes, no more lists of the dead, can it be?

# CHAPTER XV

# Liuli and Manda

1917

AS soon as the course of the war had reopened German territory to the British—that is as early as 1917—Archdeacon Johnson was given charge of the ground in which he had already been working before the war began. It may be convenient here to summarize with dates the variations of the Archdeacon's spheres of work. In 1886, he began that *C.J.* work described earlier and his parish was as much of the Lake side as he could conquer from heathendom. In 1894, work was begun on the west side at Kota Kota, but Johnson had nothing to do with that. Later, a station under a resident priest became necessary at Mponda's village, close to Fort Johnston and actually on the Shiré River, which flows out of the Lake at its south end. The priest-in-charge of Mponda's took on responsibility also from the first for the very small work the Mission was doing on the river farther south. Later, Mponda's became the base for work a little way north on the west side of the Lake. When the *C.M.* had to be built, its size made it impossible to build it in the river as had been done with the *C.J.*, and a workshop and station with a priest-in-charge was established at Malindi, right on the Lake and with deep water near, but as far down the east side as it was possible to go. The priest-in-charge at Malindi naturally extended northward along the Lake and hewed another small " Cantle " out of the Archdeacon's parish. In 1906, Augustine Ambali and Eustace Malisawa were ordained priests and each was given a parish out of the *C.M.* fields, and they worked these as curates under the Archdeacon. This left the Archdeacon with the northern strip of coast and some separated odds and ends between these other districts.

The war, as we saw in the last chapter, cut off for over two years any real work in what was German territory. In 1917, Padre Augustine Ambali was moved to Ngoo, of which he had

The variations of the Archdeacon's spheres of work from 1886-1928

1900

1906

1914
1917

sole charge under the Bishop, and Msumba, the most important station in the Portuguese area, was made a European station under Padre H. A. M. Cox (now Archdeacon of Msumba).

In 1917, the whole of the one-time German East Africa came into British occupation, though the elusive von Lettow went on playing hide-and-seek with our forces right up to the end of the war, mainly in Portuguese East Africa. This threw the Songea district once more open to the U.M.C.A., and Archdeacon Johnson, who had already more knowledge of that area than any other member of the Mission, was sent up there to reopen the work. Writing in 1920, he said :

" Do you realize that I have been isolated for five years—no white man to work with me, much less under me. I do not thirst for any of our young friends, it is true—the worst of these things is that one grows into them—I think the authorities reverse old things and the young love to have it so, for (1) ignorance of what was done, (2) love of the ordinary station and all its works. . . . Believe me, I am anxious as to this one-man show, if I could rise to it, but can I ? I have the solitary meals, but no meals ascetic—I know quite well that the natives are puzzled by it all."

It is clear that it must have been difficult to find men to work with or under the Archdeacon, and that without blaming the young men. So much in Johnson's long experience had been tried out, so many pits explored, and it is natural for age and experience to want youth to take all these tested truths as firmly established.

On the other hand, youth wants to win its own experience, to explore for itself the pits into which others have fallen, and to take nothing at second hand. Moreover, it must be remembered that there had always been strong dissent from Johnson's special policy from the earliest days, and while every man loved and admired the old man there were few, if any, who felt called to work on just his lines or who were capable of doing so. Loneliness was inevitable for such a man, just as Mt. Everest must find it lonely even in the Himalayas. The last ten years of Will Johnson's life were spent mostly in reopening bit by bit the conquered territory, starting or re-starting work there, and then, as it grew and reached the stage where a European station became necessary, the old pioneer handed the work over to a younger man and went ahead on a fresh lonely track. One would have expected the old man to settle down to the quiet

1917

regular round of work on a settled station, with nurses to tend him when sick, and ladies to look after the housekeeping and provide those comforts—gingerbread, cakes and tasty dishes—which Johnson appreciated as much as anyone, and generally to surround him with something of the comforts of a home.

His life misunderstood by partial observers

People outside the Mission, who passed through whatever place he called home for the time, passed on wondering what the Bishop was doing to treat an old man so. They even invented stories of hard and cruel things, said to have been said or done by the authorities and they were overwhelmed with pity and indignation over such a man left to such a life. All this feeling, however creditable to the kind hearts of these partial observers, was really wasted and mistaken. Johnson himself would have been furious if he had known some of the things of this sort that were said. Wasted and mistaken, because this life was not imposed on Johnson ; it was his own choice, and it was impossible to make him submit, except for short intervals, to the " cotton wool " and " clover " that awaited him as soon as he should ask for it. Nothing would have pleased the Bishop better than to have Archdeacon Johnson living the most comfortable and regular life possible at Likoma, engaged in linguistic and literary work of any kind. He could have understood an Archdeacon of that sort. But something far harder and more relentless than the most autocratic Bishop was driving Johnson as it had always driven him, and that was his intense zeal and his unflinching devotion to duty as he saw it.

No use for " cotton wool " or " clover " except for change

What it was that drove him

His Reminiscences, 1875-95

The Bishop took great interest in the suggestion that Johnson should write his reminiscences and he got him, reluctant as usual, to go home in the end of 1920, to see about publishing. The result of this visit home was that *My African Reminiscences, 1875-95* was published in 1924 by the U.M.C.A.[1] The Archdeacon took a considerable pleasure in writing these *Reminiscences*, and he produced an exceedingly interesting book, but the *Reminiscences* were definitely reminiscences of almost everything except of William Percival Johnson. It was impossible for him to write or talk much about himself, or his experiences, and it was only on rare occasions that he dwelt on his own past. If an occasion presented itself when some personal experience might help another, then he would remember and talk of it

[1] Out of print.

solely to illustrate a point. Writing to his brother Harry in 1918 April 1918, he said :

" These references to my writing my life give me a strange pleasure—I hope not all vanity, I know I have plenty of that. Look at it in this way, when Bishop Fisher talks of it, I wonder and honestly wonder, ' Does he not think it would let off some steam and not amount to much ? ' I don't mean it in any ill-natured way, but can hardly see what he can see in my past life except well-meaning but misguided ideas that have sacrified many useful lives. Sometimes I feel as if I have something to write, sometimes that, ' No, it is too thin.' "

But Johnson had no doubts as to some other matter he had collected for publication, and he was very anxious indeed to make some use of it. In this he was driven, not by vanity, not by that itch for writing which drives some men, but by his ruling passion—the desire to do something for the native people among whom he had spent his life. His active mind had been constantly at work noting, comparing, sifting and he felt quite rightly, and naturally, that he knew them better than other people, better than any of his fellow workers in the Mission. I have said " better," but that word should not be used to describe the Archdeacon's own feeling. He would have said, not that he knew them better, but that he knew them in a different way. In fact, there was no other man who had had just his opportunities. Practically no other member of the Mission had made anything like his effort to meet with them on the level, and to enter into their lives and thoughts. Some of the ladies had certainly tried to do so with more or less success ; but the men, priests or laymen, generally get caught into the machine, and, overwhelmed with details of work, find it very hard to get behind these details to the people themselves. Johnson had always cared for people first, as individuals and not as units in a total. Writing to his brother in 1919, Johnson said, " The Bishop sent me up here at a trying time to set things going and I think he ought to trust me. He took a lot of pains about accounts, but accounts for him are pounds, shillings, pence, not food, clothing, tobacco for this man or that. But he is a dear old Bishop with an awful old Archdeacon." There are so many people, even in Missions, for whom the financial details get between them and the hearts and lives of the people they want to deal with, and it is just these people who are needed to safeguard

*His notes on natives and their life and customs*

*Caring for the people first*

the Mission's interest on the material side. But Johnson wasn't of that sort and, though he constantly tried to remember how much he actually owed to such people, the inevitable conflict of opinion frequently produced friction.

Johnson's first care was to enter into the feelings of his people. Often enough he, like any other, felt the barrier that can hardly ever be broken down between men of so widely different cultures and backgrounds, but he never ceased trying and it is His locked-up store of knowledge certain that he got nearer than others. During his later years, he felt very strongly that he had, locked up in himself, a really valuable knowledge of native life and thought and custom which must perish with him if he didn't get it written down and published in a form available for use by others. His own *Reminiscences* he thought to be of comparatively little value, just talk of " old unhappy " (or maybe, happy) " things and battles long ago." He did not rate highly such narratives. But these precious collected scraps of native life, these he was very anxious to publish, not as an idle monument to himself, but as rejected by the Bishop a real contribution to the native problem in Nyasaland. He offered these notes to the Bishop for use in the Diocesan *Chronicle*, which would at least have put them more or less on permanent record. The Bishop didn't think them suitable for the *Chronicle*. The Archdeacon chafed, but continued to compile material. On his lonely treks he spent hours in camp getting from various natives confirmation and correction of his notes. True stories of native heroism He collected stories, not native folk-lore, but true stories of incidents in native life which might illustrate the teaching of our Lord. One of his favourite ideas was to collect such stories of self-sacrifice and unselfishness and helpful heroism as might give natives and Europeans some idea of the meaning of the Parable of the Good Samaritan. These have been published in Chinyanja as a school-reading book, and have been reprinted A commentary on the Psalms several times. Another idea of his was to publish a sort of Commentary on the Psalms in order to show convincingly how the Psalter really enters into the life of the people. He took infinite pains with groups of natives, getting from them light on the meaning of words and phrases, such as might be incorporated in a revised translation of the Psalms. Under all his physical disabilities he made copious notes of these talks, these " threshings out " of Nyanja words, and he took all this material home with him in 1920 and made a book out of it

which he published at his own expense. These notes also had
been offered to the Bishop for publication by the Mission Press
at Likoma and had been rejected, and it is not unlikely that
these had set up a prejudice against the Archdeacon's material
which reduced the chances of the notes on Nyasa life and
customs which had more real value. It must be confessed that
the little book of eighty pages entitled *The Psalms in Nyasaland*
falls between two stools.. It is a commentary on the Chinyanja
version without the text, obviously to be used therefore along
with the Chinyanja Psalter or Bible. But it consists of curious
comments almost entirely in English, with references to the
resemblances between some Chinyanja words and the Hebrew
word in the text, and quite often the comment takes the form of
providing alternative renderings and notes on those. It is difficult to see for what readers the Archdeacon intended his notes.
There is too much English for the Nyasa reader and too much
Chinyanja for the English reader and the aim appears to be
confused. In fact, the writer, whose mind was full of somewhat
confused matter, wanted an editor or collaborator to help him
sort it out and arrange it.

Here are two extracts, comments on verses 19b and 20b of
Psalm 35, which will serve as examples :

19b. Wink With Their Eye. Into the corner (*Ku lyunja*) shows
great hatred.
20b. Devise Deceitful Words Against Them That are Quiet.
The expression for those who are quiet in the land seems best
rendered by *wodeka*, the meek (see Dr. Scott in loc. and cf.
Arabic).

Neither of the Chinyanja words here used occurs in the
Chinyanja translation of the Psalm, and very few of the natives
have Dr. Scott's Dictionary or any Arabic works of reference.

A companion volume of only twenty-six pages, printed at the
same time at Archdeacon Johnson's expense, contains one hundred and one Chinyanja proverbs, each with a literal translation,
an explanation and the application, showing exactly how and
when the native would apply the proverb, and generally adding
a parallel proverb in English. Native proverbs are a very fruit-
ful and inadequately explored mine of native thought and this
little book has real value, even for the reader who knows no
Chinyanja. Proverb 100 will suffice as an example, though, as

1922

the literal translation is quite simple, no " explanation " is needed.

" He tied a snake up in the leaves (to hurt me or for) me."
*Adanimangila njoka m'masamba.*

*Application :* To any one who hides any (evil) report that is heard (publicly). If he had revealed it to you, you could have escaped. Here the snake represents the malice and evil devices of your enemy and this man, though your friend (i.e. under the leaves of friendship), hid it from you.

Compare *Anguis in herba*, but it takes a different course.

Value of these Proverbs

It is to be hoped that Johnson's collection of these proverbs may be studied, added to and made use of, for it is just such sayings as these that throw light on the mind and thoughts and even the customs of the native people.

These two little books appeared, the *Proverbs* in 1922 and the *Psalms in Nyasaland* in 1923, and a very limited edition of each was published.

Nyasa the Great Water

The great work that occupied the Archdeacon in 1922 was the preparation of his notes on Nyasa and the finding of a publisher. The book was published by Humphrey Milford in 1922, under the title *Nyasa the Great Water*, being a description of the Lake and the life of the people. Dr. Burge, at that time Bishop of Oxford, another old Bedford boy for whom Will Johnson had been a hero ever since 1877, wrote a Preface and Dr. Johnson's niece, Miss Bradby, did a great deal during 1921 to help her uncle to get the work into shape. Miss Bradby, who, alas, died before her uncle, was the daughter of an elder half-sister of the Johnsons who married G. F. Bradby, a master at Rugby. She is believed to have known and understood her uncle Will better than anyone else of his relatives and friends and her assistance was invaluable to him in producing this book. The sub-title gives an accurate description of its scope and aim, but none the less the book was in the main a disappointment to Johnson's friends, who wanted from him, not the wealth of native knowledge that he wanted to give them, but something of himself and his experiences. They cared far more for the man and his own doings than for the most interesting study of customs and life of the native people. Notwithstanding this, the little book should have permanent value for all students of anthropology and such as are interested in the Lake people.

has permanent value

The Bishop, as we have seen, had as far back as 1918 begun

to press the Archdeacon to write his autobiography, and he had 1924
taken, as he says : " a strange pleasure " in the idea. The
fruit of this was the volume, *My African Reminiscences, 1875-
95*, published in 1924 by the U.M.C.A. and introduced by a *My African
Reminiscences,
1875-95*
Preface from Bishop Hine, who had known Johnson longer than
any other survivor of the early days. Here, again, though the
book is of quite unusual interest and contains more of the Archdeacon than anything else he has written, it is still too detached
and impersonal to satisfy his lovers. It is, of course, just this too detached
detachment from the story of events through which he moved
and *quorum pars magna fui* that is really so characteristic of
the man. He always put his people and his cause before himself
and he wouldn't pander to the taste for sensational story-telling.
If his biographer should fail to put the work and the man in the
right relation as Dr. Johnson himself conceived it, he ought to
be haunted by an angry ghost.

These literary activities formed the lever by which his reluc- 1920
tance to move away from his beloved people was overcome in
1920, and he came back in 1921, hoping at last to return to the
steamer work from which he had been cut off since the beginning of the war. During 1919 and a good deal of 1920 the The *C.M.*
repairs
*C.M.* had been under repair. Four war years of Government
service had been a severe trial and before the boat could be
restored to Mission use the Government undertook to put its
boilers into thorough repair. Whether post-war material was
inferior or whether post-war workmanship was to blame is
doubtful, but it is certain that the repaired boilers did not stand
up well to their work and were soon in need of further repair,
which occasioned further delay in settling the *C.M.'s* future
work. Archdeacon Johnson went home late in 1920 and returned in 1921 counting on a return to the *C.M.* and to steamer
methods in so much of his old area as had not been definitely
allocated to other priests as their spheres. But the Bishop had
other plans for both the steamers. The *C.J.* was to be stationed
at the south end at Malindi, where the repairing shop secured
due attention to its failing strength—it was now nearly forty
years old—and whence it could make emergency journeys as
need arose. The *C.M.* now became the Diocesan errand-boat, its future work
with base at Likoma and making a regular monthly round of all
the lakeside stations where the presence of European resident
missionaries made a regular service of mails and stores neces-

sary. It may be asked why this work could not be combined with that maintenance of Mission work, by a floating base which had, up to the war, been the *C.M.'s* work. The fact is that the multiplication of European stations and the increase in staff, had already in 1914 begun to make heavy demands on the steamer, and the difficulty of serving the two ends had been apparent to everyone except perhaps Johnson himself. He was always ready to recognize the needs of the various stations and to do his best to meet them, but the strictly missionary work always came first ; and consequently the regularity of the monthly service, which a tidy mind like Bishop Fisher's regarded as essential, was in fact quite impossible.

**The loss of the *C.M.* to W. P. J.**

The Bishop, with whom decision rested, had little understanding of steamer work as Johnson conceived it and little sympathy with a method that belonged, in his judgment, to the conditions of a day gone by for ever. So Archdeacon Johnson " lost the steamer " and the opportunities of work that his steamer plan had always meant. His own view of this loss—or one of his views of it—peeps out here and there in some of his letters ; writing as early as 1919, when the hope of regaining the steamer was not entirely lost, he said : " I often feel we have lost the steamer because we did not rise to such an opening, such a sphere. I don't think you even guess what it might have been." It was all a sore trial to him, feeling as he did how much more he could have done in developing the northern area, as in years long past he had developed the coast-line village work in the south. He was fully content to work in the former German territory, but he hankered after at least one of the steamers as the floating base, without which the setting up of European stations was the only alternative, and he was never convinced that the vocation of the *C.M.* was to be merely the Diocesan transport boat. His loyalty was sorely tried, yet he did his best to carry on under whatever conditions were imposed.

**Work on land in the northern area**

He worked at first from Liuli, pushing northwards, and later when the quondam Berlin Mission station at Milo was given over to U.M.C.A. he took charge of that district, working it from Manda, which was in 1914 the most northern point at

**Milo**

which the Mission had a church and school. Milo is inland, only twelve miles from the Lake shore as the crow flies, but the crow would have to surmount the Livingstone Range of mountains, down which in 1881 Johnson and his handful of porters had 1921 scrambled " as down a ladder." When the explorer of 1881 was nearly seventy he had to tackle some of these difficult slopes both up and down in the necessary work of getting from village to village in that mountainous district. We should be left to marvel how, at that age, he managed it, but though he said nothing of the difficulty himself, the natives who travelled with him, Benaiah Mbiza, now a priest, Hilary, his faithful cook and *Hill climbing at 70* factotum, have told us how they managed to get him up and down with a long bamboo pole under each arm as a crutch, and with a man in front to pick out the best steps and another behind to bolster him up and prevent him from falling. How many young men are there now in England who can show such grit ? The septuagenarian Archdeacon made no song about this, for he regarded it all as part of the day's work. If he couldn't get to a village any other way, then he must get there that way. The easy plan of not getting there or of leaving such work to younger men wouldn't occur to him. However, soon after Padre H. G. Lawrence was sent up to take over Milo and its district as a separate charge, the Archdeacon, after waiting to see how he shaped at his work, did hand over to him some of the most difficult villages in the mountainous area which still remained in the Manda district allotted to the Archdeacon.

One of the great difficulties for Johnson was the systematic *The bother of accounts* keeping of accounts, and the most unusual devices had to be resorted to in order to give him the necessary help. His boy Hilary was given lessons in entering expenditure under different heads, and proved very useful and trustworthy. Padre George at Liuli, the most southerly of the northern parishes, was appointed by the Bishop to administer the finances of the Archdeacon's parish when he had charge of both Milo and Manda. Padre Lawrence, passing through Manda on his way to take over Milo, was instructed to explain to the Archdeacon that in future, with his reduced area, he must render his own accounts and send in his notes of the work to the Diocesan *Quarterly*. He asked him with a humility under which one can suspect fiery but restrained resentment, " May I advertise for a curate ? "

Johnson's Communicant registers were the despair of those *His Registers* to whom on any occasion he had to hand over a piece of work. His handwriting was difficult to read, and it must be remem-

N

bered that he had only a fraction of an eye, and in consequence his entries were bound to be irregular and untidy. But the thing that wore out the exercise books which he used for this purpose was that these records were not merely communicant registers, but family records, carrying under each name a list of children and family connections and odd notes about the person in

question. Moreover, these books were in constant use as intercession lists and when the half-page allotted to an individual was full it might happen that fresh entries were put in across the original ones. Nothing could speak more eloquently than these leaves (not infrequently " loose " leaves before they were done with) of Johnson's enduring paternal care for the multitude of his spiritual children. If his money accounts were neglected, it was by no means so with his pastoral accounts.

In the early days, as we have seen, it was possible to travel, under considerable hardships, up and down the Lake side with-

out seeing another white man. In these latter days, Liuli was a base-camp for the S.A. and Rhodesian forces operating in East Africa, and Manda, the Archdeacon's headquarters, was on a high road that saw a good deal of traffic of missionaries, officials and soldiers, for whom the entrance to the hinterland of East Africa by the Zambezi-Nyasa route was by far the easiest. The northern district, which before the war consisted of twenty-four village outposts, visited and supervised by the

steamer, was now divided into three parishes, Liuli, Manda and Milo, and each parish had more outposts than the two dozen of the pre-war days. A Benedictine Mission was working in the

same area as well, and in some cases friction resulted from the nearness of the two Missions. It is fair to say that Archdeacon Johnson always tried his best to establish friendly relations with the local heads of the Benedictine Mission, and that where Mission stations existed in close proximity he and his colleagues were always those who had been first in the field ; and they felt it their plain duty to hold the ground in which they had pegged the first claim.

Such difficulties as arose from this cause were a very real grief to Archdeacon Johnson, and the more so because he could see no way of avoiding or removing them.

One of the visitors who saw a good deal of Dr. Johnson in 1927 and 1928 was Dr. Mary Iles, and her account of his life and surroundings at Manda is vividly interesting :

ARCHDEACON JOHNSON BOARDING THE "CHAUNCY MAPLES"

ARCHDEACON JOHNSON BUYING RICE OUTSIDE HIS HUT AT MANDA

"I first reached Manda by road one morning before the Arch- 1927–8 deacon had arrived. A very large native, the Customs Officer, came A visitor's up and informed me lions were too prevalent for my proposed account of camping-place under a tree to be safe, and he showed me the only W. P. J. at place on the shore where tent pegs would hold. Presently, I saw in Manda the distance, some people approaching on foot and was told that it was Archdeacon Johnson, but as he would be very tired it would be better not to call till the afternoon. However, about noon a boy came and said he was expecting me to lunch. I found a bent, very wrinkled old gentleman, very active and with most courtly manners and conversation, only troubled that he had no guest house, and anxious to move into the vestry (a kind of apse behind the altar, perhaps six feet deep in the middle of the apse) so that I might have his house. Of course, I was to have all meals with him. His house His house was a long hut, store-room, kitchen, small room for native visitors, his own room partially divided into bedroom, and a room filled with books, files, crockery, etc., and then a semicircular verandah with a very ink-stained table, three or four upright chairs and his own little old deck-chair, where he lived. If the wind was strong a large calico sheet went up as a curtain. In front and to the sheltered (N.) side of the hut were a few feet of freshly dug ground surrounded by a lattice-work, like those surrounding the village dancing-grounds.

"Later this ground developed into a ' lawn,' hummocky and rough His lawn but real grass, and another higher fence had to be put up a foot or two outside the first, to discourage the numerous enthusiastic goats overjoyed at this oasis in the wilderness. The Archdeacon was very proud of his lawn. He had been advised by Dr. Laws how to make it. He said, ' It has cost an awful lot, but it gives me an enormous amount of pleasure and rest, and the watering does help the poor women.'

"Carrying up pots of water from the Lake seemed to occupy several women most evenings, but it was difficult to get it looked after when the Archdeacon was on tour (two or three weeks out of the month) ; a few purple flowers were also a great joy to him. When I left about five days later, his cook caught me up about half a mile out carrying a large live cock, which the Archdeacon had sent fearing I had not enough food.

"His days were very regular in Manda—Mass, 6.30 or 7, then His daily breakfast, then Hilary, a porter the Archdeacon had trained, read routine the lessons and Psalms in English and the Archdeacon followed in Hebrew or Greek ; then came interviews, and parish jobs or trans- lating of the Old Testament, first the Hebrew to be considered and then the right local words from Hilary or some teacher or boy. For recreation, a large Arabic dictionary would appear, and the Arabic word ascertained for some English one, and its relation to Hebrew

or perhaps some Bantu dialect considered, the Arab slavers having
sometimes left words as legacies.

"I asked him what made him interested in Arabic; he said,
'I must keep my intellect bright somehow.' He also believed a
knowledge of Arabic would make Muhammadans more confident, I
think. One day he said, 'I think I would belong to any sect that
could get at these people. I have seen many missions and no one
seems to have got at their heart.' He said the difference of food
made an unsurmountable difficulty; once he had tried living on
their food as much as possible, but it was no good, the poorest living
possible for a white man was luxury in their eyes, so now he didn't
bother and ate anchovy toast and anything else we could manage
to get. . . .

"Indirectly, I found he knew most things about Indian land
tenure and rowing and while ostentatiously lamenting his (lack of)
knowledge of German, read Latin and Greek and French like
English, was surprised he had forgotten some of Plato's arguments,
and delighted in St. Thomas Aquinas as a recreation. . . . About
natives he would talk very freely. . . . One time when he knew
a very hot-tempered Christian had to give evidence (in a native court)
the Archdeacon attended the Court and begged him to be restrained, whereupon the Christian declined to speak before the
Archdeacon and the whole Court departed to another house,
leaving the Archdeacon alone. . . . A native police inspector told
the Archdeacon he would like to give up Government work and
come and work as the Archdeacon's evangelist, 'but I don't know
if he meant it.'"

Dr. Iles was greatly impressed by the width and variety of
the Archdeacon's interests. During these last years he was looking to his brother in England to keep him supplied with the
latest books on subjects theological and scientific and with
magazines and reviews. He was specially keen on the *Revue des
deux mondes*, not, as he admitted, that he read it all but that
its reviews and notices and its scientific articles helped him to
keep more or less abreast of modern thought. His interest in
reunion with the Eastern Church led him to ask for the maga-
zine devoted to that subject.

Dr. Iles saw his loving devotion to the natives, saw his loneliness and isolation from his fellow missionaries, as did also other
Europeans who journeyed through his district, and she fell, not
alone, into the mistake of supposing that he was neglected by
the Mission and ill-provided for by the Bishop. "Why couldn't
this, that and the other thing be done?" they said, not realizing

that such a lonely life was the Archdeacon's deliberate choice, 1927–8
so long as he found among the new men no congenial like-
minded spirit who would share whole-heartedly in his ideas of
simplicity, and his determination to do and have as little as
possible that might increase the white man's difficulty in
entering into the native mind and life.

## CHAPTER XVI

# Dr. Johnson and Dr. Laws

1875

THE year before Johnson went first to Zanzibar the Free Church of Scotland started its missionary work on the west side of the Lake, and named its first station Livingstonia after Livingstone, in whose memory the Mission was founded. Its first head was Dr. Laws (" Laws of Livingstonia "), to whom we have found Johnson running for healing and help several times during his life on the Lake. About a year before Archdeacon Johnson died, Dr. Laws resigned and retired to Edinburgh. Thus these two men on opposite sides of the Lake both bridge the long period of transition from the days when it was still impossible to think of Nyasaland as anything other than the " open sore of Africa " to the present days of order and settled government in the very regions whence the slave trade drew its victims.

1927

Their acquaintance began in 1880 while Johnson was at Mataka's village in Central Yaoland and Dr. Laws was at the first Livingstonia near Cape Maclear. We have given some account of this first visit from Johnson's point of view. This is what Dr. Laws says of that same first visit. He received a message from the man in whose village Johnson was visiting and took out the s.s. *Ilala* to go round there and pick him up.

1880
Their first
meeting

" I found him," he says, " with a native boy. He had been at Mataka's on the hills east of the Lake, but had not only been without European food, but there was famine of native food also, and they had been able to get only one meal of beans each day. They had come down to the Lake shore and crossed in a canoe. Their whole kit consisted of a small bundle, a mat and an earthenware native pot about eight inches in diameter. As soon as possible we were back and had him safely in my house. He was in a sorry plight. Both hands and his head had severe ulcers on them, as also other parts of his body. He could not put on his coat, and he had to get his meat cut up for him at table, as he could not use his knife

198

and fork owing to the state of his hands. . . . As he got better he 1880 became impatient to be back at his work and would not wait till he was thoroughly recovered. It was the same on subsequent occasions when he came to me for treatment. Last time (1927), and their last, when over with me at Livingstonia, soon after he was able to walk 1927 about, I found him away trying to arrange for some natives to take him across the Lake in a canoe—a very risky thing to attempt. Fortunately, the speedy arrival of a steamer settled the matter satisfactorily for him. . . . I told him I had only one complaint against him—that he did not keep the Sixth Commandment, as he should by taking better care of himself. He thought ' there might be a difference of opinion regarding that.' I used to call him ' the " The Apostle Apostle of the Lake,' and he must have had a very strong con- of the Lake " stitution to come through all he endured. . . . He had very decided ideas as to what he had to do and how he should do it. This led to his working very much alone and it was best he should be so. ' This one thing I do,' seemed to be his motto, and he did it. . . . I valued his friendship highly, and during all the years we knew each other, we were always glad and ready to help one another in any way we could, and I miss him still."

Writing to Bishop Fisher a letter of sympathy on the death of both his old friends Johnson and Eyre, Dr. Laws said, " God sometimes buries His workers, but He carries on His work, and this is the strength of those who are fellow workers with Him."

In 1927, after some bout of illness, Johnson went over for the At Kondowe last time to visit Dr. Laws at Kondowe, the wonderful mission station which had been built up by Dr. Laws on the high ground on the west side of the Lake up north nearly opposite to Manda, and which remains a monument always to be associated with his name. These two Grand Old Men of Nyasa, with a hundred and three years of African service to their record between them, met for the last time, for very soon Dr. Laws was going home to Scotland, and Dr. Johnson was little more than a year from his long home. They were photographed together during this visit, and seem to have got nearer to one another than ever before. Here are some extracts from letters written by Johnson from Kondowe.

*In New Zealand.*
Behold me, tidied up about to be photographed with Dr. Laws, To M. P. J. who has under the good hand of God created this place, as far as man may reform the things of God, trifles like mountains and rivers. To one bred in these wilds of Africa, it is all a marvel—water

brought down and up from four miles off, turbines working electric lighting and many other machines. Commodious brick houses, well-furnished schools, and hospitals, all working up to the capacious College block, and a great church ; these last are not finished, but the Church is already rising, and in no ordinary sense of building elevation, and all out of nothing save the raw materials, no buying of bricks, no buying of boards, no wagon, let alone lorry, no dream of trains ; no skilled workmen, each step to be thought out, then worked out, perhaps each step had to be repeated till assured.

Certainly, hospitality is one of the things Dr. Laws has practised and realized. How many times have I realized this—scars still visible on my hands he healed some forty-three years ago. Not here, that was far south, when this was untouched by European, the site unchosen. I hope I have learnt to know the man a bit better this time—no simple matter that either, he was a regular Scot, forged by travel and time, and I was a shy Southerner steeped in a life large enough but often inarticulate. Our Master has been with us. I never felt so clearly the need of all and sundry, nor how great the need is.

N.B.—Dr. Laws declares that he never observed any trace of shyness about Johnson.

*June* 22, 1927.

Don't be alarmed, here I am in a combination of cotton wool and clover. Dr. Laws outdoing his old kindness. I feel very drawn to him.

*June* 30, 1927.

Since I wrote I have profited by Dr. Laws' *patriarchal kindness*. He is the patriarch here, though last night he told me I had cut him out as the " old 'un," here the *Mgogo*, but that might be rendered (I fear) rather as " the old chappie " than as the patriarch. All are very kind . . . they evidently share Dr. Laws' kindly spirit towards the " old man." . . . I hope I don't often bore him when busy, tired and worried, and I hope I sometimes help him a bit in following our Lord; we have much in common. It has been a great comfort to find he met me half-way when I ventured to ask if he heartily approved of my celebrating privately with my two boys.

I value being present at their prayer meetings and shall hope to be present at their Holy Communion. . . . I feel the Lambeth vision helps much. We wish you to give up no hard-won ground, but we expect the same from you, no compromise. We can't play or hold out individual hands (except in individual love). Whether the Vision was for *then* and now, only God could decide, but it clears the ground, when they and we say, " Let us pray together but not communicate outwardly, till our Lord opens the way."

DR. LAWS AND ARCHDEACON JOHNSON, 1927

## CHAPTER XVII

## Last Days

1928
Strength
failing

DURING 1928 it was becoming obvious that the Archdeacon's strength was failing and the Bishop was anxious about him, living alone at Manda. He wrote, after the end had come, to the Archdeacon's brother, saying :

The Bishop's
anxiety

" I discussed with the doctor once whether one ought—on health grounds—to insist on his living a more normal European life, but he said that while to do so might possibly add a year or two to his life, it would only make the time left utterly miserable. Short of that, all one could do was to give him a free hand, keeping sufficiently in touch to be able to come in, if serious illness came."

Precautions
and help

The steamer *C.M.* called regularly and brought medical aid for the sick people in the Manda district, generally a nurse, and at any rate, a trained hospital boy quite competent to attend to minor cases and even to perform injections where these were needed.

The priests at Liuli to the south and at Milo to the north dropped in from time to time when their work brought them near. Some time in 1928, a dispensary was established at Manda itself and one of the trained natives, Alan Smythies, was left there in charge of it. When serious illness came, Dr. Wigan was promptly on the spot and first one nurse from Liuli, then a second from Likoma were sent to help the Doctor in nursing the patient. The best account we can give of the Archdeacon's last illness is contained in the following notes written by Nurse Hall and sent to the Archdeacon's brother in England :

Sept. 1928
The last illness

The nurse's
account

" When first I went to Liuli to take charge of the hospitals there I was told that one of my duties, or, shall I say, privileges, was to keep an eye on Archdeacon Johnson at Manda and to do what I could for him and his sick people.

" Prior to taking up my duties at Liuli, I was once travelling by steamer, and, on reaching Manda, I saw crowds of people on shore who, I heard later, were sick, and many had walked several miles, hoping that a nurse would arrive to help them. The Archdeacon rushed on board, asking, ' Has the Nurse arrived ? ' but alas, she had not, and I, being ill myself, had no ' needle ' with me, also the steamer was in a hurry and there was no time. The look of sadness on the Archdeacon's face and his words, ' I could cry for my poor people,' went to my heart, thus on taking up work at Liuli I determined never to disappoint him if it could possibly be avoided, and so for the next two years the steamer never left Liuli without someone, either European or African, on board, going to do what they could for the Archdeacon and his sick friends.

" To me it was always a joy to go to Manda, the welcome of the Archdeacon and his gratitude were beyond description. He would hurry on deck saying, ' When can you come ashore ? ' and on my replying ' now,' he would take me across in the dinghy, give me a boy to attend to my wants, then, having settled me with two hours' or more good work, he would go and receive his stores, etc., from the Captain.

" Many of these sick people needed injections for yaws, and were encouraged to bring an offering towards the expense as many of them could well afford it, but to some I would say, ' From where did you get this money ? ' and they would quite frequently answer, ' From our father the Archdeacon.' Later, when the crowd was lessening he would come and try to explain to me the illness of some poor man or woman in the village who was unable to walk, and ask what he could do for them. It was just his polite way of asking me to go and see them. When I had finished this work, and had arranged to take various people back to hospital, etc., Hilary, his boy, would bring me various garments, also vestments and church linen, that needed repairing. His wardrobe was meagre, for he persisted in sharing it with his boys, or rather it seemed as though he could not keep more than one change for himself.

" It was the custom of the Archdeacon to have dinner with us on the steamer, then back he would go and spend half the night in reading and answering his mail, for the steamer usually left at 6 a.m. Sometimes, I was prevented from going (to Manda) by the arrival of the doctor or some serious case, and on my next visit he would gently chide me, saying, ' Donna, you promised, you know, to come yourself last time and many of my poor people had to go away again disappointed.' At last a dispensary was opened at Manda itself, and Alan Smythies was put in charge. He had only been there a few weeks when the Archdeacon began with his last illness.

" It was a Saturday and the Archdeacon returned from his *safari* tired and worn, but apparently well ; he took the Evening Service and prepared the people for their Communion next day ; it was not until after Alan had retired for the night that he was awakened by the Archdeacon's boy, saying that the Archdeacon was very ill and would he come. He was suffering from malaria and acute abdominal pain. Alan did what he could to ease him and remained with him for the night.

" Next morning, he seemed a little better but was unable to get up, and in the evening he had another acute attack, and Alan, without telling the Archdeacon, wisely sent word to Dr. Wigan, who was at Liuli. The note arrived late Monday night, but the doctor collected porters and food for the journey and extras for the invalid and started off to Manda early Tuesday morning. *The doctor sent for*

" The Archdeacon appeared to be getting worse and I cannot help thinking that he himself thought the end was near or he would never have consented so readily to be taken to Liuli.

" Alan procured a canoe which did not leak (an almost unheard-of thing) and putting straw and blankets in the bottom, gently lowered the patient into it, Alan himself accompanying him, while other faithful Africans walked overland taking a *machila* in case of need, and food for the journey. *W. P. J. taken to Liuli Hospital*

" The two parties (Alan's and Dr. Wigan's) met on Wednesday night and the doctor, finding the Archdeacon in a serious condition, sent on messengers to Manda with wires and cables to be sent to England and the south of the Lake.

" On arrival at Liuli he was indeed a pitiable sight, so thin, worn and tired, unable even to lift up his head. He was conscious and his gratitude, or joy, at the sight of a clean bed reminded me of the joy of the soldiers admitted to hospital after being in the trenches.

" After a few days, he began to be a little more like himself, he would smile his whimsical smile and have his little jokes.

" He was not quite sure in his own mind whether he wished to visit England again or not, and one day he said to me, ' Do you think my brother would be pleased to have me at home ? ' I replied that I was sure he would but that he must get a little stronger before he could think of travelling. He smiled and said, ' But you don't know the life I lead him when I am there ! '

" For five long weeks he hovered between life and death, but through all he was, as ever, always thoughtful for others, and he would get quite annoyed when in the night he called for Hilary and a nurse answered instead. ' Donna,' he would say, ' Go to bed or you will kill yourself ' ; it seemed a grief to him that he was taking up so much precious time which he thought might have been given to the Africans. *Five weeks between life and death*

" One day I found him on the floor, kneeling by the side of his bed ; he had insisted on his boys lifting him out in order that he

1928

might say his prayers. They did so, and then, becoming frightened at what they had done, came running for me. It was with difficulty that we put him back to bed and made him promise never to do it again without permission. He would lie for hours with arms outstretched in the form of a cross and with eyes closed would say again and again, ' Lord, have mercy upon me,' and later, as he became weaker, he would call to whoever was near to pray for him.

A peaceful end

" The end came on October 11 at 12.50 a.m. Father Benson, Dr. Wigan and two nurses were watching. It was all very peaceful. Father Benson said a few prayers and commended his spirit and his labours were over.

" The nurses lovingly prepared his body for its final resting-place and Father Benson vested him for burial. Candles were lighted and the nurses remained until morning, when the body was taken to the church by six of his old friends.

" The service was in Chinyanja and he was laid to rest at the north side of the Altar in the Lady Chapel at Liuli.

" ' We have lost our Father,' was the cry of hundreds of Africans on that day.

" May he rest in peace!

" The news was sent at once to Likoma and by cable from Manda direct to England to the U.M.C.A. Home Office, to his brother and to his beloved old school, Bedford.

" A Requiem was sung in Likoma Cathedral, when the huge building was crowded to overflowing by the Africans who loved and revered him."

Very strangely no public Requiem was sung in England, though at many altars in England and overseas the great name of William Percival Johnson was remembered and the Holy Sacrifice offered for the repose of his soul.

Postscript

Just in time for inclusion in this narrative of the Archdeacon's last days, there has come an account of him from the Rev. Benaiah Mbiza, who worked with him first as teacher, and later as deacon at Manda (Ilela), and who is now a priest working in that district. Some extracts from his account are given here as a valuable contribution from one of the later of those native friends who called Archdeacon Johnson " Father " during the long years of his work in Nyasaland.

Padre Benaiah does not know at first hand of the earliest days, because he was yet unborn when W. P. Johnson first came to the Lake, but he tells us what he heard the Archdeacon say to the Songea people when, after more than forty years, he made his second appeal to them for leave to establish Mission

stations among them. He went first in 1882 after he had met
their raiding party near Chiteji's village opposite Likoma and
he came again in 1925. Benaiah was with him and this is his
account of the Archdeacon's interview with the chiefs of the
Angoni (Magwangwara)[1] at that time.

"In 1925 when we went with him to Songea, he said to the The visit to
Angoni chiefs, ' I came here to Songea in 1882 wishing to build a Songea in 1925
station for my Mission ; your fathers were harrying the Nyanja
people whom I was teaching, and I saw that it was best for me to
teach those warriors (the Wangoni) the gospel of Jesus Christ that
they might know peace and give up their cruel ways. But your
fathers refused to let me stay among them because they were
warriors going here and there to raid and they were afraid to leave
their wives and children in their villages alone, lest other men
should come and raid them. So they said, " Go back for the time,
perhaps we might see one another again, perhaps we might not."
And so I went back and stayed at Chiteji's, the chief of the Wanyanja. Do not do as your fathers did but give me now leave to
settle here and build a mission.' They consented, but Bishop
Fisher, having regard to the Archdeacon's age, would not allow him
to be the pioneer, but he sent other missionaries and put the Archdeacon where he would have less work. You would have thought
that his work would now be less, but no, not at all. He had a very
hilly country and still he went everywhere preaching the Good
News of the Lord Jesus Christ to the very end."

Again Benaiah speaks of the conditions of the work the
Archdeacon did in the old steamer days from which we pick
out these few words as showing how it struck the native
observer.

"At sleeping times he had sometimes no bedstead ; at other Roughing it in
times he would perhaps borrow a bedstead from the teacher ; if the *C.M.* days
there was none to borrow, he just slept on a bundle of grass ; he
never considered himself at all, his heart was to consider other
people. He loved to talk with the chiefs of the country, and to try
to get them to accept his teaching. Some chiefs, such as the Yao
chiefs, refused to accept because the faith of Islam was powerful
in their lands ; but the Nyanja chiefs, though they did not quickly
believe and be baptized, yet they gave him honour and looked on
him as their great Chief."

Of course, Benaiah, like all the natives, gives great praise to

[1] Angoni and Magwangwara are respectively the western and eastern
names for people of the same Zulu origin. The names are used almost
indifferently.

the Archdeacon for his mastery of many languages, all the more amazing because the English are not generally great in this line. Benaiah says :

The
Archdeacon's
many languages

" Although he was an Englishman, nevertheless he knew many African languages. Most commonly he spoke Chinyanja so that he became like a true Mnyanja within because of his long stay in the land of the Wanyanja. It was the Wanyanja whom he knew most intimately. He knew also the Yao language because, at the time of his coming to Nyasaland he travelled greatly in Yaoland. He spoke Swahili to many people who did not know Chinyanja. He spoke Chimpoto as the people of Liuli speak it. And especially when he stayed a long time at Manda he spoke Chimanda and he knew both the speech of the Wamanda and of the Wangoni. Thus he earned great honour as one who knew many languages of the people of Africa."

When the Archdeacon was induced to go home for what was his last furlough in England in 1921 his African friends, knowing his age and seeing that his strength was failing, hardly expected to see him return again and their joy was great in proportion when he returned. Benaiah tells how the schools in his village, and in other villages, met the Archdeacon with songs of praise and dances. At Manda the song they sang in Chimanda (which Benaiah translates into Chinyanja) may be rendered in English, thus :

A Song of
Welcome

> Who is the famous one
> Gracious and merciful,
> Ever unchanging
> See he is coming!
> He went off to England, he returns to Nyasa
> Remembering the work he has worked here for years—
> Archdeacon Johnson who brought us the Gospel
> A Socrates for wisdom, a hero for courage!

I suspect that the Archdeacon himself introduced them to Socrates as a type of wisdom.

Benaiah records an instance of the Archdeacon's thoughtfulness for others during his last illness before he had been removed

His care for
others

to the hospital at Liuli. Benaiah's daughter was being married at Liuli and, of course, the father was expected at the wedding. Seeing how ill the Archdeacon was, Benaiah gave up the journey which had been arranged for. The Archdeacon heard of this and refused to let him cancel the arrangements. " Go," he said, " you must not give up this journey."

We follow Benaiah's account of the last two or three months.

" In June he heard of the death of Archdeacon Eyre, and he
said, ' My good friend has died, I hope that He will call me too.'
In August after the steamer's visit he made a journey to the hills.
He got back at the end of the month and in the first week of September he was ill. Ah! he was very ill indeed, none of us slept during
his illness. Alan, the native dispenser, helped him with medicines
but on the Sunday morning he was not able to say Mass ; on
Monday he was better, on Wednesday he set out again for the
villages of Ilungila and Mangoli and Lukanamila. He returned to
Ilela on the Saturday and that same night the illness began which
ended in his death."

The account of that last illness has already been given in the
words of the nurse, but we give here Benaiah's account of his
last visit to the Archdeacon on his death-bed.

" When we came back from Synod, the doctor allowed me to go
and see him on his sick bed. Ah! he was very weak indeed, and I
too, I had no strength, seeing the father who loved me and had led
me, on the point of death. His last word to me was this, ' Take care
of those Christians, and get from Father Dickson the money he has
and pay those that are building the Church at Ilela and tell them to
go to their homes.' I paid them and sent them home. A week later
the Archdeacon died at Liuli."

# CHAPTER XVIII

# Achievements

IN following the story of so long a life as Will Johnson's there is a danger such as must be felt by those who live with such a man, the danger of not being able to see the wood for the trees.

Now, for four years after the end of his life, one can draw away a little and form some idea of the whole without being confused by the multiplicity of detail. Of course the first conclusion we draw is that the MAN was far greater than anything he did, or than the sum of his recorded achievements. It is a great personality that we have been in touch with and the influence of such a personality is imponderable and incalculable. But it will help us to estimate that personality if first we pass in review the work done by the man.

First and foremost he is a great missionary. From 1876 until 1928 he devoted himself to Africa and the Africans. During that period of fifty-two years he went on furlough only five times and on at least two of those times he went only under compulsion, the first time the compulsion of his blindness, the second time most reluctantly under the positive orders of his Bishop and his doctor. During the whole of those years of active service he spent himself " to the $n$th " (to use a favourite phrase of his own). It is fairly easy to pile up a record of years of service if you take care of yourself, and put actual work second to self-preservation. That is what we most of us do wherever we are. That was not Johnson's way. He never spared himself or put any consideration before the work to be done. So that his fifty-two years of service are eminent not only for length but for quality.

Secondly, he accomplished a monumental work in the field of language alone. Of visible results,

> " Things done, that took the eye, and had the price ;
> O'er which, from level stand,

*The MAN greater than his works*

*A great missionary*

*His language work*

208

The low world laid its hand,
    Found straightway to its mind, could value in a trice."[1]
his language works are the most conspicuous. In preparation
for the Indian Civil Service, before he turned to Africa, he had
begun to study Oriental languages, and to the end of his days he
retained his interest in Arabic as well as Hebrew and used them
in his work. In Zanzibar he learnt Swahili, and at Masasi and
at Mataka's he learnt Yao. To neither of these did he make
any very great contribution, though he always retained his
knowledge of them and it threw light on the other tongues in
which circumstances forced him to specialize.

*Arabic, Hebrew, Swahili and Yao*

His biggest body of work as a translator or student was in
Chinyanja, the language of those lakeside people with whom he
lived longest. Into Chinyanja he translated the whole Bible,
and this not just once but with frequent revisions and re-
polishings.

*Chinyanja*

Others, lesser people, came in here and there to help to revise,
to suggest, to sift and select amid the heap of material that
Johnson's pioneer work supplied, but it is to Johnson's untiring
energy in the quest of the suitable word, the idiomatic term or
phrase, that Nyasaland owes its possession, for nearly thirty
years now, of the whole of the Bible (including of course the
Apocrypha) in the vernacular. This achievement is largely one
man's work and only those who have tried to do such work
know what an immense amount of hard work is involved even
in reaching a first complete rough version. In Southern
Rhodesia several Missionary bodies have been working for forty
years, and the first complete version of the Bible in the vernacular is still a remote dream. If Johnson had had nothing else to
do during the last forty or fifty years, this translation work
would have been a notable performance. As a matter of fact,
and as we hope this account of his life has shown, he was a man
who was exceptionally active and busy in other directions at the
same time, so that his translation work is in the nature of a
Πάρεργον, a by-product.

*The whole Bible done and done again*

In addition to these translations of the Scriptures, he has
written or translated a large number of hymns, the whole of the
Book of Common Prayer ; he was constantly preparing helps
to instruction of Christians, such as Catechisms based largely on
Sadler's *Church Doctrine Bible Truth* ; commentaries on the

[1] Browning's *Rabbi Ben Ezra*.

O

Acts of the Apostles, and other portions of the New Testament ; a Church History, together with *Padre Yohana Tawe* (translation of a Swahili abridgment of Robertson's) ; a short life of Muhammad ; the *Pilgrim's Progress* (with the help of James H. Mpila) and a curious and suggestive book on Chinyanja tense forms of special value to the student.

This is a considerable list of works to be done by one man, and it only represents what he did in Chinyanja. He also worked in Yao and translated portions of the Scriptures into that language, which is as different from Chinyanja as German is from English.

In all these languages, Swahili, Yao and Chinyanja, Johnson, though in the latter he may truly be called a pioneer, never began absolutely from the beginning without help. In very early days on the Lake he found help in a little book on Chinyanja by a Mr. Riddell of the Scotch Mission. But in the years between 1905 and 1910 he had begun to work in the then German territory in dialects which had not as yet been committed to writing by any man. In that area after he was fifty years old he began translation work in three new dialects, Chimpoto, Chimanda and Kipangwa and got the four Gospels, Matins, Evensong and the Occasional offices printed by the B.F.B.S. in Kimanda. To have acquired some mastery of six African languages, to have done a giant's work in one, and to have been the first to put at least two of them into writing is a very wonderful record for one man. One can hardly believe that the only man who has this record was handicapped for forty-four years of his active life by having only a third of one eye to work with.

*Pioneer work in three dialects after he was 50*

*Despite his eye handicap*

The amount of his language work claims for him a high place as a linguist. This claim is only intensified by the admission that in some respects he had not the gifts of a born linguist.

His ear was defective and he always had a difficulty in producing the one simple sound in Nyanja which is a little unfamiliar to English tongues.

His performance was not the easy conquest of one to whom foreign tongues come very easily, but was a triumph over difficulties. One great qualification for a linguist, an intense interest in the work, he had in abundant measure.

*Etymologies*

In later years he was greatly taken up with the subject of etymologies and spent a great deal of time in tracing connections between Bantu roots and Semitic, especially Hebrew, roots. Unfortunately, he had not the thorough equipment for this very special branch of language study and ran after will-o'-the-wisps. When he was in England in 1911, he asked me to help him to produce a clear statement of his theory for submission to Dr. Carl Meinhof, a German specialist in African languages of world-wide reputation. He appointed me " his intellectual mid-wife " and between us we got the infant into MS. form and submitted it to the expert. As I had expected, the poor little thing was knocked on the head at once and I hoped it might have decent burial. But, even in 1911, a condemnation by a German professor, instead of killing the theory in the Arch-deacon's busy brain, simply quickened it into life, and for years afterwards this will-o'-the-wisp still beguiled Johnson and led him astray. His hymns have been mentioned among his **Hymns** Chinyanja works and deserve further notice. He had already made many translations of hymns on the usual plan, i.e. by trans-lating the English words and then cutting the result up into lines of as many syllables as the metre required. In 1898 while he was in England he wrestled with another plan of much greater diffi-culty. He would make his Chinyanja hymns rhyme—a thing hitherto unattempted, and it may be added, entirely foreign to native ideas. He produced at his own cost a little book printed **in rhyme** at Aberdare, of over 200 hymns all conforming more or less to the rules of rhyme ; and a considerable number of these have found their way into the succeeding revisions of the Chinyanja Hymn Book. I am not sure that the rhymes have always sur-vived. Such a book as the Aberdare hymn book is more inter-esting as a *tour de force* illustrating Johnson's love of tackling a difficulty than as a great contribution to native poetry.

His little books, *Psalms in Nyasaland* and *Chinyanja Prov-erbs* have already been mentioned and discussed. Another work **Expositions** entitled *Sunday Lessons* was printed at Likoma in 1913 (both in Nyanja and in English), and is a very useful help towards drawing the appropriate lesson from the O.T. lessons for each Sunday. This was a central point in the Archdeacon's scheme for the instruction of the Hearers, the outer fringe of adherents. It was based on the old Lectionary and is no longer reprinted, but it still has value as an example of Johnson's way of ap-proach to the outsider who is willing to come under instruction.

Thirdly, in the first seven years that he spent between the Lake and Masasi he made a real contribution to geographical exploration, and in June 1884 he read before the Royal Geo- **Exploration**

The Royal
Geographical
Society
graphical Society a valuable paper on his seven years' wanderings. From his notes made during those years an excellent map was compiled and published together with the paper in the *Proceedings of the Royal Geographical Society* in September 1884.

The paper, which occupied more than twenty pages of the *Proceedings*, says nothing of the hardships but a great deal of the people, the rivers, the mountains, the flora and fauna. Incidentally, it settles the question of the then untraced sources of the Ruvuma and of the Lujenda, its principal tributary.

Sir T. Fowell Buxton, who was present on this occasion, referred, in a speech after the paper had been read, to Mr. Johnson's appeal in England at that time for a steamer to aid him in his work, and said, " it would be a matter of regret if the possession of the steamer kept him from wandering about among the mountains and plains over which he had travelled with such great success." As we know, Johnson's future work did not mainly lie among those mountains and plains and his object had never been merely geographical investigations, but whatever he might have done in that direction was made much more difficult, if not impossible, by the blindness that befell him before that year was ended.

Botany
In one direction, Johnson's observations in a sphere outside his mission work were continued for many years, despite the handicap of impaired sight. As he walked here and there on the shores of the Lake he always had his eye open for flowers and plants and sent many bundles of dried plants home to Kew and to a botanist friend for identification. Some of these were of species hitherto unrecorded, and with regard to the others, their collection and preservation (though only vaguely localized) gave valuable help to botanists in determining the range of such plants and the character of the flora of these little-known lands.

It is such little things as these which show the astonishing width and variety of Johnson's interests. Such a man, so deep in a missionary " rut," might so easily, does so often, become narrow and restricted in outlook. One who bore such hardships as Johnson must without his tremendous vitality have been overwhelmed by burdens and responsibilities and have become mentally repressed and crushed. To the end of his days there
His taste in
light literature
was nothing dull about Will Johnson's mind. His interests in literature were catholic, but it is impossible to imagine him

delighting in the rather sex-obsessed novels of later days. He knew and loved Dickens and would often enliven conversation or his notes in the Diocesan *Chronicle* with references to the immortal characters of that great man. Rosa Dartle's " just wanting to know " was frequently on his lips. It is a remarkable thing that the two Archdeacons, Johnson and Eyre, were both steeped in Dickens. Of the two Archdeacon Eyre's knowledge of Dickens's people was the more "extensive and peculiar," and I believe he would have had a good place in the famous Pick-wick Examination in which Walter Skeat and Walter Besant distinguished themselves. Johnson was certainly second to Eyre in this field but quite a good second, and his range of interests in literature was far wider. {.sidenote}*Dickens a favourite*

Art and music—for the cultivation of which his life afforded small chance—seem not to have touched Johnson at all deeply, but he assuredly did not come under Shakespeare's condemnation as " one unmoved by concord of sweet sounds."

One general aspect of Johnson's work, which cannot indeed be attributed solely to him, is noted by James H. Mwela, one of his native friends, a Christian of the second generation, now head native teacher in the Northern Rhodesian Diocesan Training College. He was the son of one of those plucky students who joined the " peripatetic college " under Archdeacon Johnson in 1899. *A native tribute*

He says (these are his own words, not a translation) : " We praise and thank God for his work. He, whose work is done, has left, not heathen and hostile tribes, as when he first came, but peaceful and Christian people, who will be his lasting memorial."

What shall we say of this man in conclusion ? In an appendix there will be found some few of the many appreciations of him from some who knew him best on one side and another. *Summary of his character*

Though it be like the attempt of a pygmy to measure a giant, some attempt must be made here to take a general survey of what Johnson was.

The fundamental note of his character was that simplicity (ἁπλότης) commended in the N.T., that singleness of mind and purpose, which brings fullness of light. Not in the least a man of one idea or of few ideas, he was emphatically a man of a single intention, true to that intention as the magnetic needle to its pole. *Simplicity*

Next to that let us place the note of intensity. In the pursuit *Intensity* of his single aim there was not only no wavering, no uncertainty, but there was no half-heartedness. Not for him " the unlit lamp and the ungirt loin," but rather a concentrated intensity, a flame of energy, showing itself in whatever he undertook—such as always marks the hero and saint.

> " The soldier-saints who, row on row,
>     Burn upward each to his point of bliss."

**Indomitable will**

These two notes combined explain or account for the selfless-ness which so many have remarked in Johnson ; but there was needed another gift without which all the others might in a sense have been futile and have led to nothing. You may have the finest and most powerful motor car, but without a driver it is useless. In Johnson, his indomitable will was the driver that kept all his powers on the stretch and turned all his single-minded intensity into the channel of devotion to our Lord. Fruits of this combination were the tirelessness , the fearlessness, the pertinacity, the devotion to the least of the Lord's brethren.

Such a combination might well have made a hard man and a narrow man, but it was not so with Johnson. Those who worked with him knew him for a hard man to serve, simply because he expected of them as natural what he gave himself. But they

**Tenderness**

did not find him hard in himself. To many of his friends he was known no less for his loving sympathy and tenderness than for his strenuous demands on himself and others. His capacity for love and his rejoicing in it appears perhaps most clearly in his relations with his nephews and nieces in New Zealand. To women, whether white or black, he was always courtesy and chivalry personified.

Two qualities in him that might be little suspected by those who know him only from his work and the legends that have grown up around his name are his humility and his sense of humour. It is probable that without these he could never have come through his manifold trials. Humour is always a saving salt ; it enables a man to get outside himself and to enjoy what might otherwise simply crush him. Humility is somehow more subtle and less easily identified in a world where there is so much false humility, but it is quite certain that Will Johnson had the real unselfconscious humility.

**Humility**

Bishop Fisher, in a flash of insight, saw that it was in fact Johnson's humility that made it so difficult for other men to work with him. He was quite genuinely unaware that his own powers and qualities were very exceptional, and he could never understand why other people didn't do as he did. One of his steamer captains notes that he always treated him, a much younger man of nothing like the Archdeacon's attainments, as if they were on an equality.

As we have seen from one of his letters, Johnson expected Bishop Fisher " to stoop to conquer him," as Maples had done long ago. This was no pose, but a perfectly sincere humility, that was ready to learn from any quarter. His reluctance to impose his own will on anyone who sought direction from him in any matter proceeded from the same root of humility. He would help you to see the facts of a situation but he would not take it upon him to make up your mind for you.

His humour had nothing sardonic about it and was poles *His humour* removed from mere levity. He had a great horror of any light reference to things sacred and serious. One who worked with him recalls the pain that he caused to the Archdeacon by saying apropos of some quite trivial necessity, " *For my sins*, I have to do this thing." Sin was such a reality to Johnson that these light words gave him real pain.

He was a compound of such great qualities possessed in so *of the saintly* high and heroic a degree that one has to look to the saints, to *mould* St. Francis of Assisi, to St. Francis Xavier for parallels.

To those who knew him there seems no exaggeration, no levity in saying that he was of the saintly mould, of the heroic stature.

He has left a great gap, but let us end with the simple words in which he himself ended his report to Bishop Steere on the death of Charles Janson in 1882 : " And so Janson and I are for the time parted, but I don't think God leaves gaps long in such work as this."

# CHAPTER XIX

# Appreciations

WE give below some few words culled from the many letters and notices of appreciation of Archdeacon Johnson. The attempt has been to select representative and typical words without repetition.

Bedford School expressed its feelings through its present Head Master (H. Grose-Hodge, Esq.), who said, " Bedford School is justly proud of one of the very greatest of her sons. I hope—and with confidence—that his memory will be no less an inspiration to us than his life has been." From R. Carter, Esq., who had only recently retired from the Headmastership— " We of Bedford may indeed be proud of such an old Bedfordian —the greatest example of all."

Sir Michael E. Sadler, Master of University College, Oxford, wrote : " A great and good man. One of the soldiers of Christ. In this College especially he will be remembered with reverence and honour."

Father Timothy Rees, C.R. (now Bishop of Llandaff), writing to Canon Johnson, referred to his brother's death as a " triumphant ending of such a life." He described him as " the most Christ-like man that I have ever known . . . a really great man and utterly consecrated." " It is saints we need to-day," he adds, " God grant us saints—saints like your dear brother."

Frank Winspear (Canon of Likoma, who worked the steamer with the Archdeacon for years), wrote :

" To me he will always rank as one of the great heroes of the century—a man of the same stature as Livingstone. . . . Not merely the achievements of his lifetime impress me but the man's own wonderful faith in God and deep love for Africans. . . . An African teacher once said to me ' You know it isn't only the Christians who pray about the Archdeacon, but all up and down the Lake shore when he is ill the heathen too are praying for him—he is the one man above all who has stood for them and their welfare.'

. . . The triumphal passing of a great servant to the nearer presence of the Lord."

Canon Duncan Travers, who knew him during the long years of his Secretaryship of the Mission at home, says, " there was no one like him in his heroism and enthusiasm and depth . . . the very thought of his wonderful work and noble example humbles one. I am glad he died in *Africa*."

Mr. F. B. England, who worked under Johnson as captain of one of the steamers for some years, writes of him :

" I do not think that any one who knew the man and his work would for a moment question the claim that he was undoubtedly the greatest figure in the African Mission Field since Livingstone. . . . I can see him now as if but yesterday with his worn and exhausted frame, often sick and weary in the flesh but never at heart, pressing on towards the goal. . . . How very human he was! Looking at him no one would suspect the keen sense of humour he possessed. . . . I can recall dozens of long intimate conversations with him on many matters, and the surprising thing was that though the gap of learning between us was so wide, I cannot recall any discussion in which he did not enter on terms of equality. . . . He was a great one to give you confidence and his close friendship with one so far removed from him in many ways was a very marked feature of his nature. Truly no mind so great as the really humble one. . . . The outstanding feature of W. P. J., in my opinion, was the manly side of his nature. Indifferent to personal hardship and suffering, overcoming by his iron will every difficulty that lay in his path, brave, kind and humble, he was in deed and in truth a great man."

This is a wonderful testimony from one who lived and worked with W. P. J. in the daily conflict of steamer life, of which the difficulties have been mentioned above.

Another of the steamer engineers, Mr. Philip Young, gives his impressions in words which we quote almost *in extenso* :

" I lived with Archdeacon Johnson on the *C.M.* for about two years, that was nearly thirty years ago, but his personality is just as fresh to me now as it was then.

" Curiously enough, I was also in Oxford when he took his D.D., and was present at the ceremony. I remember chiefly that I was astonished at the number of people present and at the ovation they gave him. I remember too how tremendously moved he was himself, far more than I ever saw him at any other time. Oxford meant, I think, almost more to him than anything else in this world apart from Africa. . . .

" I remember very vividly the tussles we used to have about the necessary repairs to the steamer and the necessary time off for doing them. It would be agreed between us that at the end of some trip up the Lake the *C.M.* should be laid up for say three days for over-haul, boiler cleaning, etc. ; when the time came there was always an excellent reason why we should make ' just one more trip ' before lying up. Once, when this had been deferred three or four times after definite ' one last trip ' agreements, I'm ashamed to say I lost my temper after listening to a most logical argument for ' one more trip,'—left the Archdeacon without answering and went sulking to my cabin and to bed. About midnight, I was awakened by hearing him stumbling down the companion (he was of course nearly blind) and then a half-whispered, 'Are you awake, Young ? I'm afraid I've been very trying to you and very unreasonable.' I felt, of course, full of shame and needless to say, we did our ' one more trip.'

" Of all men I have ever met he had the least regard for his own personal comfort or welfare. If he considered a thing ought to be done he would straight away go and do it whatever trouble or difficulty it might entail, and he took it for granted that every one else felt just the same. Soon after I got out there I had an accident one morning and injured my thumb rather badly, tearing out the nail. I remember that I fainted and he insisted that we should cross the Lake to Kota Kota for Dr. Howard to see and dress it. It was blowing a gale and the crossing was none too pleasant, and by the time I had been ashore at Kota and had got back aboard, it was dusk and still blowing hard, and I was looking forward to lying in the quiet water off Kota Kota as we never steamed at night except in an emergency, but I found the Archdeacon quite expecting to leave at once to cross again, and since the journey had been made for me there seemed no more to say. As a result we ran the ship on a sand spit in the dark and spent almost the whole night getting her off again—I think the most anxious night I ever spent. Passing the little chapel on deck I saw him there on his knees and there he stayed till we were off again. He explained afterwards in a charac-teristic way that he thought that was the most useful thing he could do, and no doubt he was right.

He spent hours alone in that little chapel at night. I often came up during the night to see if the anchor were holding or some such thing and as often as not, whatever the time, if I looked into the chapel, he would be there on his knees.

" Another very vivid picture of him in my mind is at the Mass. He habitually lost himself entirely when he was at the Altar. I don't think at those times that he was conscious of anything in the world. It sounds futile to say, ' He seemed to be in a trance,' but

ARCHDEACON JOHNSON IN HIS ROBES OF DOCTOR OF DIVINITY, 1911

so it was very, very often. I think too, in fact I am sure, that he counted most tremendously on saying the Mass himself every day quite apart from hearing Mass.

" I always used to think that Archdeacon Johnson's relations with the Africans themselves were in some way different from every-one else's, though it is difficult to explain exactly how. Any criticism of an African, or of Africans generally, always raised an immediate storm with him and he resented anything in the nature of a jibe against natives as though it were against himself, and yet no one was so down on their misdeeds as he was himself. The fundamental difference to him between one native and another was not so much whether a man was a good native or a bad one but whether he was a Christian or otherwise. Once a Christian he was in the Family and to be defended as such. I think, generally speaking, the natives were rather afraid of him, and often puzzled to know what he was driving at (as for that, other people were, too), but I think they trusted him and looked on him as different from other Europeans and more or less identified him with themselves.

" Another picture of him that I have in my mind is sitting as he did for hours in the evenings in the saloon doing his translation work, with his head almost on the paper, focusing his one half-blind eye in a curious way through a sort of little chink he used to make between his first and second finger. He used to work straight from a Greek Testament or a Hebrew Bible to Chinyanja.

" The Archdeacon when he was really ill was a different person altogether. Once he had been compelled to give in, he gave himself up completely. I remember being fetched to him lying on a native bed in a village hut utterly prostrated and only half conscious with dysentery, and carrying him in my arms to the boat as easily as a child. Although he had a big frame, there was scarcely anything left of him but skin and bone and that wonderful head. There he would lie inert until he was better, and when up and about again he would do twice the amount per day that anyone else did. What he loved most of all was a good argument. I remember a wordy battle between him and Padre B. as to the source of some quotation from Shakespeare, and by the time we could lay our hands on a copy they were arguing as to which had said which play the quotation came from. He had the most amazing variety of interests, the last letter I had from him was a request for particulars of trade union rules as applied to South Wales!

" He had a most disconcerting lack of distinction between his property and other people's and was quite equally regardless of what he took and what he gave. The Collections in the village churches were taken in kind rather than money (which hardly existed), and he was very keen on encouraging the natives in making their offerings in personal belongings. Rice, chickens, eggs, goats and what not went to make up the curious offertory on Sundays, and the Archdeacon used to like to add something of his own. I remember the dismay of the owner of a nice warm garment, lent to the Archdeacon to go ashore in, one chilly morning, when he (the owner) saw the said garment disappear into the Collection basket.

" The Archdeacon only talked to me once about himself and that was the night before I left, and I got a glimpse I had never had before and never suspected. He talked of seeing this life like ' looking through a funnel or the wrong end of a telescope ' and went on to speak of the endless number of people he had seen come and either die or go away again since he had been in the Mission ; Bishops, priests, laymen, ladies, all coming new to this work full of enthusiasm and often very full of criticism of what had gone before, and he felt lonely and perhaps on the defensive. I think he was a very lonely man with a suppressed craving for human love and companionship—I may of course be quite wrong, but that is what I think.

" Since those days I have known and mixed with a great variety of men but I have never met a man with the vitality and personality and above all the devotion of the Archdeacon."

From G. F. Bradby, of Rugby

Finally, we give a penetrating analysis of the Archdeacon's character and influence from G. F. Bradby, Esq., of Rugby, who, as a brother-in-law, met Johnson on terms of intimacy on those rare occasions when they were both in England. He says :

" I have been trying to think what it was that made him so extraordinarily impressive. His utter simplicity ? His unconsciousness of being great or even interesting ? A feeling one had that his spiritual experience had got beyond the stage in which it can be clothed in words ? But most of all, I think, because, wherever he was and whatever he was doing, one was supremely conscious of the presence of the Holy Spirit, and not a little ashamed of oneself— and how much he would have hated to know that one felt like that! But he always did, unconsciously, remind one of the text, ' Whoever will be great among you, let him be your servant,' and give one a glimpse of what real greatness means. I know that one ought not to write about Will like this, because he was beyond one's understanding, and it's better to say nothing than to say it wrong. But he always was, and always will be, an inspiration to the weaker brother ; and the weaker brother doesn't know when to be silent. I think Dorothy[1] did get some glimpse of the heights on which

[1] Miss D. J. Bradby, his daughter, who helped the Archdeacon in compiling his *Reminiscences* and the *Great Water*

Will's inner life was centred. Only, of course, he didn't know that they were heights ; just thought that they were the plain on which we all live. She said it was very difficult to make any progress with the book, because he was always taking for granted things which are hardly dreamt of in the ordinary philosophies of life, and which imply a quite different set of values. And whenever he told her anything about himself which was at all revealing, he always insisted that it should not go into the book. The reason why it is impossible for anybody to describe Will is simply that he *was* a saint, and a live saint is infinitely more perplexing and unintelligible than a sinner. One can only explain anybody to oneself in terms of one's own experience, and, though one can understand almost any kind of sin, one's spiritual experience is too narrow and limited to enable one to enter into the mind of a man like Will. One only knows intuitively that there are heights on which rare spirits ' continually dwell ' and where one hopes to join them some day—but not here. The Galilean fishermen came nearer to understanding Christ than any of the educated Jews, and I expect that one could learn more about Will from some of the simplest of his native friends than from any of his brother missionaries. No doubt he will become a legend in Central Africa, and the legend will grow into something very different from the real man ; but it will always be an inspiring legend. He was determined that nobody should ever make ' copy ' out of him, and the knowledge of all that he did and suffered dies with him. But I do hope that somebody who knows will give some account, not of him, but of his work in Central Africa, because he hasn't really told it in his book.

"When I try to think what I really know about Will that is not second-hand knowledge, it amounts to just this—he once lived in my house for some weeks, and I was aware that the Spirit of Christ, which is the Spirit of God, dwelt in him. He didn't frighten me in the least ; on the contrary he brought into a room the same sort of effect as sunshine. But he did fill me with a great deal of awe and made me feel very small. That is an experience to thank God for ; but it isn't communicable to others."

Nurse Armstrong nursed him many times in his various minor sicknesses, " those ups and downs we don't take much notice of," and here are some comments of hers on him during and after one such time in September 1918.

" He was very unwell with bronchitis on his return from his last ' *ulendo*,' and we persuaded him to take a month's rest, which he did. He has been away now for a month so I hope he will return again this week for another rest—a month on trek is quite long enough for him, he needs the rest at the end of that time. I think the cause

G. F. Bradby

Nurse Armstrong in 1918

of the bronchitis was his having been upset out of the canoe and his sitting a whole day in his wet clothes ; and then on the top of that cold he had a very tiring time showing the Bishop round his district. He was really very done up when he got back.

" September 29, 1918. He turned up here last Thursday, September 26, looking in splendid health after a seven weeks' round of ' *ulendo* ' work. He most thoroughly appreciates these little rests at Likoma and enjoys looking up all his old friends on the Island. I do so wish that he would settle down in one spot and give up the very strenuous and lonely life he leads. This time he says he hardly saw a white man."

In his earliest days in Zanzibar Johnson must have met the Rev. F. A. Wallis (1875-1889) and it is characteristic of him that he never forgot this old friend. Mrs. Wallis writes of this and of a visit he paid her at Oxford in 1921.

Mrs. F. A. Wallis

" He was staying not far off with some old members of the Mission and they led him to my house one Sunday evening for the sake of his loving remembrance of his old friend my husband. I have always felt more than I can express about that visit in his feebleness and difficulty in getting to me.

" He stayed with us in Birmingham (1898) and we got a big meeting with the Vicar of E. in the chair. He read up the subject for the occasion and then very eloquently spoke, comparing Archdeacon Johnson to St. Paul in his missionary experiences. We were entertaining people to tea after the meeting to meet W. P. J., but he implored my husband to go home at once. At last they got away and his first words were, ' Who was that old fool in the chair ? ' He would not be lionised or talk to any one after the speech he hated so."

Bp. Maples in 1882

Mrs. Wallis sends also a fragment of a letter from Chauncy Maples to her husband, written about 1882, which is another testimony to the dauntless character of his friend. He says : " Johnson is fighting hard at Ngofi against a bad climate and a dozen troubles, but he never loses heart."

Padre Benaiah Mbiza

Padre Benaiah sums up his impressions of the Archdeacon thus :

" Three things I have seen in the whole life of the Archdeacon, namely : (*a*) He was a man who prayed very greatly ; often, when he had no work to do, you would find him praying. (*b*) He was a very great reader ; though he had but one eye he never ceased reading ; often he would call the teachers to read with him or to ask them various questions about the Holy Scriptures, and so, because he knew the Holy Scriptures by heart, he could correct a teacher at once if he made a mistake in reading or skipped a line. (c) He was always looking after other people, especially in giving gifts to the sick, the old and those in trouble. And he constantly prayed for others, the departed, the sick and those on a journey. Also at Mass he used to remember to mention especially the name of Bishop Maples. Again with the Government he stood out for his Faith in opposition to Father Hilary, O.S.B., who denied that the Archdeacon had the true faith. The Archdeacon said, ' Ever since I came to this country I have preached Jesus Christ, the Son of God, who died for us on the Cross.' "

Mr. Bradby has been quoted as saying that Archdeacon Johnson would, of course, become a legend in the land where he worked so long, and there is evidence of that already. Benaiah, after describing the efforts to build a church at Ilela, and the rigour with which the Archdeacon forced them to rely on themselves and not on European help for this church, and after telling how, after all, their first attempt was not satisfactory, and had to be pulled down (after the death of the Archdeacon) and another built on the same place, says " The people of Ilela, in his honour and in respect for their priest call the church by his name, the Church of St. Johnson, and they remember the day of his death, October 11, as the great day of their Church." His last words are as follows : " In our prayers we remember Canon Augustine Ambali, who was the teacher to begin work here with Archdeacon Johnson ; Yohana Abdallah, priest of the Wa-yao, of a great name in the land of the Wa-yao ; Leonard Kamungu, the first Mnyanja priest, who died at Msoro in Northern Rhodesia ; and so we do not fear to call the Archdeacon St. Johnson, Physician of the soul, Archdeacon, one of us Wanyanja, who clave to our people, and himself preached to us the Gospel of God. God will repay every man according to his work."

To parallel these words from Padre Benaiah, here are words from Canon Travers, who knew Johnson as well as most people over a long period. He says : " He ought to be described with a halo round his head ; he must have St. before his name."

# CHAPTER XX

# Extracts from W. P. J.'s Letters

## I. Mainly Thoughts about Religion

*Dated October 25, 1897.*

Letters
To Miss M. E.
Woodward
Have you seen Bishop Maples's Life? Miss Maples kindly sent me a copy, I have not read much yet. May we but only live in our Lord and so learn to face these awful realities of change of state!

*Written from the Waiting Room of the Medical Board of the Mission at Dr. Oswald Browne's, September 20, 1898.*

With a roomful here ready to go out if accepted, I feel drawn to you who have so often proved your readiness to go out if not *called* elsewhere, and so I can write a word of sympathy from my heart. (*Miss W. was called to stay home to care for her mother.*) Sometimes it seems, to one like myself without magnetic gifts of winning confidence, there are masses of suffering hearts and bodies, too, all round one of which one knows nothing—of course it is easy enough to think that one is full of sympathy, which may after all be quite selfish, a wish to be in it and to have company, but when you write of your trouble, right or wrong it does seem as if the atmosphere is cleared a little. It sometimes seems as if we can talk of sin and guilt, etc., and yet it has not come home to us with the terrible grip of life and death.

We need not think quite meaningless whatever brings us to a truer sense of what life means to most of our Lord's servants. We cannot know what our guilt really is, it is a matter for the Judge, and any real trouble may bring us to His feet who alone bore our sins, may it not? Remember that a real call to service at home must have its real trials just as a real call to service abroad. Perhaps we everyday people are extremely annoying at times and then we have got so accustomed to the idea of forgiveness that we expect no malice or criticism to remain even in those who make no profession of forgiveness.

I often feel two-minded, but then find that the only remedy really is crying to our Lord, He becomes the only life, the only way, in a sense not realized before.

*March* 9, 1911.

As you say, Chauncy was much in my thoughts at Oxford. What
I need and hope I shall be given is a heart more adequately alive to
such things, and our Lord alone can give such a heart towards Him
and in Him towards these dear ones. I want you to realize that I am
so cold and so cold-blooded and our Lord can use you to help me
onward. If we can trust Him for such miracles, trusting Him for
those He has taken will not be hard.

To Miss
Maples

*June* 7, 1911.

I know that you must often have made an effort, feeling a disappointment ; one gets hopes which perhaps *cannot* be satisfied,
and sometimes *are* not through someone else's fault. Honestly I am
thinking now chiefly of the former, as I am sure that we are being
drawn on through the very fact that we cannot be satisfied in our
great losses by anything short of Him who gave us the loved one
and the very love we had and he had. I am feeling something of the
bitterness of those times past just now, but after a long course of
them, surely let us go on, not back, till we really get to know more
of Him whom I fear to name glibly, have named too glibly, but
surely not too often.

*May* 1918.

I fear as I see the waves of Modernism, I believe whole-heartedly
in the Virgin Birth and the literal Resurrection of the Body of our
Lord, but I should deprecate any condemnations which appear to be
one view against another view, when often enough the owner of the
condemned view has seen so much more of some sides.

To his brother,
Canon H. R.
Johnson,
On Modernism

*November* 3, 1918.

You may imagine we do indeed need your prayers. Our Lord
" in full day " the only hope, the only meaning in it all—but, as
Archdeacon Glossop said of the Admiralty, " I do not ask for any
better authority," so we may say, I feel, of our Lord. . . .

Please God, you will be led on, even pulled or shoved on, that is
what I pray ; I not infrequently get " lights " in the early morning
or midnight (but, thank God, I sleep admirably)—at such times I see
some things, e.g. my reading, in a different light. I spoke of it once
to dear —— and he said, " Oh, you have rats too ! " I felt " No, it is not
that," but it would be, if it were not for our Lord, nothing I do is
even tolerable, if stuck to apart from Him. Any denying of oneself
is so beside the mark, or ends in some subtle form of self-pleasing,
unless He has been with us all through. . . . I have lately felt off
and on a resting in Him thankfully when very tired, it is a great
gift and a very necessary one to rest in Him.

P

*January* 19, 1920.

After an illness  I came round quick, thank God, but I am feeble still, working south to meet the s.s. *C.J.*, due 28th. I get lots of milk and eggs and fowls and not a little kindness, some of the teachers have been touched by my severe illness. I came on in a good canoe hired up here, yesterday it was a bit rough coming round the last point. I find a new or at least a modified experience, the entire effort to be in the Lord's hands, no plea but He himself and so leave it. I don't think it is mere funk but keener imagination and, I trust, a truer view of things, given of absolute mercy.

*February* 3, 1921.

To Mrs. Cooke  This letter is just as a sign that, if submerged, I am still full of old
(Miss Maples)  memories and young hopes in Him who has guided us so far and so gently.

*From Southampton, October* 27, 1921.

I suppose it is right in some ways that a man in my position should look at how he stands all round boldly, whereas a man in the calling in which he primarily looks to Duty to the King, to the Republic, may rightly take a simpler view—I should venture to say a more one-sided view—and deliberately close his eyes to many doubts and dangers. Yet I hardly dare to write thus as I feel what sufferings, what fears must face myriads from the prince to the stoker who go out and hide their feelings in their vocation. Yet again it is our duty to face the future and realize what absurd pygmies we are unless HE goes too.

*From Beira, December* 1921.

To his brother  I have been studying the First Epistle of St. John again and I find the " If we confess our sins, etc." very helpful ; however much one has been pig-headed, gone astray, He is faithful and just to forgive us. We can start again, only trusting Him more, even here at this Savoy Hotel.

There were, they said, some 800 English at Delagoa Bay, ready to help the Church with money but not to worship—we reflect on the bad example of the Portuguese, but I wonder how it compares all round, English sailors, soldiers, etc.

*Dangers of Mariolatry, March* 27, 1923.

I ask the Bishop to consecrate the Liuli Church " The Church of the Annunciation." He fears the advanced teaching as to the B.V. Mary.—Yes, but that is the reason to bring out what we have been given.

*Asking for advice, July 30, 1928.*

So far (*i.e. with regard to "advanced" practices among some* To Bishop Hine
*younger brethren*) I feel neutral, critical but sympathetic, but what
does alarm me is the putting the Blessed Virgin Mary in juxta-
position to the Persons of the Blessed Trinity and the Holy Name
of Jesus in thanksgiving after the Eucharist. . . . Positive honour
to the B.V. Mary, by itself, seems to me different, but here it is
simply parallel and almost identical with the Godhead.

*On Hearing Confessions, February 9, 1897.*

Some came to see me in church. Pray that I may never go to To Miss
such work alone, it seems like being the goat of atonement driven Woodward
out into the wilderness to God only knows what mysterious fate.

*December 2, 1926.*

Living as I do, and not very "winning," I perhaps see a truer To his brother
view of the people from one angle. To get any personal element is
an aspiration of a lifetime, bringing together East and West or
something more divided still, and I feel absolutely the inestimable
boon of looking to our Lord alone, otherwise you get up an inch
only to fall. Oh, but Harry, Harry, are you nearer than they?
Sometimes "things" seem to open, certainly praying for the
departed grows a greater comfort—may he or she or the tiny "it"
rest in peace, by the mercy, by the mercy sheer and simple of God,
may he by the Blood of Jesus come into Thy presence and then in
the heart of Jesus pray for us. What matter if he prays for others
far away, our Lord knows that power goes out of Him, and it will
come to the very distant, obscure, with no claims. . . .

I generally seem to look on, you and D. now are the protagonists. Trials of
I feel my life is led on so gently, your love throws in the lights and sickness
shades, but our Lord only knows if there is anything real here or
with you, but specially here.

There is a reality of the Cross in having "a heart" and in an Jan. 3, 1927
operation. God guard you from minute to minute!

Lent begins to-morrow. What possibilities! How I am blessed, Lent
yet I feel that you will very likely gain more than I. Oh this Love!
I read Tennyson's *A Lover's Tale* yesterday. No room for Hate and
Love in the same house.

*Quinquagesima Sunday, February 19, 1928.*

How different it seems now! At one time one seemed in a world
of perfect machinery, or even a world automatically run by one's
own power ; now we seem supported, carried along, kept alive by the
only power that counts. "Underneath you are the everlasting arms."
You know more of love—see the collect to-day—and as I read, that
is what covers sins and proves forgiveness. Tell me of your thoughts,

fancies, anything and everything ; I feel such a failure and yet a growing sense of being carried, like the tiny things that clutch at my heart (or substitute for a heart) as they rely on Mother and are miserable out of her sight.

*Von Hugel on the* UNINCARNATE *God.*[1] *July 30, 1928.*

To Bishop Hine    Von Hugel's *Lectures on the Philosophy of Religion* I find very helpful, but some very hard reading—some very clear. But I want your help (who else ?) as to what he says of the Unincarnate God working in the world, and the Incarnate God. I speak out of an abyss of ignorance, yet just there one sticks to a buoy. . . . I feel that I was brought up believing with the Alexandrian divines that our Lord, i.e. the Second Person of the Trinity, illuminates all, e.g. Socrates, Plato, etc., etc., etc., down to Frank Chepe of Likoma. Would not this cover all that v. Hugel objects to, rather than his Incarnate and Unincarnate God ? The person of Jesus is the Second Person of the Blessed Trinity, is " Jesus."

*August 6, 1928.*

To his brother    You always seem so looking at our Lord and the Beyond and yet so sane. Waggett contends that this combination is a great test, a great encouragement—God does not play the fool.

In the 51st Psalm it seems as if what first comes as physic proves in the end our Lord and Power. My goodness! it has some brass-cleaning, even sewer-cleaning, to do first in W. P. J. even now!

*God's Hand in Trials, March 1, 1927.*

Truly I have been very very blessed in health, December, January and February alike, so I can think in awe of our Lord and you ; you write bravely. I used to think Bishop Temple wrote too boldly of God's hand in these great trials, but yesterday I read again and found it " Bible " truth, but how grasp it ? One must be very near to Him or rather He to us—but He can take care of that—one longs for some grace and power to praise and not simply imbibe like a jellyfish.

*July 21, 1925.*

To Miss M. W.    If I could enter into a mother's love, root and branch and all in
Bulley    all, I should know what HIS love is *in ovo*.

*Undated, written in England.*

To Miss E.    This neighbourhood is very attractive although as I say I don't
Kenyon    know what people do in such changes who have not our Lord's feet to flee to. Some would think my feelings feeble ; let them ; I

[1] Von Hugel's " Lecture on the Apocalyptic Element in the Teaching of Jesus," p. 134 in *Lectures on the Philosophy of Religion.*

should rejoice to tell them where I get help so many millions must need. He sends such friends as you to defy changes.

1923.

St. Mary Magdalene at the grave is indeed an inspiring subject, and here all realize it is the sister, the woman, who is absorbed in the mourning—Where have they laid Him? . . . Our Lord must have been wondrous patient with all our stupidity, our idiotic dialects and my murdering of them. Yet in a way it brings Him (no one else HIM) before us, are we mad or drunk or do we believe in Him, Him, HIM? . . . Pray for us to be reverent, less like a great dance.

## II. On Mission Methods, etc.

*The Question of Girls, November 1, 1892.*

The girls are still a great crux, an unread enigma. Dr. X was after *To Miss* his manner scandalized at their lack of respect, we need not be so, *Woodward* yet we feel here is a hard thing. I don't think any mere methods will do the thing, the girls have a perverted standard, prayer and the Sacrifice of the Church can alone bring our Lord's saving light to them, and one fears, some terrible outside lessons too.

*The Reading of the Commandments, February 9, 1897.*

Perhaps a certain spirit of contrariness helps me to appreciate saying the Commandments in the Communion Office, where many seem to think them at least superfluous. But *here* there is something ineffably solemn in praying to be given to keep the great laws that are defied on all sides—something specially sacramental ; and perhaps you now are staying to support your mother in part in answer to our prayers that in spite of ourselves we may keep this law. Such great laws do not at once make a primrose path for this or that individual like myself, and one may find oneself in the self-convicting position of thinking each law an impertinence.

*The Question of Vocation to Mission Work* [1]

Fancy Miss Q. carried off by the gallant German Captain! One *Vocation* little point comes out here, it is but something to be expected if we are to ask people to come and not emphasize the need of the " religious " element ; people will come out to cook and nurse and make themselves agreeable like Miss Q. and then suddenly draw the line there. Miss Q. has been a really admirable specimen of a woman of the best intentions, good heart and unique abilities, coming out *in a vague way to do her best* and make us all comfortable, special

[1] The U.M.C.A. rule is that members are pledged to celibacy as long as they continue in the Mission.

vocation, special crosses, tradition of Mission, all put in the background—May God bless her in her new life!

*The Question of vocation to mission work or to marriage considered again twenty-five years later, February 15, 1922.*

Mission work or marriage

I found much kindness at Likoma—the engaged lady, Miss X, is very sweet, all melt towards her—but here I think the Bishop's attitude is not right. How can the whole thing be left to drift? I understand he actually said *tête-à-tête* with three or four senior ladies that any one who disapproved was a case of the fox and the grapes. I feel to differ here *in toto*—though Mr. Jeaffreson, whose letters I am reading, thinks that often those who have missed an offer of marriage may do very, very good Church work. It is awful to me to look on any one of the very few women we meet as a possible mate, still more awful if the girl looks on men so and has no power of realizing it. Coming here is practically a dedication with the majority of our ladies—I expect these marriages make the lives of many of the other women much harder, I mean just the women we need. I am not thinking of those who get married when on furlough, when providence, rather than special vocation, gives you your circle of choice or possible vocation to marriage.

*Liturgical changes, May 4, 1922.*

To his brother Liturgy

I think anxiously of Synod, how mad we may be, changing our Liturgy seems to me sheer madness, like your rural deanery of Cardiff changing the Liturgy—no pretence of natives wanting it and we are all paid from England!

*July 15, 1922.*

The Liturgical changes sometimes paralyse me, not as to doctrine, that, thank God, does not come in at any rate directly, only that some hardly seem to see it *is* there under all the verbal fighting and ought to be prominent in any question of reunion—but to use a document written by young men at Likoma, not used anywhere else, to learn it all and forget the Prayer Book—but yet good discipline.

*January 21, 1922 or 1923.*

To the Rev. H. A. M. Cox

Again the proposed Liturgical changes puzzle me. We are like a tiny rural deanery and why have a liturgy all to ourselves? There seems no idea, no pretence that we represent the native mind, and here we shall be different from everybody, Rome, Greek, Anglican etc., etc. An Uganda *Boma* man who came to our Eucharist on board coming out and was able to worship at Uganda too, heartily, said with feeling, " Can't we have one use for the native converts everywhere ? " True, if the Liturgical Committee of the Lambeth Conference recommended some improvements all round it would be different—but changes in Liturgical usage are not to be lightly emprised (not refused simply on that account) but again why shake native confidence unless it is necessary ?

*February* 10, 1922.

I feel that each of us, however strong or gifted (as e.g. X) is also so one-sided, e.g. X looks most to confessions, counts them, is comforted by them, cites them, etc. (though he has depths in himself far deeper and all-round, still this holds as his view of his work). He does not examine ABC, etc., and gets quite cross and puzzled when I try to take a view of the teachers' mind.

To B. H. B.
O.T. Lessons

I used (of course wholly abnormally) to refuse School Syllabus, taught Hearers O.T. Sunday Lessons, Catechumens and Christians the Sunday Gospel. Why ? Because I was an absolute jackass ? Perhaps partly, but mainly because I could not teach at random (especially Hearers), felt if I wandered I got vague ; and still more that the teachers do.

*December* 2, 1926.

We have been " argifying," not to say squabbling, to-day too. One teacher I meant to go home and his wife simply because I have no place for them down on the Lake and they won't, partly can't, go to the hills. He was to go and did not and there's no way home for five weeks more and a long, long way home. There is a fallacy that I ought to find a place for a friend, rather than find a friend for a place and its people that need him. Our white ideas, especially W. P. J.'s white ideas, and theirs are not identical. Then I remember how can He stick all my comfort when the poor people round are suffering. I alone, observe, in some ways worse than the different class selfishness.

To his brother

*August* 21, 1928.

I am very keen on a school (whether called central or not) of brick (now the Likoma people build well and rapidly) with *big* bricks sun-dried. I want three classes there.

W. P. J.'s last letter

1. From the lakeside villages, they are in the running and ahead.

2. From *these hill schools* who are left out in the cold and drift off to the coast [the Indian Ocean Coast], the Coast villages [i.e. lakeside villages] will, I pray, rise to help them and me.

3. Lower class for backward hill villages.

All these boys, if from another village, to be helped with food and cloth, and to read hard and have competitive entrance examination each two months. I am not clear which village is best for this.

This trip in a hammock (*machila*) is very helpful—I get more time and the six men help (esp. the *capitao* Benjamin, who has just had a little daughter).

At this village *where I write* nearly all the school have gone off to the Coast. . . .

I am hoping to get an interview with the Superior O.S.B. near Manda about each two months to ask as to any friction (Bishop Hensley was urgent on this). Fr. Hilary, the present Superior, is going home. His English is faulty, but, I am ashamed, I am ashamed, my German is practically nil. Oh spirit of Dr. Steinmitz and my foolish waste of time!

Education      I was much struck by Bp. Frank Weston's notes on Education near the end of his book (pp. 257, 258). The Editor thinks them not thought out, but they seemed very suggestive and true—even if not worked out as he might have done ultimately. The key to them seemed to me to be, Does our educating fulfil the old root laws of native thought and life (cp. our Lord, " I have come to fulfil the law ")—work, marriage, family life, respect to father and mother ; greater eagerness for and understanding of work in its widest sense (just some bit of a job for some man quite unbeknown, for objects unbeknown, to get necessary coppers, can't help). I think if Canon Scott Holland groans over the mechanical work of clever London boys, what about these ? Even our Lord's teaching would challenge this test, how much more education which claims to develop just the intellect as working here below.

To Bishop Hine, on ritual changes, in 1900    Here follows a letter addressed to Bishop Hine in January 1900 on the subject of some ritual changes introduced at that time by the Bishop. It must be remembered with regard to Johnson's attitude on matters of ritual that he had left England in 1876 and that from then till the end of his life he had lived under pioneer conditions, trekking and working in villages where the simplest accessories of worship were for the most part lacking and where such as could be procured easily from home were utterly foreign. The Archdeacon stinted himself in candles because his teachers were unable to get them ; and on the same ground, as he says in this letter, he did not always feel that it was edifying to use them on the altar. He was not at all un-reasonable in his attitude to the ritual changes and wrote be-cause he felt it a duty as a senior priest to voice the feelings which he shared with some others. In Nyasaland as elsewhere a great deal that some objected to thirty years ago has now become accepted as part of the ordinary course. The letter which follows was in answer to questions addressed to the clergy of the Diocese by their Bishop, and must not be read as a cantankerous criticism that was unasked for. The tone of it throughout illustrates what has been said of Johnson's unswerving loyalty at all times.

*Likoma, January 17, 1900.*

I feel it only the clear duty of any one of your staff here, after learning of the misconceptions rife in England as to our relations here, to express his sorrow that such misconceptions should have arisen and to declare how manifestly groundless they are. I feel sure that each member of your staff would bear the same witness as I do to our unshaken loyalty to you. If no difficult questions had to be settled under your governance, and if no decisions ran contrary to anyone's personal prejudices and opinions, the above testimony would be meaningless. It is on one such point that, if I am not mistaken, you would be not unwilling to listen to a one-sided view, for the value of which I plead. This point is that of Ritual. Let me first say how I agree with my whole heart with much which you read to us last night, e.g. (1) setting aside such obviously wrong ideas of the use of Ritual as something to draw congregations ; (2) claiming a liberty in our infant Church here as heir of the whole Church, and not bound by the conditions of our Mother Church in England ; (3) more than this, I feel the ideal of such worship is worthy of such an infant Church. While I feel this, as expressed by the Bishop of Font du Lac, and I believe our friends in England would heartily agree, I feel also that such independent action of the infant Church ought, at any rate in matters of ritual and in the infant stage, to originate with your Lordship. You approve what is Catholic, and, as you believe, draw from our heritage what is adapted to the needs of our infant Church. You have the responsibility and the corresponding grace and guidance  If your Lordship does not represent and put in action the healthy potentiality of a Church (which is in no province),[1] there is a danger of being carried along by a current in the form of a majority, who are irresponsible  and may represent some unhealthy tendency, as for instance to or from Rome, as an end in itself. After reading Canon MacColl's book I have my fears confirmed as to such a danger existing.

In further answer to what you said to us, I would point out that I believe that, as you say, you have not advanced on what Bishop Smythies practised at Zanzibar, and yet it is true, doubtless owing

[1] The dioceses of U.M.C.A. are missionary dioceses under Canterbury even now (1933), but a Province of East Africa is likely to be formed before long.

to the Church here having been in her early days, that very much now practised at Likoma, and much referred to in your charge comes as something quite new to me personally. This hardly needs explanation but I cannot ignore my position as a matter of fact nor would you wish me or others to do so.

*Still* at all our stations on the mainland we only use the minimum of ritual you refer to with a few exceptions, e.g. Mr. Eyre uses linen vestments, I have ceased to do so for some months, I think since I came back, possibly for too frivolous reasons, certainly not on the ground of conscientious scruples. I seldom use lights on the altar, as at most places we get morning winds and candles are consumed in a wasteful way, while for months our teachers have not been able to buy candles for use in services and for reading in their own houses, in part owing to the block of our goods down the river. Partly my outlook lies in a firm conviction that the idea that very big stations like Likoma, Magila, etc., are necessarily in advance of stations such as Msumba, *qua* the growth of a native church, is a mistaken one. This does not seem to me to be affected by the lowest view of the latter. Of course I am not venturing to speak of inner growth and spiritual life, but of the manifestation of certain principles very vital to a native Church, if we venture to hope for a miracle, as such miracles have been worked in all countries when the Church has gathered in her children. Thus I feel it difficult to allow that the Church, in any station where a number of Europeans, workshops, etc., form an important objective for European eyes, is necessarily or probably a better field for a more elaborate worship. Have the people learnt to provide more or to provide less for their own worship? To distinguish more or less between work for God and work for man? To this it might well be answered that the Europeans are more able in point of means and in point of understanding to carry out a more elaborate worship; but to this I answer that no elaborate ritual is carried out with the Europeans but with and through the natives. Serving at the altar, censing, etc., is not set forward as the privilege of the richer and more intelligent class but as part of the elaborate service that surrounds Europeans in plenty quite independent of worship.

Thus, not seeing any valid reason for thinking the native Church at larger European centres more fitted for elaborate ritual than those at such places as Msumba, I have to ask myself the question whether such ritual would edify the Christians there, if it were possible; and secondly what the effect of ritual at Likoma may be on them if not practised there as well.

Turning for a moment to look at the places of worship, Bishop Steere urged on us that our places of worship should be superior to our own and other dwellings around, and that we should look at that, and not at what would be fitting in England. So may we not take a misleading standard of dignity of worship ? The furniture, dress, etc., must certainly be better than is used around, but, to give any idea of education, surely there must be a difference of degree rather than of kind, not the mere witnessing of what foreigners may introduce. I fear our ritual may act as an incentive to the native to improve his ritual as little as our steamer encourages him to improve his canoes. What he does himself and how he may improve step by step seem the important points. Hence I cannot feel that altar hangings, numbers of lights, numbers of candlesticks, cassocks, surplices, etc., even if possible, would build up the native Christians in any ambition to make their worship more outwardly decorous, or that it would make their worship more heartfelt. They would more and more be taught that all this, if it is to be done, must be done for them. Their strength and their weakness, at present, is in their sense of being admitted to one body, and I should imagine our aim ought to be to foster this : bringing out their individual responsibilities and duties and share in worship. I cannot think that this is done by their seeing a few take a prominent share in gorgeous ceremonies with, to them, gorgeous clothes, while they understand nothing. For instance, I suppose they may understand the priest going to the altar, but if the choir sing an introit and nine out of ten do not know it, it so far seems to exclude them, and irritates or, more probably, teaches indolence and alienates. Some few points of ritual, e.g. the position of the altar, the direction of attention to the Blessed Sacrament, I can believe that they appreciate, but not any movements hither and thither or anything complicated or difference of colours or number of lights, when one sees how indifferent they are to flowers and beauties of landscape, etc.

So I should again put before myself and urge on myself the endeavour to lead all to feel they *must* take a part, in hearing, in understanding, in responding and, of course, most of all in inward worship ; to leave the one object of worship as clear to all the congregation as position and simplicity of all between them and it would permit.

Another consideration comes in, among much vagueness as to their feelings, they are utterly unaccustomed to play at anything in the way of scenic representation,[1] and while I think it may be very useful to teach them to move in procession and realize they are playing the part of Christian soldiers, yet it is all so new to them, that any introduction of such things in connexion with the Blessed Sacrament seems to threaten their reverent worship at its root. I

[1] The Archdeacon is surely wrong here. Many native games and dances are of the nature of primitive drama.

am thinking of the congregation as a whole, as one said, their impression of a procession must for long be " *Wazungu wango-yendayenda* " [" Those Europeans just go here and there "] : surely other times are better suited for training their minds in such matters than at a celebration of the Blessed Sacrament.

Secondly, what effect would more elaborate ritual at Likoma have, say, at Pachia ? I cannot help thinking that much of a ready adaptability to divine worship is rather apparent, when the majority all follow one way and no one of the people likes to be out of it. One often finds mere imitation, as of the wall behind the altar in the old Church at Likoma which happened to be built in a pointed form to follow the roof : this was copied in *cloth* at Pachia. Those who have been taught that hangings are the right thing would cover Parian marble with any tawdry hangings. Perhaps from lack of teaching they seem to pick up quickly enough the value of orna- ments, candles, etc., in worship, without any corresponding value of the question who pays for them.

There is much which may be wholly wrong in this view, much owing to misconception, but we have to see matters as they are. No one seems to have any idea that a neat bowl offered by the native Church would be more pleasing to God than a gilt bowl offered and made by a foreigner, looked at with regard to the native Church : or neatly sewed calico worked by Amy, Eustace's wife, be of more value than something which a native cannot apprize or imitate. From the principles given above as to houses we should all agree that a European presiding over such worship ought to affect such standards, still more a body of Europeans living around and sharing in Church worship, but I doubt if this will seriously affect the question before your Lordship.

At the risk of appearing to leave my particular watch-tower, I would suggest, might the ideal of a Catholic worship be brought forward once and again at the Easter season, and all the Europeans show that *that* is how they would worship, if they had not to remem- ber the condition of their native brethren.

In conclusion let me assure you that I am not unconscious how like dry bones these statements must appear when you are looking for light and truth. We look to you, and rely fearlessly on your having both sufficiently for our needs, even if dimmed by our sins.

Yrs. affect. and obed. in O. Lord,

W. P. JOHNSON.

### III. Miscellaneous Extracts

*Just after the fires at Likoma, November* 1892.

To Miss Woodward

The new big school makes a capital church, and they got it ready so quick that we had choral Evensong and sang " Te Deum " the day of the fire. It was a mercy that the new stone houses were spared, a wonder too. I could not stand near that side of them, the heat was so intense, and the iron bars of the new carpenters' place were hot long after. The people came up from all round and helped well. Our biggest loss was the Library. You should have seen the flames flickering between the leaves of the books which long remained intact, and even the print quite clear as the books lay half open.

*October* 1892.

Please pray for us. I do not get better at this work, I am terribly ignorant of the faces of many Christians, this principally owing to the difficulty of getting them to talk to in a good light ; in a half-lighted church I see little of any one.

*November* 5, 1896.

I have been " gallivanting " to Unangu and even think of doing Unangu so again as " a great door is opened " there. I had a good time, rather tired on the hills and not a very graceful or agile, rather a ploughman-like, figure crawling up, but none the less it was good for one. The flowers were beginning to come out and a perfect bramble spray, fruit (red) and leaves, stands out as if photographed on my eyes as I saw it over the waterfall not far from Njiri. . . .

You will think of what I feel as to our new Bishop after our long Bishop Hine yoke-fellowship ; well, few men have a character of which one may hope more than of Bishop Hine. I feel sorry only as far as one system is approved versus another in which I believe to the very tips of my finger-nails (after backwood wandering too), but I have learnt that no system is THE thing. Mr. Margesson is another *person* who teaches me to value persons, as do Messrs. Eyre and Auster.

*October* 28, 1897.

Why affect to think me very busy and with no time to write to you, or uninterested in your news, etc., etc. We ought to be able to beat old soldiers who have fought side by side out of sight in common interests. We look on as well as back, and can get help when we do feel a chill come over us to whisper and cheapen our life.

*From the College on mainland opposite, complaining of loneliness,* To Miss
*September* 1900.                                                    Schofield, at
Dear Miss Schofield,                                                  Likoma
    There was an old man and a College
    Both wanted where there is no knowledge ;
        So they sent him a cake
        But they crossed not the Lake
    To that poor old man at the College.

Many thanks for such a cake, a thing to dream of with marriage feast and song when we celebrate the Marriage Feast of the Church.

*From New Zealand, 1901.*

To Miss
Woodward

I suppose one cannot have everything at once and it is a great thing for an old bachelor uncle to have a lot of nephews and nieces to play with—he has to go through a great deal of mental as well as bodily gymnastic which is good for him.

*October 11, 1902.*

To the Rev.
Duncan
Travers

Portuguese
troubles

" Joy cometh in the morning," and so after the Portuguese at Kobwe had assaulted me and of course frightened my two natives, and things seemed pretty black, the Senor Lima at Mtengula rises to a fine fury of indignation and goes up, sacks the offender and makes peace with Mataka, in full war paint, cocked hat, spurs, etc. He seems really a good sort of man *qua* friendly feeling and orders from Ibo. . . . X here, I think, hardly understands the conditions

Difficulties

of the problem. On our side we stand between Muhammadan millions from the Jordan to Mozambique, from India to Ujiji, and the rawer natives with whom the Scotch deal (on the West) ; at Likoma and along a good strip of coast they did welcome us, but we have yet to see them do it at Malindi or Kota Kota. S.W. our converts are surrounded by (1) Muhammadan dances and teachers, (2) Yao initiation ceremonies, (3) Nyasa do., (4) heathen in service with Europeans and bearing all sorts of Christian names without baptism.

*From Sydney, returning from New Zealand, February 14, 1902.*

To Miss Maples

I have, thank God, been given a good share of renewed animal strength in N.Z. and I can look to you for no stinted sympathy in my fellowship with my dear brother there, and in him with his family too—a new revelation of life to me. Thank God I have the firmest belief in family life as our Lord's ; is it too much to say that St. Paul seems to have been led on to dwell on this side in the Pastoral Epistles, even so one must get some heart-aching in sympathizing with so much life, often on such different terms to our simpler hope. . . . I often think of how Chauncy was one of the influences which warded off the intense loneliness of our service at times. Yes, intense loneliness just because there is always life and hope there, enabling one to measure the apparent outlook and see something of both the realities of loneliness and sympathy there in spite of all.

Now Bishop Hine is going through Spain, I suppose, where indeed I have been in Crockett's " Firebrand," where the idea of the " Angel of Death " visiting the outposts struck me. May God in His mercy guide both of us to do His will, and not to think less of the life we have seen, but to see the Source more and more clearly till our perspective is a little less hopelessly like that in Hogarth's famous picture.

*The* **C.M.,** *May* 1902.

Now we are trying to get our new steamer life into full blast. Certainly I have never had such a ship before or such a band of workers and daily we all join in the Eucharist and look forward to the battle. We need it—the Portuguese and burnt villages up north ; the English and solid Islam down south! Thirteen Ki-Islam teachers in a village we visited yesterday. This sort goeth not out save by prayer and fasting—perhaps still true *pace* Revisers and Medical Boards.

To Miss Woodward

Power of Islam

*W. P. J.'s debt to Bedford,* 1907.

It seems to me a wonderful thing, like a fulfilment of the prophet Isaiah's words " Who hath brought me forth all these ? " when a quiet missionary like myself finds people taking up the wonderful work in spite of his shortcomings and insignificance ; and I know of few or none who bring this out as you and our friends in Bedford have been given to do. Greeting to all the brethren *Unter den Linden* or near the old bee-haunted limes and John Bunyan's statue, Pray for us!

To Mr. Wm. C. Toll, of Bedford

*January* 1909.

So willingly I acknowledge my debts to you and to all in the old town. As one ages I have been told and seem to find it true that the time of boyhood looms out strongly and with it the Ouse and the old haunts continually recur and live again.

*March* 6, 1912.

Another of your wonderful lists telling how Bedford has played up. Bedford always *does* play, but that it should play up in this particular direction is very wonderful and you must feel that your kindness and enthusiasm have not been in vain. Bishop Hine was temporarily house surgeon at the Bedford Infirmary, Bishop Trower's father was curate at St. Peter's when the Bishop was still trouserless, Bishop Fisher was born at Kempston, so Bedford ought to send another man to look after us.

Links between Bedford and U.M.C.A.

*March* 24, 1913.

" A quarter of a century of hearty co-operation! " May it remain a ground of happy remembrance as the years roll by. Ought I to feel sorry for lack of power in the past to realize all such help as

Twenty-five years of help from Bedford

yours means, or rather feel drawn up to the Master who lets us play and help around His feet ?  Anyhow you and yours, Bedford town and school, Kimbolton Road and Fosterhill Road, St. Peter's Green and Church, will form a big part of the background of both our lives. Mr. Hart Smith called home—all our Nyasa Bishops with some Bedford link—all come in as strands in the rope, so may the Lord graciously bind us up in the bundle of life as one feels more and more His undeserved help and presence even when one least expects it.

*January 29, 1925.*
Such as Bedford friends, such as you, and all the interest and prayers at home . . . are a sign, a rainbow, if only a very modest moonlight rainbow, reflecting our Lord's life in our church at home across our waste of waters here.

Bedford and W. P. J.

These references to Bedford and the Archdeacon's long connection with the town and the school are assembled here because this connection was really a very important thing in Johnson's life. Mr. Toll, his correspondent, for many years acted as the local secretary in Bedford for the U.M.C.A. and he kept Johnson in touch with the school. The boys took great interest in the work on the Lake and to the end of the Archdeacon's life sent an annual sum which had originally been counted as providing the uniform and keep of the native crew of the *Ousel,* one of the boats which the school put on the Lake. The name " Ousel " kept the memory of Bedford and the Ouse green among many on the Lake who otherwise knew it not.

To B. H. B.

*B. H. B. had been helping to standardize the final version of the Gospels, December 15, 1908.*

The " privilege " of translation work

I am most thankful to you for your toil and skill, we are rowing in the same heavy boat against the same long swell in the teeth of a *mwera* [the trying S.W. monsoon of the Lake] and have no time to be thankful, but we can unclasp one hand at intervals to take the strain off the weary muscles, or get some change. . . . So now you have done the Gospels, I can see much good in this but hardly think even now that you ought to have left your valuable work ;  I think the Bible Society and S.P.C.K. are all given wrong ideas about the size of our needs, though I feel again that, when we look at things as you and I do, we feel such standards of numbers and cost an impertinence.  Our Mistress grows and we follow, feeling it a unique privilege to translate the living oracles into a living speech, even if only the *kungu*[1] fly used it, if they too had souls.

[1] The *kungu* fly, a species of tiny gnat seen in clouds on the Lake.  See *Nyasa the Great Water,* p. 9.

*Sympathy with her on leaving Nyasa, 1910 or 1911.*  **To Miss Schofield**

You will be spared much pains, I believe, in looking back in **Opportunities** feeling that you did not waste opportunities. It is not so much the gross idleness, etc., which comes back on one, but the failure to rise to what might have been, what might be, which one only gets hints of round corners as it were ; or again what one has lost by temper, letting miles of carefully veiled hate run out and grieve our Lord. Surely you have been saved from this last failure, is it not so ?

*The " Tea and cake danger," January 3, 1911.*  **Tea and cake**

I still by order take quinine and two or three times " a wee drap of whisky " and so am quite fit. You will know we need not fear the whisky danger, please God. But I do fear the tea and cake danger. I half laugh, half cry when I feel how *big* a comfort they are and yet perhaps I ought rather really to be thankful and like a child. Yes, our Cathedral is grand, and yet much anxiety to any priest-in-charge there, and indeed to the Mission.

*On seeing her brother Archdeacon Woodward (who died June 17, 1932,*  **To Miss**
*after fifty-seven years of service in Africa), December 14, 1910.*  **Woodward**

It was indeed a pleasure to see your brother, a real old veteran and so peaceful, it did me good. I had no need to come home, I had no illness, only one of the little downs (and ups) we don't think much of.

*On his being offered the Degree of D.D. by Oxford, February 18, 1911.*  **To Miss Maples**

This degree is a graceful tribute to the Mission, much like having  **The D.D.** Chauncy's picture in University Hall. I do indeed hope to have  **degree** some talk with you which may, please God, help me and may, I hope, help you too ; Chauncy could, dare I say can, give out so much sympathy. . . . It was good to hear E. B. [Canon E. F. Brown of the Oxford Mission to Calcutta] enthuse about Chauncy.

*June 7, 1911.*

I so often feel absolutely lost as to what may reach people's hearts  **Preaching** and help them, all the more because I don't feel at a loss as to what interests me, and then learn afterwards that one shot at random.

*Eve of the Epiphany in England, January 5, 1911.*

At such a season as this you and I would be boiling over to get  **To B. H. B.** somewhere and do something supposed in a mysterious way to spread more light of our Lord in honour of the Epiphany—if we duplicated or got swamped or sat up to 12 midnight so much the better ; but now I am sitting before a comfortable fire and shall not get up till 7.30 nor go any whither. May our Lord Himself lighten

Q

the hearts of those dear ones who seem always so far away and yet so near.

*February* 5, 1911.

The last month before I came away, I think I must have had a presentiment of change. I went out nearly every evening to villages round to try and get at least one word in ; and now where am I ? One voice says, " Resting, run down two stone, old, toothless, wrinkled " ; another says, " Get out, you lazy beggar, have only black people souls ? " . . .

Please remember me in your prayers that I may not live as " a heathen man and a publican " in England, nor trample on pearls, or otherwise " jolly well " take the cake as swine, as the *babu* in *Kim* might say.

**To Lawrence Chisui**

*On the eve of his Ordination as a Deacon (Translation)*, 1911.

Dear Lawrence. What, have you forgotten me far away in England ? But I haven't forgotten you a single day ; now I hope you

**On his ordination**

are near to your ordination, and I pray our Lord that you three may help one another. I have no doubt that you have learnt a good deal through being with Yohana and Petro, but I hope that they have gained something through being with you. You became familiar with the work in the villages when the s.s. *C.M.* was going

**Our hope**

about from village to village. You know how we hope that the Lord Jesus will not refuse to enter into our villages and into the hearts of the people that they may have His life and His Spirit and so have strength in all their ways. I entreat you, do not throw away this hope that the Lord Jesus will be with you so that in your ordination you may be given power to help in worshipping Him well in the Eucharist, and in ministering to the sick and poor, as He is by His Spirit in all Christians that they may be saved from

**Love all men**

their sins and do the works that God has given them to do. Do not forget me on your ordination day that we may love all men, yes, even the Wa-Islam. Our Lord loves them and has given us the work of serving them. Truly we English are burdened with many customs, but the Lord cannot fail, He can help us and help you too. I see that God has given us many blessings here in England, but He will call us to account for them. So I want most of all knowledge and love. He alone loves all, our mothers and us young people, Wa-yao, Wa-Islam and *Wazungu*.

**Miss K. H. Nixon Smith**

*The Work of the Printing Office, March* 5, 1912.

Endless little things printed, useful in their way, but no big things and regular bossing. The Bishop has a passion for printing this and that and so rescuing the Diocese from its heathen darkness and lack of method, but one is at times tempted to chuckle as Bishop Trower used to do at the triumphs of Africa versus the white man, e.g. white ants versus jodolite—" Keep them off," he said, " Why, the stuff is a dinner bell to them "—even though we suffer in the process. . . . I hope this letter won't show signs of rollicking—we are rolling up the Lake on the s.s. *C.J.* much as in old times—I feel what infinite mercy I need as I realize all that has passed on this boat and with the scene of Maples's death and our "handling" at Makanjila's both in sight, and now these *new* and dear workers on board the old boat. . . .

The Bishop would not hear of *our* using the College [on the mainland] as I wanted—anything to keep our Portuguese work in full swing and not allow the idea of *nkondo* [war] between the English (i.e. the Mission) and the Portuguese to gain head.

NOTE.—This was written some months after the shooting of Padre Douglas, Principal of the College, by a Portuguese official. The Bishop removed the College to the British island Likoma and refused to establish in Portuguese territory any permanent stations for European workers (with ladies) for many years after. The Archdeacon was naturally anxious to make some use of the buildings at St. Michael's College even if the original use was inadvisable.

*Memories of the Angoni Raid on Uchesi, October* 3, 1911.          To B. H. B.

On the other side the old school-church-dormitory with all my baggage, school things and my cook and 7 boys (northerners at that) last night recalled somewhat too vividly some of our camping experiences, only that the northerners have less clothes and less bathing. God bless them, their life eats into mine. I have been looking at a few poles left where their forebears lived for years. The headman told us to-day that he was taken by the Angoni as a   Link with the food-carrier when about 15 (i.e. about the age of his son now in   past school here), he thus went down with them to raid Uchesi,[1] when I was first at Chiteji's and remembered my coming to meet the Angoni. I like the chap very much but he has 6 wives, that is rather a hindrance to his advance. How we long for some real guidance and spiritual strength, a grasp on life.

1914.

What you say of more co-operation with other whites ought to   Co-operation come home to me. But does it? To be in a minority of one is proverbial, but misleading if it means a climax ; what if you are the national assembly, majority and minority in one, and fancy if you are not penitent. Surely such a one needs your kindly and skilled help.

1917.

I have economized candles and read names at dinner and after   To H. A. M.
Cox

[1] In 1881.

An evening's work

till 7.30, then Class for Communicants (generally only schoolboys owing to (1) darkness, (2) lions, (3) tiredness), and then talk with boys and meditation in evening, lighting up 9-9.30.

*Rearrangements of work and districts, July 27, 1917.*

To Miss Nixon Smith

I seem likely to find myself like a "jinn" in the *Arabian Nights* bottled up in a very small Muhammadan flask (seven very small villages) at the bottom (i.e. the south end) of the Lake. Never mind, *you* couple us all up in a satisfying system of sympathy.

*October 11, 1918.*

To his brother

Just a line by my canoe which should go south to-morrow and leave me to go on afoot as a bigger and better man did long ago. . . . I have quite a lot of cloth, owing to you at home and your liberality, plus Brother Sargent, plus the Bishop. I find the latter a very effectual help in business, if he says it will come, it does and vice versa.

*From the Base Camp at Mbamba Bay, April 10, 1918.*

A base camp

Still at the old "Chester" but, unlike the Roman camps, these base camps soon begin to fade away and I have but now written an order by which men will draw on these huts to build our little mission buildings in three villages. As it is, long rows of grass, reed and stick buildings remain empty and cattle with their calves wander about.

*Sympathy needed, October 11, 1918.*

I have always relied very much on the sympathy and support of the Church at home and I often feel a rift with sympathy out here ; one wants to sift it and be put right and join up.

*November 1918.*

To Miss Nixon Smith

Granted that the "elect" will shine with wonderful fires in the sight of God like the spirits Dante saw in Paradise, those who have in them the Spirit of the Gods, yet why not say explicitly that men like Westcott have poured the jewels through their fingers and scooped them out and found in their humility that many an old woman and young child was doing the same in the form of drinking of some brooklet ? If you don't "mew" thrice after this, my name is not Jack Johnson!

*His attitude towards changes of work made by authority, February 21, 1918.*

Please don't speak of all as finished and gone (e.g. at Likoma or anywhere else). True it may be bits cut out of a man or woman to be

left more wholly in our Lord's keeping, but never less lost. I have
had to look at it squarely many times, one is apt to resent the
action of someone who has the cutting off to-day and even talks
glibly of the responsibility being his or hers—so it may well be, but
as often in a sense little dreamed of, or again in a sense that means
little more than use of them like a hammer or cutting machine.

*About going home, January 22, 1919.*

I have settled, as you will have read ere now, to come to England   To his brother
after Easter and then D.V. to New Zealand, but ? as I come up
here [Mbamba Bay] I cannot feel it clear, often I cannot feel it
right. What do I go to do or get? Health, strength—they are not
to be ordered at Whiteley's or even the Army and Navy Stores.
Believe me, I am not answering pigheaded, I feel awestruck, and
long to be guided, and there is much to cheer but much to make one
think.

*Appetite, June 1, 1919.*

When off, I lust after the fleshpots in an absurdly coarse way—
and yet very much fear that I am often over- not under-fed, now.

*Padre Cox had been recently put in charge of Msumba, one of the
Archdeacon's old places, September 22, 1919.*

Now I try and picture you in the old scenes, familiar and yet I   To H. A. M.
expect changed everywhere—the old church which was a great joy   Cox
and yet a great trial, in its later stages it dragged heavily. I am
like our friends at home, I should like to know what time you rise,
what soap you use, how many eggs, etc. Do you ever read? I think
I see some new historical book worth its weight in gold in these
parts. Do you read the *Church Times* or the *Guardian* or both or
neither? I dip into Browning and more than dip into the Psalms,
W. P. J. his *magnum opus*, recalling Archbishop Benson's *St.
Cyprian* which he wrote between his wonderful works as Archbishop.

*July 20, 1919.*

I am very critical when I hear praise (is it jealousy?), very much   To Miss Nixon
the other way, when people are run down (is it cussedness?).   Smith
  Jealousy and
  cussedness

*February 2, 1920.*

Pray for us. I am in cotton wool again. Indeed we are blessed   To H. A. M.
in people like Miss A. and Miss S. (*After thanks for teachers sent up.*)   Cox
I am looking at my own little garden patch and all its calls but,
believe me, not indifferent to yours. . . . I should value seeing
you and W. but have followed a rule and as so much begins to
swim and old landmarks shift, and especially now when I am

howling for cash, I had better follow the old track back to the sheep as soon as may be (much the line you have followed for the last two years), sleep in a native village (as you do at Msumba) unless prevented by sickness or war.

*April* 27, 1920 *or* 1921.

My dear Cox. Drop the " Archdeacon " and live in peace with all men. . . . How can dear Miss X. Y. resign ? If she can, who can't ?

1923.

I must think and pray over your Chapel of the Blessed Sacrament. I am not tempted to judge as far as I can see, but do not see my way clear as you do, D.G. I feel so deficient (alas! alas! alas!) in realizing our Lord in the Baptized and the Faithful. Anyhow HE will lead us on, very likely I am culpably blind.

To Miss Nixon Smith

Locke's *Mountebank*

*Easter*, 1921.

I have been ashamed after reading Locke's *Mountebank*, his discipline and how he could see the good and profit in it.

To Mrs. Cooke (Miss Maples)

His sight

*Written in England, August* 20, 1921.

You must not put me under a ban as mannerless and ungrateful, rather sympathize. I put a letter down and am lucky if I find it after many days ; e.g. I heard from Bishop Burge and put that down as the breakfast bell rang and can find no trace of it. Now after a systematic taking of stock I find yours and feel uncomfortable—not to say silly—but really it is only my half eye.

*Fears of the journey, October* 27, 1921.

Mr. B., a Durham man, was to go with me but, poor chap, is again unwell. I am indeed the loser, and again I am not afraid to say I rather fear the voyage—white faces so many, so little known, so imperfectly seen, but so many of you at home have taught me to expect kindness. . . . I wonder if Mr. C. will be kind enough to think out my needs on this voyage, or up there with men no longer feeling the spell of English civilization. If he will, a few prayers may rise up and help us perhaps as well as a less critical sympathy.

To his brother

*Lions about, March* 27, 1922 *or* 1923.

A last word before it is dark, it is dank, rain heavy, continuous— and by all accounts dangerous too as lions are about or said to be. They have provided us with a rickety old door and bars and have cleared off, i.e. the residents—reminding me of the people at Songea long ago when my cook Thomas was taken. Very likely lions are no nearer than 20 miles, but everybody carries assegais, clubs, billhooks, etc. But don't pity me, dear man, for there has been much to help at Nasungu this morning and here to-day.

### " Gareth and Lynette," June 5, 1922.

You dear old brother, I would rather be with you at the bottom of a class than with most people at the top. I have been reading " Gareth and Lynette " (Tennyson's *Idyll*) and there the outward armour of the Evening Star (i.e. of an *old* man) soon gets knocked off, but our ingrained hide is the real fight.

### *His books and his vanity, July* 15, 1922.

I felt a little pang that Longmans did not accept [his *Nyasa the Great Water*, published by Milford]. It is awful the sidelights I get on my vanity which needs (and has in part had) a garden roller to keep it down. I am very glad about the *Psalms* and the *Proverbs* too, it all seems some sort of progress and encouragement to fellow workers. See p. 189

### *Changes of Districts, December* 6, 1922.

I have very much to be thankful for. George followed me to Likoma and now behold me (i.e. from January 1) launched on the northern part, i.e. from Liuli to Milo, a new budget which ought to suffice mine alone, and George's that is Liuli alone. It is happy leaving Liuli as Miss W. writes warmly and I think Miss F. feels kindly and George is very good and helpful and now nothing else to disturb. A man who is go-ahead like him naturally has his own ideas which one may cross without even knowing it. Now my work is simple and straightforward though a little overwhelming.

### *At Sea, September* 20, 1921.

I hope and pray you have weathered the " sore " trouble, such an old enemy to us all, e.g. Maples and myself. I recall Belcher, the bright-eyed Captain of the *C.J.*, leading off with some idea that a clean-gentle-man would not get sores, much less smell of iodoform, but alas, the " blains " broke out on his own hand. It helped one to sympathize with the magicians of Egypt. I hope you sometimes think of me, not only at the altar—if chiefly there. I say " Amen," but not as if a magical thing, only the gate of heaven for the currents of our life. As I swagger down the first-class staircase to a goodly banquet, and see young men and maidens, mothers and kiddies, etc., I feel that God, having given me hope in our Lord, can and will give them a like hope. I think my life for years has made dreams of wondrous life and sympathy a possibility—even if often a fool's paradise. . . . I played and won a heat in the bucket quoits, not so bad with half an eye. To H. A. M. Cox

Sores

Bucket quoits

*Dr. Laws of Livingstonia, February* 10, 1922.

To B. H. B.    Have you read *Laws of Livingstonia* ? I feel very humble after reading parts—not that it seems such a glorious ideal, but it does seem an ideal realized as it went along.

*A Feast at Manda, July* 21, 1925.

To Miss M. W. Bulley    You, a σύνδουλος, can picture last night's dinner table here (or rather three combined tables), five sat down, each in *his* own arm-chair. Plates only one each, so intervals for washing, lamps low and not too many or too bright, so you could not see if the boy Frazer offered potatoes or scones or what. . . . These celebrations are a glory, a privilege, a danger. To-day the others have got off and here I am in my jungly hut beloved of my soul. . . . Think of the Church in England and London,

> They laugh and talk in Sion,
> They sit them down in Sion,
> They meet and " tea " in Sion,
> They bus and tram in Sion,
> *Ni ine ndeka ndeka ndeka !*
> [And I alone, alone, alone!]

*Shall he retire and come home ? June* 3, 1926.

To his brother    Your words of welcome home rejoice me. Bacon said truly that Univ.'s kindness[1] would warm my heart, true indeed, but your words more, and yours mean stopping with you.

Still I hope and pray to see the way and feel nearly always that leaving my daily calls here, when in unusually good health, is tempting Providence.

George, Lawrence and Glossop all agree [against going home] and obedience is not so clear ; our Bishop is hard pressed and needs men now to-day and not merely sent next year. I feel to welcome rest and work with you, if so it will be, or here. . . . The home you offer is my life-blood and a bright comfort if I break down, as it has been a glory in the past as I look back. God is very good to me.

I value these visits of a man like Dr. Wigan ; his outlook is quite different, and yet not too much so not to be helpful.

He goes round and gets many true views of the Mission work, and must find me difficult to fit in. It grows more and more on me that I do not fit in, only our Lord can carry me through at all, there is often much comfort in that.

*December* 2, 1926

I owe you much in letters but your three this time seem more helpful even than usual. Partly ? because of your hearty sympathy,

[1] University College, his own old college, had just made him an Hon. Fellow.

partly because your own share in the Cross casts its shadow, a
blessed shadow. When I read the kindness, overflowing even to this
obscure and distant spot, and then see how I am surrounded by
conflicting currents, where it seems impossible to catch any sympathy, I wonder which is I ? Is the W. P. J. of dear Bishop Hine
and of your affection a myth, or is the angular Angle of Hampshire
a will of the wisp ? True, I have gone down in weight, I am thin,
but alas! the angles are very very real. You will answer, yea, I
answer myself : You try and see what our Lord would see, and there
is also what one must fear. Dear brother, your heart has done so
much work, it may well need rest, yet there too will come in the
contrast. I storm and fly round and then melt and turn ; you
sympathize, a divine gift, till wearied you turn back into yourself.
Let us in His mercy find Him as He will. " Thy will be done "
seem the most helpful as the most awe-inspiring words.

*December* 2, 1926.

It seems clear, as time goes on, two men, say Dr. Wigan and I,
get each more and more incorporated in a different outward world,
i.e. I think native, he thinks white, neither necessarily better or
worse for it, but it needs something Higher to unify, and that insists
on unifying, and that means a continual effort. . . . Dr. Wigan has
his visions and rays of light, quite as clearly as mine.

*Gaps in the bridge, April* 24, 1927.

On Thursday Frank George came to my most southern station to
see me, 3 p.m. that day, he walked ? 17 miles to do it, through any
amount of water and mud, a very helpful fact. . . . I valued seeing
him. I think he really tried to help me, only once or twice there
seemed a gap in the bridge. Perhaps he has his " gaps " as certainly
I have. He is very down on the R.C.'s. I think that the country
certainly needs *both* unless we are supported in a wholly different
way.

*May* 24, 1927.

I have a comforting assurance that you will find some clear calling
in all your really terrible trial ; you have always been given it
hitherto, and you have always cheered me feeling the value of
*different diverse* callings, often unexpected.

*Other people's views, July* 30, 1928 ?

Would I could repay your interesting notes by cross-cuttings from
current events *here* but (1) I have not the gift, (2) the events are in a
tea-cup, not in London or even Cathay. After another Synod and
Conference there is no heart in me as I return to my own country, I

To Bishop
Hine

Synod worries

hope spices and some gold were extracted from me, as from the Queen of Sheba, willy-nilly. Certainly I feel that there are possible other views (yes, even right views) of many a question on which I once could see only one view, W. P. J.'s view. Dear old Bishop Fisher appears in possible new lights, a real chairman is a vision to me. I dare say you are a real chairman but I haven't seen you in that part. Sixty-odd Europeans (" all sober," as Eyre used to say) all eating, sleeping, talking, laughing, is another vision. Yes, and all praying—but yet *qua* corporate body, scrapping all the outward garb of such divine worship as we (may I say *we*?) regarded as sacrosanct. And why? Because any native wanted it? not a scrap, no pretence of it (except a real loyalty of men like X to what he believes a native will find helpful *where* the new converges on and threatens the old).

Matins and evensong

I confess I find I am always going back to a forty years' custom of rejoicing to say matins (and evensong) where possible with my people. This has gradually been made impossible. (1) In Bishop Trower's time, on the plea that even senior teachers ought not to say matins (i.e. in absence of priest) and so new books were introduced ; (2) *now*, snippets of matins all we can get in new dialects and very few of them ; (3) *now* radical change of matins even on Sundays (where no priest) ; we shall soon have no book in native dialect containing matins, etc. *Eheu! eheu! On not being consulted in language revisions.*

I should feign a humility which I do not feel had I acknowledged that I was out of date.

*Conscious of failing strength, August 7, 1928.*

To his brother
Near the end

I am not certain of my strength since Easter. It is a great treasure to know you are willing to take me in, an untold treasure, often a source of bodily health. I have good hopes that I can go on   Humanly speaking I am hardly likely to be able to come home, get strong and not more out of touch and come back again. Yet I often feel that getting new people in and a simple solidarity with the natives is very rare.

Cox is better than I am, George very good, but with side-shows, building, and a Captain's way of looking at things,—admirable, enviable but one-sided,—Hicks very good as a forward but otherwise a dark horse,—the Bishop knows nothing of the native as I do, but I feel it may be equally true that I do not know as he knows. Therefore, dear Harry, pray for us and for me as you know how aggravating I can be,  I question whether of Eyre, old sailor, George, architect, W. P. J. translating, each does not lose more than he (severally) gains in these talents, hobbies, etc. Only can our Lord save us and give you to pray us out of the danger. Follow the Lord whithersoever.

*The Bishop's burdens, September* 21, 1928.

I deeply feel with our Bishop, his burdens and his puzzles—Now what can he do, what ought he to do to fill (or leave unfilled) Eyre's place? I should think the engineers, good as many are, are enough to drive him mad. The native clergy are good, but very difficult, let alone us Archdeacons. He often seems to aim at making our billets palatable (or less unpalatable) to ordinary young men and yet just where I criticize, I feel that *in a sense* he succeeds with me—the food and other things *now* are a great comfort (and temptation).

*From W. P. J.'s last letter*

*Difficulties in approaching some people, August* 1928.

X too I hover round, and we talk of native things, of persons, of this and that, but he will not close—he wearies of the life, but shrinks from England. I feel lacking as to him. He harks back to witch-craft and *outré* things ; I feel such an ass without religion that I always want to hark back. Didn't we wear the Cross, the blue and gold, very obviously on the river ? I repeat and repeat, one has so the greater strength to go on, withal an obvious job.

*A lay friend*

*" Going on "*

*Native soldiers going to the Coronation,* 1902.

Some twelve of the native soldiers are going home to the Corona-tion to help to establish the throne of King Edward VII. . . . One has to keep one's eyes open to recognize old friends, these soldiers are our old friends the Yao youth who despised labour of all sorts and were not very susceptible to religious influences. Now they are fêted and taken home : e.g. one who went with a Lieut. P., a second cousin of mine, boasted that he had been one of the men at Makanjila's to try to tie me up. So I am continually recognizing little Mission agencies *of sorts* where boys are living with Europeans just as they do with myself or Mr. B. ; we all have great faith in the vague influence of ourselves *qua* Wazungu, possibly *qua* gentlemen—What does it come to ?

I feel quiet confidence as to the steamer but cannot tell how long it will be to select the first *corpus vile* of would-be teachers on which to experiment. . . . After this knocking about one feels how much more we might make of our common life, our common hopes, our common Lord.

*To Miss E. Kenyon*

*October* 8, 1902.

I always seem as a friend seemed last year, trying to get work done, yet always behindhand with it,—but thank God if, as you say, we are only led to realize the elements of our faith,—that our Lord is working a real hope and life just when we break down.

*From South Wales during furlough, January* 30, 1911.

Indeed, I am very happy and blessed in being with my brother and in a hundred other things, and yet I confess rather out of my bearings ; what can one do when nearly everything is changed, temperature, hours, food, colour, etc., etc., etc. Yet our Lord is at hand and makes it all seem right and real, instead of a mere " illusion and turning on the wheel " as we read the lama says in *Kim*. . . . I am very much obliged for Miss F.'s subscription and the other lady's, but I dare not receive any subscriptions. I have not had money for years and years. I fear I am rather like Mr. Harold Skimpole in *Bleak House* in my powers of spending money and yet knowing nothing about it.

*Like Harold Skimpole* — *(margin note)*

*February* 2, 1923.

It was something to thank God for to meet you again. It certainly helps a feeble critter like I am to find a fellow soldier (of either sex) who is simply following HIM and gives one credit for doing the same. True, you often rate one too highly, but it is the regiment, the reign of the Lord you look at and it humbles while it encourages one. I am off again, as people would say " by himself," but I hope with Him and with the natives.

*The Birds in the O.T., September* 19, 1923.

A long cry to birds—do you remember helping me about birds ?[1]— and now I am back at them again. The natives seem sometimes to know nothing of natural history, and then again if you can strike the note they know much and I am collecting their imitations of birds ; just as one might collect their mimicry of Europeans they have known. What do you think of publishing the latter ? Chap. I. Bishops, II. Priests, etc.—Do you sleep at night now as you ought to do ? Or pray as perhaps I ought to do or meditate on the years that are past and on His love ?

## A FEW EXTRACTS MAINLY ON NATIVES

*On Lenten observance, Lent* 1927 ?

*To Miss Nixon Smith* — *(margin note)* My boy casually mentions at lunch that he has resolved in Lent to eat " *nchima* " ([their staple food]) only on Sundays. I only hope his flashes of natural sharpness will not vanish under this rather indefinite dieting. I hope it does not mean " resolving " on no buttons on my clothing when they come off, while Lent lasts.

*The Choice of an old heathen.*

I was struck in the hills by a coincidence. I had taught the Bwinali boys that perhaps Adam gave way to Eve in the matter of

---

[1] In 1900 at Likoma.

the forbidden fruit, because she (his wife) was already entrapped. I have my misgivings but it is at least possible. *Next day* I had an interview with an old man who was an outsider and a witness to a marriage. As usual I asked him, " Why do you not follow the Way? " He was unusually emphatic in a negative sense, " No, I am an outsider,"—" Yes, so we all were, but *now* ? " " No, my son-in-law may follow new ways but I am an outsider. My old wife is lost, and one daughter is ' lost '." [*He used a word which means either literally " lost " or euphemistically " dead."*]

I spoke of " being lost." He assented, " Yes, I should not say that, one who is ' lost ' may be found but not so the dead. My wife is *dead* and I shall remain an outsider." You may imagine my feeble protest, to which he answered in set terms, " If my wife has followed a bad way, I will follow the same," Oh Father Adam, Father Adam! I felt weak and helpless in myself as one struck these bed-rocks of human nature ; one can but turn to Him.

I went this morning to see an old lady—imagination might connect her, sitting upon her mat and her head covered, with Saul—She is blind, and her grandson came this morning to say she was talking of hanging herself as his mother (her daughter) was killed by " fire from God." This was on Feb. 1, the boy's mother Maria had been killed by lightning. The old lady, deprived of her stay, finding speech said, " What could this bit of a man-thing do to take his mother's place ? Can he bring firewood, pound flour, cook or comfort ? He is in your school, etc., etc." *A blind old woman in despair*

### Funeral Customs, January 1909.

At one village, alas, many had joined in the sacrifices at a headman's grave. Fancy you and me being tempted to put a pint pot on some of the honoured mounds in St. Peter's churchyard! It is unthinkable, but not so here. One very advanced printer who had been at Johannesburg fell into this, and pleaded that I didn't know what it was to be regarded as a wizard by my kindred. This was true enough but didn't seem to elucidate the matter much. At another village the river had swept away the reredos and altar and I knelt at the communicants' step and could look down a 12 ft. bank where the altar had been. Our new school had been taken out to sea altogether before we had paid for the thatching. A man in huts which had escaped, though hard by, said they got the womenkind out of the way and then they were prepared if need be to climb on their roofs and so go out to sea till picked up, but it did not come to that, the river was very capricious. It was like most of our other enemies here—you don't know when they will take you. *To Mr. Toll, of Bedford*

*B. H. B. now in Johannesburg and in touch with a number of Nyasa boys there. A warning, February 3, 1912.*

To B. H. B.　　Hurrah, you are at Johannesburg, thank God for that! Pardon me if I warn out of all these years that, alas, many canker-worms have got fat on, be on your guard with these natives full of *virility*. Virility is not, as Yohana said of a brass cooking-pot, a sin, but it is not a charm against sin and I think we Europeans are often drawn by the weight of virility and need a decided watch and guard. It is a hard task to steer just right, not hate too much nor love too much (you can't *love* too much but one can feel an attraction too much) ; I am an old idiot, you will say, and bless me, crossed in love and in everything—yet I feel more trusting to-day, much of the future unknown.

*Daily Bread, May 24, 1927.*

To his brother　　I went to see a leper girl this morning and said the Lord's prayer. What a difference between her daily bread and mine (capital scones, butter and *an appetite*), still her people like having her. She shrinks from going to the leper settlement even at Liuli where they have some great advantages but no family life.

# INDEX